The Global Student Experience

There are 177 million students in higher education throughout the world today. This book provides some indication of what they are learning and of their wider experiences. It also outlines the changing global context of provision for undergraduate students as countries and universities respond to what they anticipate will be new demands for virtual and more traditional learning in and across subjects of study. *The Global Student Experience* brings together contributions from a range of authors to focus on common themes combined with descriptions of the student experience in national higher education systems. Providing insight into what students can expect from emerging patterns of provision worldwide, it also informs institutional decision makers as they attempt to meet changing international student demand within their own national circumstances of retrenchment or expansion in competition with private, public, and for-profit rivals at home and abroad.

The editors present this panorama of provision through a team of expert contributors who relate their experience and knowledge of shared global concerns. Thus, they combine the big picture of economic and political globalisation with examination of its various aspects, such as:

- cultural differences in learning
- distance provision
- the globally connected undergraduate curriculum
- academic literacy and language development
- the assessment and 'employability' of graduates.

At the same time, in an increasingly open market there are also restrictions upon student travel and residence in many polities, and increasingly variable fees for home and international students. *The Global Student Experience* combines these pan-global themes with an overview of 'Western' higher education, including the US and UK systems of higher education contrasted with systems in different cultural contexts, such as Europe, Africa and South America, as well as the new giants China and India.

Camille B. Kandiko is a Research Fellow at King's Learning Institute, King's College London.

Mark Weyers was a Senior Teaching Fellow in the UCL Centre for the Advancement of Learning and Teaching at University College London.

International Studies in Higher Education
Series Editors:
David Palfreyman, OxCHEPS
Ted Tapper, OxCHEPS
Scott Thomas, Claremont Graduate University

The central purpose of this series is to see how different national and regional systems of higher education are responding to widely shared pressures for change. The most significant of these are: rapid expansion; reducing public funding; the increasing influence of market and global forces; and the widespread political desire to integrate higher education more closely into the wider needs of society and, more especially, the demands of the economic structure. The series will commence with an international overview of structural change in systems of higher education. It will then proceed to examine on a global front the change process in terms of topics that are both traditional (for example, institutional management and system governance) and emerging (for example, the growing influence of international organisations and the blending of academic and professional roles). At its conclusion the series will have presented, through an international perspective, both a composite overview of contemporary systems of higher education, along with the competing interpretations of the process of change.

Published titles:

Structuring Mass Higher Education
The Role of Elite Institutions
Edited by David Palfreyman and Ted Tapper

International Perspectives on the Governance of Higher Education
Steering, Policy Processes, and Outcomes
Edited by Jeroen Huisman

International Organizations and Higher Education Policy
Thinking Globally, Acting Locally?
Edited by Roberta Malee Bassett and Alma Maldonado

Academic and Professional Identities in Higher Education
The Challenges of a Diversifying Workforce
Edited by Celia Whitchurch and George Gordon

International Research Collaborations
Much To Be Gained, Many Ways To Get In Trouble
Melissa S. Anderson and Nicholas H. Steneck

Cross-border Partnerships in Higher Education
Strategies and Issues
Robin Sakamoto and David Chapman

Accountability in Higher Education
Global Perspectives on Trust and Power
Bjorn Stensaker and Lee Harvey

The Engaged University
International Perspectives on Civic Engagement
David Watson, Susan E. Stroud, Robert Hollister, and Elizabeth Babcock

Universities and the Public Sphere
Knowledge Creation and State Building in the Era of Globalization
Edited by Brian Pusser, Ken Kempner, Simon Marginson, and Imanol Ordorika

The Future University
Ideas and Possibilities
Edited by Ronald Barnett

Universities in the Knowledge Economy
Higher Education Organisation and Global Change
Edited by Paul Temple

Tribes and Territories in the 21st-Century
Rethinking the Significance of Disciplines in Higher Education
Edited by Paul Trowler, Murray Saunders, and Veronica Bamber

Universities and Regional Development
A Critical Assessment of Tensions and Contradictions
Edited by Rómulo Pinheiro, Paul Benneworth and Glen A. Jones

The Global Student Experience
An International and Comparative Analysis
Edited by Camille B. Kandiko and Mark Weyers

The Global Student Experience

An International and Comparative Analysis

Edited by Camille B. Kandiko and
Mark Weyers

LONDON AND NEW YORK

First published 2013
by Routledge
2 Park Square, Milton Park, Abingdon, Oxon OX14 4RN

Simultaneously published in the USA and Canada
by Routledge
711 Third Avenue, New York, NY 10017

Routledge is an imprint of the Taylor & Francis Group, an informa business

British Library Cataloguing in Publication Data
A catalogue record for this book is available from the British Library

Library of Congress Cataloging in Publication Data
The global student experience : an international and comparative analysis
/ edited by Camille B. Kandiko and Mark Weyers.
  p. cm.
  Includes bibliographical references.
  1. Education, Higher. 2. College students. 3. Education and
  globalization. I. Kandiko, Camille. II. Weyers, Mark. III. Kandiko,
  Camille. Students in a global market.
  LB2322.2.G546 2012   378.1'98--dc23
  2012038591

ISBN: 978-0-415-80926-9 (hbk)
ISBN: 978-0-203-59016-4 (ebk)

Typeset in Galliard
by Bookcraft Ltd, Stroud, Gloucestershire

Printed and bound in the United States of America by Publishers Graphics,
LLC on sustainably sourced paper.

Contents

Figures and Tables

Figures

Tables

Contributors

Fatima Adam works at the Zenex Foundation, a donor agency that supports the development of mathematics, science and technology education in South Africa. Her experience straddles both the public and private sector and encompasses a variety of activities, including project management, strategic planning and research. Whilst she started her career as a scientist, most of her recent work has focused on higher education development. Prior to taking the position at the Zenex Foundation she worked at the Open Society Foundation, the Joint Education Trust and the University of Johannesburg. She has a BSc in Chemistry, a Postgraduate Diploma, Honours and Master's degrees in Education and a PhD in Higher Education. She holds a visiting position in the School of Education at the University of the Witwatersrand.

Lena Adamson is Associate Professor of Psychology holding a position at Stockholm University (SU), Stockholm, Sweden. Her original research interest has dealt with adolescent development including issues such as self-concept, future orientation and adolescents' contacts with adults. In her recent work in this field she has also focused on positive youth development programs, and prevention and effectiveness studies. Since 2004 she has also worked with issues concerning teaching and learning, quality assurance and the Bologna process at positions as, Director for The Centre for Learning and Teaching at Stockholm University, head of The Department for Social and Cultural Studies, Stockholm Institute of Education, Secretary General at the Swedish National Agency for Higher Education and contracted expert on quality assurance, teaching and learning for creativity and innovation to the European Institute of Innovation and Technology (EIT). She is currently engaged as Higher Education Consultant to Council of Europe and as independent higher education expert to the Swedish Green Party. She was the main author of the handbook for *the EIT Quality Assurance and Learning Enhancement System – Quality for Learning* http://eit.europa. eu/education/eit-labelled-programmes/ and has been invited as a speaker at a number of seminars and conferences on issues concerning learning outcomes, aligned teaching, student centred learning and quality assurance tied to these concepts.

Gaby Atfield is a Research Fellow at the Warwick Institute for Employment Research (IER). Her research focuses on skills development and differential access to education and employment. She has worked on the longitudinal

Futuretrack project, where she has taken a particular interest in the role of higher education in overcoming inequalities of opportunity. Gaby is a mixed methods researcher with a background in social geography.

Raúl Atria Benaprés holds a degree in Law and in Sociology from the Catholic University in Chile, and doctoral studies from Columbia University, New York. He was a regional advisor for the United Nations at the Economic Commission for Latin America and the Caribbean (ECLAC). He is a professor at the University of Chile, where he heads the Sociology Department at the Faculty of Social Sciences. He has been a consultant for public and private agencies in Chile and other Latin American countries, on population studies, regional development, higher education and quality assurance, and has been invited to act as an external reviewer in many universities in Chile and abroad.

Judy Backhouse is Head of the School of Economic and Business Sciences at the University of the Witwatersrand, Johannesburg. Her expertise in higher education is wide-ranging. As Director: Advice and Monitoring at the Council on Higher Education, she was responsible for drafting policy advice to the Minister of Higher Education and Training as well as the national monitoring of higher education. Prior to taking up her current position, she headed the School of Information Technology at Monash University's Johannesburg campus. She consults on and researches the use of information systems in universities, doctoral education and research development, as well as under-graduate teaching and learning. She worked for twelve years in the information technology sector in management and technical positions, developing a deep knowledge of both information systems and organisations. She oversaw the implementation of several large systems for telecommunications and medical insurance companies and was particularly successful at facilitating understanding between business and technical staff. Professor Backhouse has a PhD in Higher Education, an MBA in Technology Management, and an MSc in Mathematics.

Heike Behle works as a Research Fellow at the Warwick Institute for Employment Research (IER), University of Warwick. Over recent years, Heike has mainly worked for the Futuretrack project (go.warwick.ac.uk/ Futuretrack) and was especially interested in the higher education experiences of international students and their transition to the labour market or further study. Heike is a quantitative sociologist and works mainly with longitudinal or panel data.

Daniel S. H. Chan is a Professor in the Department of Electrical & Computer Engineering at the National University of Singapore. Over the past three decades, he has taught courses in semiconductor materials and devices at the undergraduate and graduate levels. His research interests are in the physics and technology of semiconductor devices, and techniques for failure analysis and reliability studies of these devices. He has published over 250 journal and conference papers and graduated twenty doctoral students who now work as academics, technology entrepreneurs and researchers and leaders in industry. He is currently involved in the redesign and development of the undergraduate programmes in his department and chairs its accreditation committee. At different times, he has served as the Head of the Department of Electrical & Computer Engineering and as the Associate Provost overseeing graduate education in the university.

Chng Huang Hoon has degrees in Philosophy (Honours) and English Language (MA), both from the National University of Singapore, and in Linguistics (PhD, University of Texas-Austin, USA). She is an Associate Professor in the Department of English Language and Literature, National University of Singapore. Her research interests include gender, ideology and identity construction. Her publications on the subject of gender include the book, *Separate and Unequal: Judicial Rhetoric and Women's Rights* (2002, John Benjamins, Amsterdam) and several articles including '"We women aren't free to die": Transacting sexualities in a feminism classroom in Singapore' (2004, *Critical Asian Studies*), 'The politics of representation: Negotiating crisis in a feminism classroom' (2007, *Australian Feminist Studies*), and, more recently, 'Developing social literacy: Assessment strategies in a feminism class' (2012, *Developing Literacies through Alternative Assessments*), and 'Interrogating Gender' (forthcoming). She has also contributed articles on identity construction, including '"You see me no up": Is Singlish a problem?' (2003, *Language Problems and Language Planning*) and 'Celebrating Singapore's development: An analysis of the millennium stamps' (2004, *Systemic Functional Linguistics and Critical Discourse Analysis*, Lynne Young and Claire Harrison, eds.), and, most recently, on education, 'Mentorship in teacher training' (2013). She is currently the Associate Provost (Undergraduate Education) and can be contacted at pvochh@nus.edu.sg.

Priti Chopra has a PhD in Education (King's College, University of London) and an MA in Language Studies (University of Lancaster). She has worked in the UK and in India as an education practitioner and researcher for over eighteen years. She is, currently, an International Coordinator and a Senior Lecturer in Education at the University of Greenwich. Her research interests are in the areas of: borderless higher education and the internationalisation of higher of education; intercultural learning and inclusive curriculum development; multilingualism and second language acquisition; technology enhanced learning and digital literacies; global education policy and practice; and widening participation and social justice.

Gráinne Conole is Professor of Learning Innovation and the director of the Beyond Distance Research Alliance at the University of Leicester, UK. Prior to this, she was Chair of E-Learning at the Institute of Educational Technology, The Open University, UK. Gráinne has research interests in the use, integration and evaluation of Information and Communication Technologies and e-learning and impact on organisational change.

Savita Datta has a PhD in Physics from the University of Delhi and has held the office of the Principal, Maitreyi College since 2004 along with the additional charge of Director, Campus of Open Learning, since 2006 and visiting faculty at Institute of Informatics and Communication, University of Delhi since 1998. She has several papers/publications to her credit and is supervising PhD students. She has conducted training workshops to familiarise university teachers with content creation for e-learning and has been a resource person at several faculty training programmes. She led a delegation from the University of Delhi to The Open University, UK, to initiate a Blended-Learning Project under the UKIERI Programme which she is supervising as director. She has also initiated a partnership with Edinburgh's Telford College, Scotland, to design and develop a course in media and animation with provision of exchange of students. She is the National Coordinator of Pan African e-Network Project of the University of Delhi, and a member of the Academic Council of Centum Learning Limited, Distance Education Council (DEC) of India, Industry Advisory Council of NIIT, Governing Body of Cluster Innovation Centre of the University of Delhi and CBSE and National Committee of Education of CII.

Rosalind Duhs is a Senior Teaching Fellow at the Centre for the Advancement of Learning and Teaching (CALT), University College London (UCL). She works with the School of Life and Medical Sciences supporting the professional development of university teachers. She also runs courses across the university on a range of pedagogical approaches, including some for new teachers and teaching assistants. Rosalind has worked in higher education in Stockholm, Sweden, and helped to set up a centre for the development of teaching and learning there, designing a range of courses on teaching and assessment. She is bilingual and in close touch with Sweden. She is particularly interested in the assessment of student learning and the provision of feedback to students on their work and is a practitioner of the Association for Educational Assessment, Europe. She holds a Master of Education in post-compulsory learning (The Open University, 2001). Her PhD thesis was a comparative study of academic staff at research-intensive universities learning to teach in higher education in England and Sweden.

Anders Flodström is the Vice-chairman of the EIT, the European Institute of Innovation and Technology Governing Board and the Chairman of .se, the Foundation for the Swedish Internet Infrastructure. Professor Anders Flodström is a former University Chancellor at the Swedish National Agency for Higher Education (HSV). Since 1985 he has been a Professor in Physics at the Royal Institute of Technology (KTH) in Stockholm, Sweden. He has been the Secretary General of the Swedish Research Council for Engineering Sciences, President of the Knowledge foundation and the President at Linköping University, Sweden. He was the President at the Royal Institute of Technology (KTH), Stockholm Sweden until mid-2007 when he was appointed as the University Chancellor for Sweden. He is member of the Swedish Academy for the Engineering Sciences (IVA) and Swedish Engineering Academy in Finland (STV). He is honorary doctor at Riga Technical University in Latvia, honorary doctor at the Aalto University in Finland and honorary professor at Dalian University of Technology and Zhe Jiang University, in China. He is a member of the advisory board of Tallinn Technical University in Estonia. Anders Flodström has written about 300 articles in international scientific journals and a number of books. He has supervised almost forty PhD and numerous Master students. He is a referee for Physical Review and Surface Science. Anders Flodström started his career in Palo Alto, USA, as researcher at Xerox PARC. He has been a guest professor at HASYlab in Hamburg, Germany, and at National Bureau of Standard in Gaithersburg, USA. He was the first Director of MAX synchrotron radiation laboratory in Lund Sweden.

Camille B. Kandiko is a Research Fellow at King's Learning Institute, King's College London. Her research focuses on international and comparative higher education, with areas of interest in curriculum and the student experience, interdisciplinarity, PhD supervision, and developing the use of concept mapping. She co-convenes the Student Experience Network through the Society for Research into Higher Education. Before taking up her post at the Institute, she was project associate at Indiana University- Bloomington (USA) working on the National Survey of Student Engagement (NSSE). Camille holds a first degree in English and Classics from Cornell University (USA) and a Masters degree in Higher Education Administration from the University of Pennsylvania (USA). She was awarded her PhD by Indiana University-Bloomington (USA).

María José Lemaitre, sociologist with graduate studies in education, is currently Executive Director of CINDA, a network of universities in Latin America and Europe. She is the current President of the International Network for Quality Assurance Agencies in Higher Education, INQAAHE, and past president of the Iberoamerican Network for Quality Assurance in Higher Education, RIACES. She is a member of the Advisory Council for the International Quality Group of the Council for Higher Education Accreditation of the United States (CHEA) and of the Advisory Council of

ANECA, the quality assurance agency in Spain. She was in charge of the design and implementation of quality assurance processes in Chile between 1990 and 2007; has published many articles; and has provided consultancy services to governmental agencies, higher education institutions and international organisations in South and Central America, the Caribbean, the Middle East, Africa, Eastern Europe and Southeast Asia.

Shuiyun Liu works in Faculty of Education, Beijing Normal University (China) as a lecturer. Her main research interests include higher education, quality assessment, and educational policy. Dr. Liu got her PhD from the Institute of Education (IOE), University of London in September 2011. Her doctoral research was funded by the Centenary Scholarship at the IOE. Prior to this, she studied at the University of Oslo, University of Tampere and University of Aveiro for a MPhil degree in higher education, which was funded by the Erasmus Mundus Programme of Europe. Her latest publication is a book chapter in *Accountability in Higher Education: Global Perspectives on Trust and Power,* entitled 'Accountability in China: Primitive attempts' (2010, pp.73–92). She also published a paper in *Higher Education Management and Policy,* entitled 'Quality assessment of undergraduate education in China: A policy analysis' (2008, vol. 20, pp.79–96). In addition, she has recently contributed a chapter to the book, *External Quality Audits: Has it Improved Quality Assurance in Universities?,* which is going to be published soon.

Veena Mishra is Deputy Dean, Foreign Students, at University of Delhi holding the post for more than a year. She is Associate Professor in Physics in Maitreyi College, University of Delhi. She has experience of over twenty-three years of teaching physics to undergraduate students. Dr. Mishra was a member of the organising committee of the national workshop on 'Quality Assurance' sponsored by University Grants Commission, India. She has been the coordinator of the physics strand in a UKIERI project on Blended Learning, initiated by Delhi University. She has worked on a blended learning project related to laboratory work in undergraduate physics. She has been a reviewer in 'Mathematical reviews'. Dr. Mishra has published a few papers on physics in reputed international journals. She has presented papers and attended national and international workshops. Dr. Mishra has a master's degree and a PhD in Theoretical Physics from University of Delhi.

Gabriel B. Reedy is a Lecturer in Higher Education at King's Learning Institute, King's College London. His teaching and research focus on the intersection of technology, pedagogy, and higher education, especially in practice-based disciplines and fields such as business, healthcare, and education. Prior to this, he was a Curriculum Innovation Fellow at The Open University, UK, designing technology-enabled blended and distance learning courses.

Arlys van Wyk holds the position of Head of the Unit for Academic Literacy at the University of the Free State in Bloemfontein South Africa. She has been working in the field of academic literacy and student access for the past sixteen years. Her research focuses on academic literacy development and the language needs of English second- language students.

Thushari Welikala is a Research Fellow in Participatory Research at Liverpool Hope University, UK. Before joining Hope University, she was a Senior Research Fellow at the University of Nottingham and previously, worked as a Research Officer at the Institute of Education, University of London. She has contributed to a number of research projects funded by major funding bodies: Leverhulme Trust, British Academy, Higher Education Academy, European Union and Leadership Foundation for Higher Education. Her main research focus is on internationalisation of higher education and the mediation of culture in learning. Thushari's research experience extends to higher education curricular and pedagogy, inclusion, lifelong learning and teacher education across different contexts. She co-authored the book *Improving Intercultural Learning Experience in Higher Education: Responding to Cultural Scripts for Learning* (Institute of Education Press 2008). Thushari holds a Masters degree in Education and International Development and a PhD in higher education from the Institute of Education, University of London

Mark Weyers was a Senior Teaching Fellow in the UCL Centre for the Advancement of Learning and Teaching at University College London. His area of expertise is in the learning sciences, with a specialisation that revolves around advanced and innovative approaches to course and curriculum design. His previous roles have involved working with university academics to develop strategies and implementation plans that focus on enhancing the student learning experience across an institution. At UCL he designed and led a UK Higher Education Academy (HEA) accredited continuing professional development scheme for UCL staff and postgraduate students. He has worked with a large number of university departments and programme teams to redesign their teaching and assessment systems to enhance student learning and satisfaction and has led on the design and development of a number of learning technology innovations. He holds undergraduate and graduate degrees in education, psychology, educational psychology, neuropsychology, educational leadership and management and has a professional qualification in e-learning. His previous research interests have focused on how students' perceptions of the teaching–learning environment (teaching, assessment and environmental factors) influence their approaches to studying. In addition, his work has involved looking at how classroom-based activities and assessments can be designed to encourage students to engage at a deeper level with their course (i.e. problem solving; critical thinking). His book, *Teaching the*

FE Curriculum: Encouraging Active Learning in the Classroom (Continuum, 2006), focuses on practical techniques, based on scholarly research, for actively engaging students in the classroom. Mark now works at the International Institute of Academic Development (IIAD) and is the founder and director of the virtual academic development centre at the IIAD. He has worked with academics, colleges and universities in Canada, Ireland, UK, The Netherlands, Australia, New Zealand and across the Middle East running academic development programmes in teaching, e-learning and leadership and he has run workshops for institutions on the design, development and strategic implementation of accredited professional development schemes and staff support that supports an institution's strategic priorities for teaching and learning.

Nan Yeld holds the position of Dean: Centre for Higher Education Development at the University of Cape Town. Her research has focused on the development of widely used assessment instruments aimed at broadening access to higher education, and theoretical studies of test validation in relation to educational provision in higher education, focusing on the challenges of diversity and educational disadvantage.

Preface

Higher education is indeed a global business. There are millions of students studying all over the world outside their own countries. Rather than studying at home they choose to go abroad to get a degree in a foreign university. Others remain at home but take a degree awarded by a foreign institution in one of their own country's universities. Some countries are large exporters of students; others are mainly recipients of students from other countries. This international trade in both undergraduates and postgraduates has grown greatly in recent years, fuelled by rapid economic growth in countries with large populations, in particular China and India. In these countries, the growth of a middle class, which aspires to educational success for their children and perceives the added benefit of a university degree from well established, high status, higher education systems such as those of the USA and the UK, has made a rapid expansion of this global market possible.

This fascinating collection of essays sets out to chart the development of what the editors call the global student experience. Part 1 of the book defines the boundaries of the global market and considers such questions as cultural differences in learning, the nature of graduate attributes and employability, and the development of global online learning in higher education, and moves towards a globalised undergraduate curriculum. Part 2 consists of a number of case studies of the student experience in various countries. It also includes a chapter on the EU and Bologna.

Undoubtedly the development of English as the world's most important language and the realisation by ambitious young people, whose mother tongue is not English, that fluency in writing and speaking it, is a key to their advancement in a global world is central to global higher education. Moreover, it is one of the reasons why the English speaking countries of the USA, Canada, the UK and Australia have been able to bag a large share of the international market. The governments of Australia and the UK, in particular, have invested in the marketing of their education systems around the world seeing higher education as an important export which could generate large returns for their economies. As the Minister responsible for developing what was known as the Prime Minister's Initiative under Tony Blair, I was astounded by how successful it was in reaching our targets for international student recruitment well in advance of the deadlines we set. UK universities were fleet-footed and entrepreneurial in promoting their degree programmes under the national banner of a newly branded British higher education system, which was persuasive in its marketing techniques. The Australian government's campaign was also highly successful in tempting foreign nationals to study there.

In continental Europe the share in the market has been much lower, although the authors of the Bologna chapter in this collection make clear that the pursuit of a larger share was not the prime motivator of the Bologna initiative. However, as a participant in both Bologna and the Sorbonne Declaration the previous year, I believe it was a factor in the search for a common framework for higher education across Europe. European Ministers were only too aware of the danger of missing out in the competition to recruit more students from outside Europe. Nevertheless the main thrust of the debate was to promote intra-European student mobility through a common framework to be adopted by each country participating. But it is not true that to promote Europe as a destination for students from elsewhere was entirely absent from the thinking behind Bologna.

In the years since the Bologna process was initiated the emphasis has shifted somewhat towards discussion about Quality Assurance and new approaches to learning. These focus on learning outcomes which emphasise skills and competencies, creativity and the ability to innovate. This contrasts with the traditional approach of many European systems which focuses on discipline based acquisition of knowledge. In this sense Bologna has succeeded in a way I never anticipated at the time to move European Higher Education closer to the needs of the knowledge society. Knowing things is no longer enough. How to use knowledge and apply it to the problems we face has to be central to what students learn. As this became accepted national boundaries may become of diminishing importance. But are we really ready to move towards a European degree as the authors imply? I doubt it. After all there is still no such thing as a British degree: the variety in content, form, teaching and outcomes is very extensive.

I welcome this book. It is a timely reminder of the scale of globalisation in higher education. I congratulate the editors on putting together such a rich range of essays. It deserves to be widely read by everyone interested in higher education around the world. The authors do not speculate on whether the trends of recent decades will continue with ever more growth in global student mobility. Investments in new universities in countries such as India and China may lead to a levelling off. There will need to be another volume of this kind in 2020 to review just what has taken place between now and then.

Tessa Blackstone
December 2012

Series Editors' Introduction

This series is constructed around the premise that higher education systems are experiencing common pressures for fundamental change, reinforced by differing national and regional circumstances that also impact upon established institutional structures and procedures. There are four major dynamics for change that are of international significance:

1   Mass higher education is a universal phenomenon.
2   National systems find themselves located in an increasingly global marketplace that has particular significance for their more prestigious institutions.
3   Higher education institutions have acquired (or been obliged to acquire) a wider range of obligations, often under pressure from governments prepared to use state power to secure their policy goals.
4   The balance between the public and private financing of higher education has shifted – markedly in some cases – in favour of the latter.

Although higher education systems in all regions and nation states face their own particular pressures for change, these are especially severe in some cases: the collapse of the established economic and political structures of the former Soviet Union along with Central and Eastern Europe, the political revolution in South Africa, the pressures for economic development in India and China, and demographic pressure in Latin America.

Each volume in the series will examine how systems of higher education are responding to this new and demanding political and socio-economic environment. Although it is easy to overstate the uniqueness of the present situation, it is not an exaggeration to say that higher education is undergoing a fundamental shift in its character, and one that is truly international in scope. We are witnessing a major transition in the relationship of higher education to state and society. What makes the present circumstances particularly interesting is to see how different systems – a product of social, cultural, economic and political contexts that have interacted and evolved over time – respond in their own peculiar ways to the changing environment. There is no assumption that the pressures for change have set in motion the trend towards a converging model of higher education, but we do believe that in the present circumstances no understanding of 'the idea of the university' remains sacrosanct.

Although this is a series with an international focus it is not expected that each individual volume should cover every national system of higher education. This would be an impossible task. Whilst aiming for a broad range of case studies, with each volume addressing a particular theme, the focus will be upon the most important and interesting examples of responses to the pressures for change. Most of the individual volumes will bring together a range of comparative quantitative and qualitative information, but the primary aim of each volume will be to present differing interpretations of critical developments in key aspects of the experience of higher education. The dominant overarching objective is to explore the conflict of ideas and the political struggles that inevitably surround any significant policy development in higher education.

It can be expected that volume editors and their authors will adopt their own interpretations to explain the emerging patterns of development. There will be conflicting theoretical positions drawn from the multidisciplinary, and increasingly interdisciplinary, field of higher education research. Thus we can expect in most volumes to find an intermarriage of approaches drawn from sociology, economics, history, political science, cultural studies, and the administrative sciences. However, whilst there will be different approaches to understanding the process of change in higher education, each volume editor(s) will impose a framework upon the volume inasmuch as chapter authors will be required to address common issues and concerns.

This volume in the series is edited by two emerging scholars, Dr Camille Kandiko and Dr Mark Weyers, who throughout its preparation respectively held posts at King's College and University College, University of London. Through its in-depth conceptual analysis, combined with detailed empirical investigation, it represents a very sophisticated approach to higher education research. Moreover, with its focus upon the student experience it addresses what many would consider to be the most critical topic in the study of higher education. The student experience is placed in a global context, critically examining how it assumes different meanings in contrasting national and regional environments. At the same time it traces the forces that are reshaping the student experience with particular reference to the pressures of globalisation. Is the student experience becoming more homogenised or more diversified over time? The volume is truly international and comparative in scope with examples of the student experience drawn from nearly all corners of the globe. The editors and authors embody the complex and dynamic flows of academics, students and policies that are part of the increasingly international higher education landscape.

David Palfreyman
Director of OxCHEPS, New College, University of Oxford

Ted Tapper
OxCHEPS, New College, University of Oxford

Scott Thomas
Professor of Educational Studies, Claremont Graduate University, California

1

Introduction

The Global Student Experience

CAMILLE B. KANDIKO

This book investigates the national and international strategies, agendas and trends in global higher education to understand how these factors directly impact the student experience. This book has a solid empirical scope and is organised around national agendas and themes that are prominent in global higher education. However, what internationalisation and globalisation mean around the world vary immensely. Perspectives from the West are not universally shared throughout the world, and there are multiple regional spheres and networks of globalisation in higher education, such as growing education hubs in the Middle East and South East Asia. Furthermore, countries' participation in the global exchange of students varies, such as India being a low importer of students but a high exporter, China educating large number of students from the East Asian region, and the UK sending relatively few students abroad, whilst being known as a global hub of internationalisation.

Following a global trend, what is termed 'home' and 'international' student differs across countries, and in many ways does not reflect the real experience of higher education for large numbers of students. Across various countries differences in class, ethnic origin, religion, first language or gender play a much larger role. Many of the challenges of educational epistemological backgrounds and frameworks that traditionally arise in the context of international students are significant issues for many home students as well. While taking a broad perspective, we acknowledge that discourses that homogenise student experiences are not useful, and in the book each chapter explores aspects of 'the global student experience' in individual and unique ways.

There are 177 million students in higher education throughout the world today (United Nations Educational, Scientific and Cultural Organization [UNESCO] 2012). This collection provides some indication of what are they are learning and of their wider experiences. It also outlines the changing global context of provision for undergraduate students as countries and universities respond to what they anticipate will be new demands for virtual and more traditional learning in and across subjects of study. It brings together contributions from a range of authors to focus on common themes internationally, combined with descriptions of the student experience in national higher education systems. This affords insight into what students can expect from emerging patterns of provision worldwide. It also informs institutional decision makers as they attempt to meet changing international student demand within their own national circumstances of retrenchment or expansion in competition with private, public and for-profit rivals at home and abroad.

This panorama of provision is designed for a worldwide readership through a team of expert contributors who relate their experience and knowledge to shared global concerns. Thus, the big picture of economic and political globalisation is combined with examination of its various aspects, such as cultural differences in learning, the role of academic literacy, its distance provision and quality in the context of competition, what a globally connected undergraduate curriculum can offer, and the shift of the role of higher education in the assessment and employability of graduates. At the same time, in an increasingly open market there are also restrictions upon student travel and residence in many polities, and increasingly variable fees for home and international students. These pan-global themes are combined with perspectives from Western higher education, including several chapters by authors who are themselves international academics, contrasted with systems in different cultural contexts, such as Southeast Asia, Africa and South America, as well as the new giants China and India. This international and comparative approach works to move beyond the 'false dichotomies' (Ryan and Louie 2007), such as those between Western and Confucian thought, that can polarise the study of internationalisation of higher education.

This book aims to explore themes that affect mobile students around the world, and the experiences of students in different countries – students in their home countries, students that leave to study abroad and incoming international students. This approach, although acknowledging a Western-influenced point of departure, is designed to take a wider, more global perspective. Hopefully this will instigate more international, comparative and global research into the study of students in higher education.

The Higher Education Context

Recent policy developments are putting even more power and control of higher education in the hands of students, raising issues about the quality, diversity and outcomes of the student experience. The global shift towards mass higher education coincided with the economic period of neoliberal expansion, now entering a new period of austerity. During this economic period, the US student experience has been generalised to many parts of the world where it has largely superseded previous dual track academic and vocational systems, although European exceptions remain. In the period of consolidation that can be anticipated there may be some return to these systems, while some countries – notably India and China – are developing their own national higher education systems but with reliance upon either importing teaching and accreditation expertise – in some cases whole 'offshore campuses', like England's University of Nottingham in Ningbo, China – or upon exporting students.

Nevertheless, there are over 4.1 million tertiary students studying outside their countries of citizenship, representing a fivefold increase in the last thirty-six years and a 99 per cent increase since 2000 (Organisation for Economic Co-operation and Development 2012). This widening participation in higher education has had both convergent and divergent effects within higher education systems. Therefore, there is even more need for students to consider their choices of institutions in which to study, and for many students this includes regional, national and international options. Also, it is important for institutions to consider their investments in distance and overseas' provision, as providers of international student services and as gateways for student and staff exchange. This widening of participation, growth in locations, shifts in provision and the increasing diversity of students is moving the traditional binary of 'domestic' and 'international' into a much more fluid, dynamic and complex world. We use the term 'global student experience' to capture the diversity within the experiences of students in higher education around the world. Rather than acting as a homogenising force, we adopt a 'global' view to signify the mutual trends of convergence and divergence within globalisation theory, and to explore what that means in specific aspects of the student experience and across different countries and regions in the world.

As higher education shifts from being considered a public good to a private good, the future of the student market is extremely uncertain. Changes in national higher education funding, tightening immigration laws and supra-national collaborations are likely to significantly alter the global movement of students. The degree to and directions in which it may develop are the subject of intense speculation. This book informs these discussions with the authoritative chapters of its contributors who examine various aspects of the global student experience without losing sight of the very basic questions of what the 177 million students are learning and how or whether their qualifications contribute to their future employment and other prospects as well as to the cultures and economies of their home countries.

Like the growth in trade during the recent expansive phase of globalised capitalism, there have been winners and losers in the international exchange of students and the global knowledge economy. Over half of all international students study in five countries: the US, the UK, Germany, France and Australia (OECD 2012). Over half of all internationally mobile students are from Asia (OECD 2012). There are varied flows of higher level knowledge communicated via new information and communications technology. This has posed questions of validity that have both undermined and reinforced the positions of the dominant authorities and their quality regimes across governments and institutions. What developments can be anticipated and how will these present themselves in a recessionary economic climate or in the conditions of a new recovery? In either case, the uninterrupted growth of educational goods and services is unlikely to be maintained at its previous levels. What forms of consolidation of markets and institutions can be anticipated internationally and how will these be experienced by students and staff of the new global higher education scene?

The Student Experience

There is no universal 'student experience' or 'international student experience'; there is great diversity in what is even meant by such terms. In diversified mass higher education systems, students often lack common experiences, teaching practices or assessments, and there is a resulting challenge to measure or evaluate the range of outcomes from higher education (Chatman 2007). However, 'the student experience' has been adopted around the world as an umbrella term for student-related aspects of higher education. For example, the UK Quality Assurance Agency for Higher Education (QAA)'s (2012) research into the student learning experience focused on the following areas: teaching of courses; feedback and assessment; student engagement; student representation; public information and informing student choice; complaints and appeals; academic support; and other aspects that help form a high quality experience. The UK Higher Education Policy Institute (HEPI) report (Bekhradnia 2012) on various aspects of the student experience included the amount of contact students have with their staff, the size of teaching groups, the overall number of hours they devote to their studies and perceptions of value for money. The US Student Experience in the Research University project at University of California Berkeley explores:

> how students of diverse backgrounds and with varying economic pressures and competing obligations organize their time, define their academic purposes, respond to the curriculum and the extra-curricular opportunities for intellectual development, and make use of the resources of the institution.
>
> (Center for Studies in Higher Education 2011: 1)

Two dominant aspects of research on the student experience are collecting feedback from students themselves on their experience and the institutional commitment to enhancing the student experience.

The US Association of Public and Land-Grant Universities commissioned the Kellogg Report on the student experience, which reported:

> We can invent quite different institutions if we reaffirm three broad ideals and adhere to them tenaciously, following their implications faithfully

wherever they lead: (1) Our institutions must become *genuine learning communities*, supporting and inspiring faculty, staff, and learners of all kinds. (2) Our learning communities should be *student centered*, committed to excellence in teaching and to meeting the legitimate needs of learners, wherever they are, whatever they need, whenever they need it. (3) Our learning communities should emphasize the importance of *a healthy learning environment* that provides students, faculty, and staff with the facilities, support, and resources they need to make this vision a reality.

(Kellogg Commission 1997: vii–viii)

A recent study into the student experience in world-class universities in China, following on from Projects 211 and 985, affirmed this notion of the nexus of the institutional approach and the experiences of students, finding that the 'college environment (academic, campus, and interpersonal) affect students' learning and living experience, and b) students' learning and living experience impact the development of creating world-class research institutions in China' (Chan 2012: 1).

Across research into the student experience, there is a noted danger of 'quantity underwriting quality' (Hellstén and Prescott 2004: 351), with more attention paid to marketing and recruiting than learning and teaching. Ainley (2008) calls for research into the student experience of both what is taught and what is learnt, across diverse groups of students. For example, foreign language speakers may be learning multiple new languages, in terms of an 'everyday' new language, but also the language of the discipline and of the host higher education context.

Ryan (2011) describes three phases, beginning in the early 1990s, of approaches to teaching and learning for international students across UK and Australian higher education. The first was to 'fix' students, and to get them to adapt to the Western educational context. This was followed by a shift to 'fix' teachers and institutions, and for them to accommodate international students, and augment their learning experiences. The current phase adopts a broader perspective on integration of international students into the teaching and learning experience. This is seen through calls for social and academic integration of students (Montgomery 2010), greater intercultural fluency across the curriculum (Ramsden 2008) and the promotion of global citizenship (Gacel-Ávila 2005). The phases Ryan (2011) describes highlight the tension in educational responsibility for students and their learning experiences. The chapters in the first part explore themes that raise common educational challenges across countries. Some of these use case studies from Western institutions, others highlight issues from a distinct perspective, such as academic literacy and language in the South African context, and some move to new stances, such as the global consequences of virtual education.

This book aims to show the similarities and diversity of experiences, policies, challenges and systems around the world. There are perspectives from Western contexts, looking within the complexity and diversity of such systems, and wider perspectives from regions around the world. This is mirrored by the chapters which highlight the global flow of international students, which goes beyond a Western-intake model. There is also acknowledgement that the US-style student experience is not universal, nor is the funding model; globalisation has led to both a convergence and divergence in policies and realities on the ground. Many countries have maintained dual track systems, particularly in European countries such as Germany and The Netherlands. Many have not adopted neoliberal funding models, for example Finland, Iceland and Norway (and until 2012, Sweden) have not charged international students tuition fees and many countries operate largely insular higher education systems, as seen in Chile (UNESCO 2012). However, the global flow of students is increasing, and in dynamic ways, with large swings in enrolments across countries from year to year based on political and economic shifts; regulatory policies, particularly those around student visas; and high profile incidents involving student safety.

From the International to the Global Student

In much of Western higher education, the dominant discourse on internationalisation is founded on a globalised economic agenda that positions higher education as an export sector. In the policy sphere internationalisation is often considered for economic reasons, and within higher education institutions as a necessary challenge in terms of structures and governance (de Wit 2002) and its financial implications (Larsen, Morris and Martin 2001).

Although globally there is focus on competition within the internationalisation agenda, (Marginson 2006), there are critiques of the marketisation of internationalisation (De Vita and Case 2003; Kehm and Teichler 2007; Mok 2003). Alternative perspectives on internationalisation identify how it can be used as a vehicle to support diversity, access and equity for all learners (Montgomery 2010). To this end, the lenses of interculturalism and inclusion help to identify a precise tension between internationalisation being part of a global capitalist agenda, or being a means to move towards 'global understanding' (Teichler 2004).

Within the dynamic landscape of higher education, internationalisation is often used to gesture to calls for increased diversity. However, this diversity is itself maintained within strict discursive limits. As the 'international student' emerges as an increasingly familiar archetype within much of Western higher education, there is a concern that, at an apparent moment of recognition, significant swathes of an international student population are occluded. However, internationalisation can be used to recognise wider indices of diversity (Banks 2002).

There are calls for more study into the diversity within the international student population (Harrison and Peacock 2010), and an increasing blur between the boundaries of 'home' and 'international', concepts that fail to capture differences across the student body in many countries. At present, rather than promoting inclusion, conceptual frames emerging in the internationalisation literature can polarise and homogenise 'home' and 'international' students. A danger in higher education is that international students and other minorities are regarded as the 'diverse ones', 'leaving the majority identities unmarked and unexamined. This is highly problematic because it reproduces invisibility and normalcy of the majority identities and thus the privileges associated with being free of such critical examination' (Laker and Davis 2009: 254).

Practically, many staff and students are concerned about misconceptions, stereotyping or lack of knowledge, but find these issues difficult to discuss because of their political, personal and sensitive nature. This can lead to tensions in classrooms and can negatively impact on the student learning experience, for all students. This speaks to gaps in our knowledge of how universities frame their understanding of internationalisation, how academics construct meanings of inclusive practice and the conditions that actually make a difference for diverse and international student groups. As the notion of internationalisation gains increasing (pedagogic) credence, it becomes necessary to engage with the term critically in terms of the student experience.

Overview of the Book

The chapters in this book investigate internationalisation and globalisation and their relation to the student experience, curriculum and pedagogy. Specifically, the chapters engage with international students' experiences within and beyond the classroom, and, for some students, beyond the walls of institutions altogether. The chapters draw on a range of case studies, empirical studies, interviews with students, official statistics and expert research. Throughout the book, the meaning of 'international' students is challenged. For example in the UK, it is useful to problematise the boundary between international, and 'domestic/home' student. English is not the first language for a significant number of home students. Competing issues around the globe include: the current policy context for internationalisation; changes in funding and regulatory policies; student identities; and curriculum frameworks in diverse societies. The book seeks to investigate an inclusive internationalisation agenda that encompasses wider forms of diversity, understanding and attention to the student experience for all students. Outcomes of this include: models for inclusive classroom practice; the development of institutional-level curriculum policy; and national and international debate and development of higher education.

This book promotes attention for more global and diverse students and a curriculum framework for greater understanding and inclusion for use inside and outside the classroom. Such frameworks look very different around the world, and need to address specific local issues, as well as linking in with wider student support functions. This identifies a number of tasks for leading and managing a diverse student body including fostering new meanings about identity and internationalisation; promoting inclusive practices and learning environments; and developing relationships between universities and the communities in which they are situated. Such a framework also provides diverse students with capabilities and skills necessary in the modern global workforce. To this end, the book is divided into two main sections. The first part, 'Emerging issues of the global student experience', presents the overarching themes that are exemplified in subsequent examples of national, regional and international provision. Each chapter covers an introduction and overview of the theme; differences, challenges and opportunities for international and home students; the role of the theme within the student experience; and international issues and comparisons of the theme.

The second part, 'Exploring the student experience: International perspectives', presents examples of institutional, national, regional and international provision. These chapters cover an introduction reflecting upon the major themes of the book and how they relate to the student experience in the country; the context of the country's higher education system; the student experience in the country, the experience of international students in the country, and the experience of country students internationally, including destinations, the quality of experience, and the role of international degrees within and beyond the country. Each chapter concludes with a reflective prognosis.

The concluding chapter draws the above chapters together comparatively to consider whether the international student experience is becoming increasingly homogeneous or whether new divergences can be anticipated. What new forms of international provision and collaboration can be predicted?

References

Ainley, P. (2008). The varieties of student experience. *Studies in Higher Education*, 33(5), 615–624.

Banks, J.A. (2002). *An introduction to multicultural education* (3rd ed.). Boston, MA: Allyn & Bacon.

Bekhradnia, B. (2012) *The academic experience of students in English universities*. HEPI Report. Oxford: HEPI.

Center for Studies in Higher Education (CSHE) (2011). Student experience in the Research University (SERU) Project Mission. Available at: http://cshe.berkeley.edu/research/seru/mission.htm.

Chan, R.Y. (2012). Students' learning and living experience at world-class universities in China: a comparative case study of the University of Hong Kong (HKU) and Shanghai Jiao Tong University (SJTU). The 56th Annual Comparative and International Education Society (CIES) Conference, 24 April 2012, San Juan, Puerto Rico.

Chatman, S. (2007). *Institutional versus academic discipline measures of student experience: a matter of relative validity.* University of California Center for Studies in Higher Education, Research & Occasional Paper Series: CSHE.8.07. Berkeley, CA: CSHE.

De Vita, G and Case, P. (2003). Rethinking the internationalisation agenda in UK higher education. *Journal of Further and Higher Education,* 27(4), 383–398.

de Wit, H. (2002). *Internationalization of higher education in the United States of America and Europe: a historical, comparative and conceptual analysis.* Westport, CT: Greenwood.

Gacel-Ávila, J. (2005) The internationalisation of higher education: a paradigm for global citizenry, *Journal of Studies in International Education,* 9(2), 121–136.

Harrison, N. and Peacock, N. (2010). Cultural distance, mindfulness and passive xenophobia: using Integrated Threat Theory to explore home higher education students' perspectives on 'internationalisation at home'. *British Educational Research Journal,* 36, 877–902.

Hellstén, M. and Prescott, A. (2004). Learning at university: the international student experience. *International Education Journal,* 5(3), 344–351.

Kehm, B.M., and Teichler, U. (2007). Research on internationalization of higher education. *Journal of Studies in International Education,* 11, 260–273.

Kellogg Commission. (1997). *Returning to our roots: the student experience.* Washington, DC: Author.

Laker, J.A. and Davis, T.L. (2009). Continuing the journey towards multicultural campus communities, in McClellan, G.S., Stringer, J., and Barr, M.J. (Eds.). *The handbook of student affairs administration* (pp. 242–264). San Francisco, CA: Jossey-Bass.

Larsen, K., Morris, R., and Martin, J.P. (2001). *Trade in educational services: trends and emerging issues (Working Paper).* Paris: Organisation for Economic Co-operation and Development.

Marginson, S. (2006). Dynamics of national and global competition in higher education. *Higher Education,* 52, 1–39.

Mok, K. (2003). Globalization and higher education restructuring in Hong Kong, Taiwan and Mainland China. *Higher Education Research and Development,* 22: 117–129.

Montgomery, C. (2010). *Understanding the international student experience.* London: Palgrave Macmillan.

Organisation for Economic Co-operation and Development (OECD) (2012). *Education at a glance 2012.* Paris: OECD.

Quality Assurance Agency for Higher Education (QAA) (2012). Student engagement projects: research into the student experience. Available at: http://www.qaa.ac.uk/Partners/students/projects/Pages/Strand-1.aspx.

Ramsden, P. (2008) *The future of higher education. teaching and the student experience.* York: Higher Education Academy.

Ryan, J. (2011). Teaching and learning for international students: towards a transcultural approach. *Teachers and Teaching,* 17(6), 631–648.

Ryan, J. and Louie, K. (2007), False dichotomy? 'Western' and 'Confucian' concepts of scholarship and learning. *Educational Philosophy and Theory*, 39, 404–417.

Teichler, U. (2004). The changing debate on internationalization of higher education. *Higher Education*, 48, 5–26.

United Nations Educational, Scientific and Cultural Organization (UNESCO) (2012). *Global education digest 2012*. Paris: UNESCO Institute for Statistics.

Part 1
Emerging Issues of the Global
Student Experience

2
Students in a Global Market

CAMILLE B. KANDIKO

Global forces affecting higher education, which include mass enrolment and issues of access privatisation and affordability, decentralisation and accountability, can be united through the process of globalisation. For Bloom (2004), 'globalization refers to the process whereby countries become more integrated via movements of goods, capital, labor, and ideas' (59). The view of globalisation as an intensification of relations between the local and the global is shared by many as a holistic definition (Held 1991; Wiseman 1998). It has been argued that in education globalisation leads both to convergence, which emphasises homogenisation processes, and to divergence, which emphasises different, pluralistic and localised responses to global forces (Vaira 2004).

Education, particularly at the post-secondary level, is entering the global economic market. The discussion surrounding the inclusion of education in the General Agreement on Trade in Services (GATS) through the World Trade Organization (WTO) has shifted higher education from the public to the private domain (Altbach 2004). In turn, the political and economic repercussions of globalisation can be seen in higher education. The resulting changes include declining public funding, a concentration of research funds in the science and technology fields and expanded relationships with corporations (Slaughter and Leslie 1997). 'Globalization has brought the free market into universities but with serious ramifications and significant costs' (Currie and Newson 1998, 6).

Although there are many facets of globalisation, neoliberal forms of globalisation concentrate on the political and economic aspects that most strongly affect education (Morrow and Torres 2003). The neoliberal theories focus on the role of the market and the reduction of the social welfare state (Friedman 1981, 1991; Olssen and Peters 2005). Neoliberal theories help to explain changes in education policy, the role of faculty, and student behaviour and attitude in response to global forces. The repercussions of these theories are seen in higher education. The resulting changes include declining public funding, a concentration of research funds in the technology and science fields, and expanded relationships with corporations (Slaughter and Rhoades 2004). This chapter uses neoliberal theories to explore the changing nature of the student experience, particularly the relationship between academic staff and students in higher education.

Neoliberalism

Rhoades and Torres (2006) argue that globalisation is the vehicle of neoliberalism, which in turn has marked the character of globalisation, although this relationship is not inevitable. Rather, it is the consequence of political and economic decisions. A neoliberal account of globalisation is:

> A discourse about progress and a rising tide that lifts all boats, a discourse that takes advantage of the historical processes of globalization in order to valorize particular economic prescriptions about how to operate the economy (through free trade, deregulation, and so on)—and by implication, prescriptions about how to transform education, politics, and culture.
>
> (Burbules and Torres 2000, 13)

Neoliberalism is an ideology based on individual economic rationality and the idea that a weak state is better than a strong state, and what is private is necessarily good and what is public is necessarily bad (Apple 2000). This ideology calls for a dismantling of the Keynesian welfare state and the withdrawal of the state from the economy (Hay 2004; Marginson 1997). Neoliberalism promotes the policies of deregulation (freeing capital mobility), privatisation, and liberalisation (including weakening trade protection and tariff reductions) (Stromquist 2002).

The modern development of globalisation and neoliberalism are closely intertwined. Neoliberalism developed as an alliance of theories and interest groups centred around cultural conservatism and economic liberalism under the governments of Margaret Thatcher in England, Ronald Reagan in the United States, and Brian Mulroney in Canada (Morrow and Torres 2003). 'Neoliberal governments promote notions of open markets, free trade, reduction of the public sector, decreased state intervention in the economy, and the deregulation of markets' (Morrow and Torres 2003, 97). The goals of the neoliberal ideology are to reduce fiscal pressure on public enterprises by privatisation and to deregulate practices of the state (Hay 2004; Torres and Rhoades 2006). It is important to distinguish between globalisation as a process of increased connectedness and communication and a conception of neoliberal forms of globalisation that incorporate market ideology and business practices. This chapter uses the term 'neoliberalism' to encompass the political and economic aspects of globalisation that are affecting higher education.

Globalisation, Neoliberalism and Higher Education

The influence of globalisation on higher education can be viewed through neoliberal ideology; this encompasses ideologies of the market; new institutional economics based on cost-recovery and entrepreneurialism; accountability and new managerialism (Ball 1998). Neoliberalism manifests in three major trends in higher education: privatisation, commercialisation and corporatisation (Kezar 2004). Neoliberal economic policies in higher education are characterised by the growth of capitalist and corporate influence (Chomsky 1998). 'In the neoliberal model higher education is ideally integrated into the system of production and accumulation in which knowledge is reduced to its economic functions and contributes to the realization of individual economic utilities' (Morrow 2006, xxxi).

Much current research in higher education revolves around changes wrought by neoliberalism, including: recruitment of international students (Jiang 2008); academic stratification of the disciplines (Gumport 2000; Rhoades and Slaughter 1997); knowledge transfer (Gaffikin and Perry 2009); privatisation (Ehrenberg 2006); the rise of managerialism in higher education (Deem 2001), particularly the adoption of practices and values from the private sector such as accountability; corporatisation (Rhoades and Rhoades 2005); commercialisation of athletics, research, and the educational process in higher education (Bok 2003); students as consumers and customers (Naidoo 2003); and a global trend of increasing consumerism and corporatism inside the classroom (Boyles 2007). Neoliberalism is also related to recent shifts in higher education funding towards the hard and applied sciences (fields close to the market) and away from the social sciences and humanities. Torres and Rhoades note:

> Knowledge is now evaluated with the language of finance, and universities are measured by their efficiency in awarding degrees and certificates. Academic leaders are replaced by managers with business backgrounds, and the university shifts from an educational institution to just another business with a bottom line.
>
> (2006, 32)

The neoliberal economic agenda is leading to a decrease in funding for public services around the world; in education, this agenda attempts 'to weaken public control over education while simultaneously encouraging privatization of the educational service and greater reliance on market forces' (Berman 2003, 253). This coincides with large-scale changes in the economics of academia. There is a contemporaneous shift from positioning higher education as a public good to a private good. There is a global trend of cost sharing in funding higher education, which places a greater burden on individual students (Johnstone 2004).

Slaughter and Leslie (1997) coined the phrase, *academic capitalism*, to explain governments', institutions' and professors' market (like) efforts to secure external funding in response to global political and economic changes. These responses interact with a global push for the development of a well-educated citizenry and surging increases in enrolment.

Students in a Global Market

All higher education students exist in a market. According to UNESCO (2012), there were 3.6 million internationally mobile students in 2009, up from 2.1 million in 2002. Nearly 60 per cent of those students were studying in North America and Western Europe, with 20 per cent in East Asia and the Pacific and another 10 per cent in Central and Eastern Europe. Countries compete to recruit international students, and it can be a volatile market. Due largely to changes in visa policies and several high-profile incidents involving international students, Australia's applications for student visas fell 23 per cent from 2008–09 to 2010–11 (Australian Bureau of Statistics 2011). Many countries also struggle to retain their own bright students. There is also an emerging market in distance and virtual education, where the traditional notion of an 'international student' becomes increasingly blurred.

The market for students exists in a competitive financial context, raising the interest of governments and businesses. However, more the focus of the chapters in this book, competition also emerges in the educational context. Institutions need to be sensitive to cultural differences in learning and also pay attention to academic literacy and language differences. Educational challenges vary across countries and regions in the world, as do the challenges faced by students within different systems and for international students that cross educational systems.

Students are consumers of education, and often pay substantial sums, but they are consumers in more than a financial sense. Students seek a high quality experience, and are savvy about researching and comparing their options. Students place importance on teaching and learning practices and are increasingly attuned to assessment and feedback practices. Institutions are realising the importance of what they offer students, leading to increasing interest in the curriculum, and the role of distinctive curriculum offerings (Blackmore and Kandiko 2012). Around the world, students seek information on employability, across countries, fields of study and institutions. There are related patterns of stratification across disciplines, with student interests often in contrast to those of government and industry. For example, students often choose humanities and social science fields over science, technology, engineering and mathematics (STEM) subjects.

Academic stratification and academic consumerism, along with academic management, are leading to academic restructuring of higher education institutions (Gumport 2000). Academic stratification involves both students as consumers and faculty as managed professionals. Full-time faculty, particularly those who are research-only and research-active, are concentrated in strategic fields, which may or may not coincide with student demand. Contingent faculty are used to fill in supply gaps (Bradley 2004). Stratification occurs between both disciplines and institutions, where the rich are getting richer (Bastedo and Gumport 2003). Neoliberal theories predict greater differentiation within academic disciplines, caused by competition, student demand and market potential.

Changes in Faculty Roles, Responsibilities and Relationships with Students

Although neoliberalism is affecting many aspects of higher education, its influence on faculty roles, responsibilities and relationships with students may be the most pronounced. For example, it seems that globalisation has decreased the value that teaching receives (Marginson and Rhoades 2002; Slaughter 2001), particularly in relation to research, and also increased the fluidity and volatility of the profession (Altbach and Chait 2001). There is increased pressure on academics to pursue outside resources (mostly through external grants), consequently they are less available to students (Slaughter and Rhoades 2004; Sporn 1999). Faculty are measured by hourly productivity, number of students and classes taught, and amount of external research dollars brought in to the institution. This trend manifests in various research assessment schemes that have been adopted by governments to award research funding, such as those developed in the UK, Australia and Denmark, often concentrating funds in a few select research-intensive universities in the process.

The shift to market-like behaviour by faculty and institutions is altering the relationship between faculty and students. For example, neoliberal practices in higher education may discourage interaction between academics and students (Marginson and Considine 2000). As nations try to maximise their development of human capital through educating a larger number of students at a lower cost (Apple 2000; Slaughter 2001), one way to cut costs is by limiting the number of full-time faculty, hiring more contingent faculty and increasing class size, particularly in low-cost fields of study. Faculty in research institutions are encouraged to pursue externally funded research (Slaughter and Rhoades 2004). The increased role of commercial activities has reduced the share of faculty time and resources devoted to students and teaching (Ehrenberg 2006). Such policies are leading to a consistent devaluing of teaching and service (Altbach 1979; Fairweather 1996; Marginson and Rhoades 2002; Slaughter 2001). These changes to the academic profession are occurring despite the documented importance of student–faculty interaction on student performance and attainment (Astin 1993; Feldman and Newcomb 1969; Pascarella and Terenzini 2005). The effect of neoliberal polices on students, faculty, institutions and countries is not uniform. Different government and institutional reactions to globalisation have led to variations in the type and degree of response to global forces.

The changes in faculty roles and responsibilities are in contrast to the overwhelming research on the positive effects of student contact with faculty members. Student–faculty interaction was thoroughly investigated in early higher education research (Astin 1977, 1993; Bean 1985; Bean and Kuh 1984; Ewell 1989; Feldman and Newcomb 1969; Pascarella 1985; Wilson, Gaff, Dienst, Wood and Bavry, 1975) and has been reemphasised in more recent literature (Anaya 2001; Cotten and Wilson 2006; Kim and Sax 2009; Kuh and Hu 2001; Kuh, Kinzie, Buckley, Bridges and Hayek 2006; Pascarella and Terenzini 1991, 2005). However, some recent policy trends in higher education are acknowledging the importance of contact hours and student–faculty interaction. These include the National Student Survey (NSS) in the UK, which has led some low performing programmes to lower their student to faculty ratio.

Policy Implications

There are concerns about the divergence between academic disciplines based on their economic potential (Slaughter and Leslie 1997). Increasingly, this includes a programme's ability to attract international students. In the current age of academic capitalism, 'academic disciplines gain stature almost exclusively through their exchange value on the market, and students now rush to take courses and receive professional credentials that provide them with the cachet they need to sell themselves to the highest bidder' (Giroux 2002, 432). Rhoades and Slaughter (2006) note the privileged fields in the research marketplace are physics, biomedical and life sciences, biotechnology and information sciences; left out are the social sciences, humanities, and fine arts. Palmer (2001) notes the push for research in interdisciplinary centres, relegating the task of educating undergraduates to discipline-based departments. This does not portend well for undergraduate education as government funding increasingly follows research opportunities and not student demand.

A focus on the market value of disciplines ignores important variations in how knowledge is conceptualised and presented to students differently in a range of academic fields (Lindblom-Ylänne, Trigwell, Nevgi and Ashwin 2006). Economic-based logic is only one of many ways of knowing and thinking. There are important civic, cultural and political dimensions of higher education that should not be ignored. Further neoliberal-influenced policies include the shifting financial burden from governments to students and their families, a focus on learning and development outcomes, and questions about whether the current curriculum is providing students with what they need in the new knowledge-based economy (OECD 1996a, 1996b), which 'requires workers with the capacity to learn quickly and to work in teams in reliable and creative ways' (Morrow and Torres 2000, 33). Moreover, many fields of study that are in the strategic interests of governments and industry have low student demand and enrolment.

The study of neoliberalism in higher education is confounded by the often unintended effects of neoliberal policies. In a World Bank report on higher education, Johnstone (1998) noted that neoliberal policies of autonomy, deregulation and privatisation often lead to a convergence of institutional forms and missions, rather than market-inspired entrepreneurial strategic differentiation. Similarly, recent reforms in British higher education, designed to encourage competition and market differentiation, have faced largely uniform reactions from the sector. The push for accountability and quality assurance at regional, national and global levels is leading to the adoption of similar policies in higher education. Such policies affect students around the world, and, along with many facets of globalisation, are leading to both convergence and divergence in higher education and the student experience.

Convergence in Higher Education

National and regional higher education systems have always had a mix of international influences and local variations. This can be found in the US research university system, traditionally seen as a mix of the British residential college and the German research institute; local variations are seen in various grading, honours and degree schemes within and across different countries. One aspect of globalisation is that universities, and higher education systems, are adopting many similar policies. Drivers for this include: opportunities for regional and international cooperation; a desire to be globally competitive; a push to make institutions easier to manage and more transparent; as well as adopting effective and beneficial educational practices.

Regional initiatives such as the Bologna Process are driving standardisation across Europe. However, a large number of countries and regions around the world are also adopting tenets of Bologna to work towards a 'global standard'. International league tables, rankings and institutional groupings lead universities to compete on the same metrics. Global drives to be a 'World-Class University' lead to a convergence of institutional structures, policies and practices. There has been simultaneous attention to 'The Student Experience', often conceived as some sort of global norm.

The processes adopted often have a significant impact on the curriculum, including the modularisation of courses and associated set credit hours and liberal arts-style 'general education' requirements, often two years of a four-year degree with a two-year 'major', in a particular discipline, and often a 'minor', or secondary, area of study. Such trends often include the adoption of increased breadth across the curriculum. The associated award scheme of a grade point average (GPA) (on a four-point scale) has become increasingly popular, and been adopted by universities in the UK and discussed in Hong Kong. In another convergence trend, Japanese universities, starting with the University of Tokyo, are debating moving the academic year start date to autumn to coincide with many leading systems of higher education. Overall, convergence leads to the standardisation of educational structures, processes and outcomes.

Divergence in Higher Education

Although the trends towards convergence can seem inevitable, there are strong counteracting forces as well. Competition at global, national, regional and local levels can lead to specialisation, positioning and stratification. Some governments, such as the UK, are focusing research funding in areas of excellence. Many governments look to the mapping of a 'system' of higher education, as detailed in the California Master Plan of 1960, particularly in the way such initiatives can thwart 'mission creep' and 'academic drift'. Local university cultures are preserved through unique histories, locations and links with local communities; there are also niche degree, programmes and institutional structures. Many institutions have, and many are adopting, distinctive curricula, both across entire institutions as well as within specific courses. This can include interdisciplinary offerings, 'place-based learning' or making particular use of the location of an institution and unique programmes, often at the Master's level. Many institutions have adopted distinctive approaches in response to local conditions and needs.

Converging on Distinctiveness

Through the dynamics of globalisation, there are interesting intersections of trends of convergence and divergence. As noted, many institutions are adopting a 'distinctive curriculum'; however, across the world from Hong Kong to Scotland, South Africa to Europe, similar 'distinctive' offerings are being made. These include: interdisciplinary options; work-placed learning; service-integrated and community-based learning; research-integrated teaching and research-based learning; local and civic engagement; global connectedness; and promotion of diversity and diverse learning experiences. Further, many initiatives offering more flexibility in the curriculum and increased student choice are tightly bounded by university requirements and regulations.

Although many of these curriculum features have long been part of universities, they are now key aspects of how institutions are marketed to students, particularly international students. Many universities have specific website portals for domestic and international students, with customised services for each group. Several countries, including the UK, are exploring ways of offering 'enhanced transcripts' that cover both formal curricular degrees and co-curricular activities.

Globally there has been major expansion of branch campuses, international partnerships, and multi-institution joint degree options. Several initiatives are often based on 'East-meets-West', through mixing staff and students, sharing locations around the world and adaptations across the curriculum. The latter can be found in multilingual programmes, bringing together canon texts from different cultures, and considering multiple historical traditions and practices in science and medicine. Less common are 'North–South' collaborations, although there has been increasing interest with the BRIC countries (Brazil, Russia, India and China).

In summary, there appears to be a global trend of 'converging on distinctiveness'. This is not limited to major research universities; many institutions without a traditional global reach are adopting such practices, branding and positioning. Although there are many superficial aspects, diverse institutional cultures abound. In an early report on a project looking at how to promote distinctive institutional identities (Gwinnett 2011), the primary distinction of any institution was the 'unique student experience'. It remains to be seen whether a convergence on distinctiveness leads to more homogenisation in higher education or towards individual interpretation and practices. Although there have not been dramatic shifts in how undergraduate higher education is offered, technological improvements, changes to student visa systems and the global financial climate all have the potential to instigate radical change.

Global Students, Neoliberalism and Higher Education

Reflecting more broadly on the effects of neoliberalism, it is useful to look at some of the theoretical assumptions of the neoliberal ideology. Neoliberalism is not necessarily good or bad; there is nothing wrong with neoliberalism itself (Rhoades and Torres 2006). Advantages of the increased movement of higher education into the marketplace include the specialisation that stems from increased competition and within the free-market model; the ability of consumers (students) to choose the best product (institution); and devolution of power from central governmental control to individual units (colleges and universities). The theory and logic of neoliberalism are valid and have great potential. Neoliberalism posits that increased competition improves quality.

However, the advantages that stem from economic and political models are based on theoretically 'perfect world' scenarios, which assume consumers are rational, have full freedom of choice, are receiving all the available information to make decisions and that institutions are adapting and responding to consumer preferences. However, due to market constraints and political dynamics, the theory of neoliberalism does not translate into reality. Higher education, particularly public higher education, does not exist in a free market; the reality is regulation through state and federal governments, limits on global student mobility, price restrictions (currently seen in tuition freezing and capping), course offerings and admissions standards. The predominance of economic rationality is in contrast to many fundamental aspects of higher education and students' experiences.

Many of the benefits of neoliberalism, such as consumers choosing the best product and competition leading to quality improvement, are not apparent and the negative impacts are amplified, such as declining public funding without available resources to pursue other areas of revenue, high recruitment of international students without appropriate training and resources for staff and higher education funding shifting towards high-return potential research rather than to undergraduate education. Rather than blaming current challenges in higher education on neoliberalism, the issue is with the current constraints that higher education institutions face, in the pretext of market settings, that is leading to an erosion of quality higher education.

In higher education, problems arise in the gap between the theory and practice of neoliberalism. For example, neoliberal theories would suggest that through increased competition, students would select the highest quality programmes and institutions, or those with the greatest economic payoff. In turn, such colleges, universities and disciplines would be rewarded with increased funding. However, due to enrolment caps within institutions and programmes, this process is not occurring. Furthermore, students who are not accepted into the high-demand programmes are funnelled into low-cost, 'cash-cow' programmes – which results in a market mechanism that rewards low-demand programmes.

Trends of convergence and divergence will continue. The market for international students is changing, with the emergence of education hubs in the Middle East and South East Asia, development of South–South collaborations (such as those between countries in South America and Africa), more formalised East–West partnerships and increased tuition fees and visa constraints across North America and Western Europe. However, many of these developments are based on similar models and structures. The student experience, a particular point of convergence and divergence, is gaining attention across all higher education sectors; competition between institutions to offer a high quality, and distinctive, experience for all students could enhance higher education.

However, as competition between institutions increases, often instead of increased quality there is a push for cost reduction that affects hiring practices of academic staff and may lead to fewer contact hours and interaction between academics and students. As Torres and Rhoades (2006) note, there is a danger that higher education is becoming just another business with a bottom line. There is a need to identify factors that lead to increased quality of the student experience, and promote them to governments, institutions and – most importantly – students. As detailed in the following chapters, there is great diversity in the student experience around the world, but the student voice is growing in strength, most especially from the globally mobile student.

References

Altbach, P. G. (1979). Comparative higher education: Research trends and bibliography. London: Mansell Publishing.

Altbach, P. G. (2004). Higher education crosses borders. Change, 36(2), 18–25.

Altbach, P. G. and Chait, R. (2001). Introduction. Higher Education, 41(1–2), 1–2.

Anaya, G. (2001). Correlates of performance on the MCAT: An examination of the influence of college environments and experiences on student learning. Advances in Health Sciences Education, 6(3), 179–191.

Apple, M. W. (2000). Between neoliberalism and neoconservatism: Education and conservatism in a global context. In N.C. Burbules, and C.A. Torres (Eds.), Globalization and education: Critical perspectives (pp. 57–77). London: Routledge.

Astin, A. W. (1977). Four critical years: Effects of college on beliefs, attitudes, and knowledge. San Francisco, CA: Jossey-Bass.

Astin, A. W. (1993). What matters in college? Four critical years revisited (1st ed.). San Francisco, CA: Jossey-Bass.

Australian Bureau of Statistics (2011). Australian social trends, Dec 2011 (4102.0). Canberra: ABS.

Ball, S. (1998). Big policies/small world: An introduction to international perspectives in education policy. Comparative Education, 34(2), 119–131.

Bastedo, M. and Gumport, P. (2003). 'Access to what? Mission differentiation and academic stratification in U.S. public higher education', Higher Education, 46, 341–359.

Bean, J. P. (1985). Interaction effects based on class level in an exploratory model of college student dropout syndrome. American Educational Research Journal, 22, 35–64.

Bean, J. P., and Kuh, G. D. (1984). The reciprocity between student-faculty informal contact and the academic performance of university students. Research in Higher Education, 21(4), 461–477.

Berman, E. H. (2003). The political economy of educational reform. In R. A. Arnove and C. A. Torres (Eds.), Comparative education: The dialectic of the global and the local (2nd ed.) (pp. 252–291). Lanham, MD: Roman & Littlefield Publishers, Inc.

Blackmore, P. and Kandiko, C. B. (2012). Strategic curriculum change: Global trends in universities. London: Routledge.

Bloom, D. E. (2004). Globalization and education: An economic perspective. In M. M. Suárez-Orozco and D. B. Qin-Hilliard (Eds.), Globalization: Culture and education in the new millennium (pp. 56–77). Berkeley, CA: University of California Press.

Bok, D. C. (2003). Universities in the marketplace: The commercialization of higher education. Princeton, NJ: Princeton University Press.

Boyles, D. R. (2007). Marketing sameness: Consumerism, commercialism, and the status quo. In J. C. Smart (Ed.), Higher education: Handbook of theory and research (Vol. 22, pp. 537–582). New York: Agathon Press.

Bradley, G. (2004). Contingent faculty and the new academic labor system. Academe, 90 (1), 28–31.

Burbules, N. C., and Torres, C. A. (2000). Globalization and education: An introduction. In N. C. Burbules and C. A. Torres (Eds.), Globalization and education: Critical perspectives (pp. 1–26). London: Routledge.

Chomsky, N. (1998). Profit over people: Neoliberalism and global order. New York: Seven Stories Press.

Cotten, S. R., and Wilson, B. (2006). Student-faculty interactions: Dynamics and determinants. Higher Education, 51, 487–519.

Currie, J., and Newson, J. (Eds.) (1998). Universities and globalization: Critical perspectives. Thousand Oaks, CA: Sage Publications.

Deem, R. (2001). Globalisation, new managerialism, academic capitalism and entrepreneurialism in universities: Is the local dimension still important? Comparative Education, 37(1), 7–20.

Ehrenberg, R. (2006). The perfect storm and the privatization of public higher education. Change, 38(1), 46–51.

Ewell, P. T. (1989). Institutional characteristics and faculty/administrator perceptions of outcomes: An exploratory analysis. Research in Higher Education, 30(2), 113–136.

Fairweather, J. S. (1996). Faculty work and the public trust: Restoring the value of teaching and public service in American academic life. Boston, MA: Allyn & Bacon.

Feldman, K. A. and Newcomb, T. M. (1969). The impact of college on students (1st ed.). San Francisco, CA: Jossey-Bass.

Friedman, M. (1981). The invisible hand in economics and politics. Pasir Panjang, Singapore: Institute of Southeast Asian Studies.

Friedman, M. (1991). Monetarist economics. Cambridge, MA: Blackwell.

Gaffikin, F. and Perry, D. (2009). Discourses and Strategic Visions: The US Research University as an Institutional Manifestation of Neoliberalism in a Global Era. American Educational Research Journal, 46 (1): 115–144.

Giroux, H. A. (2002). Neoliberalism, corporate culture, and the promise of higher education: The university as a democratic public sphere. Harvard Educational Review, 72(4), 425–463.

Gumport, P. J. (2000). Academic restructuring: Organization change and institutional imperatives. Higher Education, 39(1), 67–91.

Gwinnett, A. (2011) Distinctiveness as a route to sustainability for higher education institutions. Society for Research into Higher Education (SRHE) Annual Research Conference. 7–9 December 2011, Newport, Wales.

Hay, C. (2004). The normalizing role of rationalist assumptions in the institutional embedding of neoliberalism. Economy and Society, 33(4), 500–527.

Held, D. (Ed.) (1991). Political theory today. Stanford, CA: Stanford University Press.

Jiang, X. (2008) Towards the internationalisation of higher education from a critical perspective. Journal of Further and Higher Education, 32 (4), 347–358.

Johnstone, D. B. (1998). The financing and management of higher education: A status report on worldwide reforms. Washington, DC: World Bank. Available at: http://www.worldbank.org/html/extdr/educ/postbasc.htm

Johnstone, D. B. (2004). The economics and politics of cost sharing in higher education: Comparative perspectives. Economics of Education Review, 23(4), 403–410.

Kezar, A. J. (2004). Obtaining integrity? Reviewing and examining the charter between higher education and society. The Review of Higher Education, 27(4), 429–459.

Kim, Y. and Sax, L. (2009). Student–faculty interaction in research universities: Differences by student gender, race, social class, and first-generation status. Research in Higher Education, 50, 437–459.

Kuh, G. D. and Hu, S. (2001). The effects of student-faculty interaction in the 1990s. The Review of Higher Education, 24(3), 309–332.

Kuh, G. D., Kinzie, J., Buckley, J. A., Bridges, B. K. and Hayek, J. C. (2006, July). What matters to student success: A review of the literature. National Postsecondary Education Cooperative (NPEC) Commissioned Paper.

Lindblom-Ylänne, S., Trigwell, K., Nevgi, A. and Ashwin, P. (2006). How approaches to teaching are affected by discipline and teaching context. Studies in Higher Education, 31(3), 285–295.

Marginson, S. (1997). Markets in education. Sydney: Allen and Unwin.

Marginson, S. and Considine, M. (2000). The enterprise university: Power, governance and reinvention in Australia. Cambridge: Cambridge University Press.

Marginson, S. and Rhoades, G. (2002). Beyond national states, markets, and systems of higher education: A glonacal agency heuristic. Higher Education, 43(3), 281–309.

Morrow, R. A. (2006). Foreword – Critical theory, globalization, and higher education: Political economy and the cul-de-sac of the postmodernist cultural turn. In R. A. Rhoades and C. A. Torres (Eds.), The university, state, and market: The political economy of globalization in the Americas (pp. xvii–xxxiii). Stanford, CA: Stanford University Press.

Morrow, R. A. and Torres, C. A. (2000). The state, globalization, and educational policy. In N. C. Burbules and C. A. Torres (Eds.), Globalization and education: Critical perspectives (pp. 27–56). London: Routledge.

Morrow, R. A. and Torres, C. A. (2003). The state, social movements, and educational reform. In R. A. Arnove and C. A. Torres (Eds.), Comparative education: The dialectic of the global and the local (2nd ed.) (pp. 92–114). Lanham, MD: Roman & Littlefield Publishers, Inc.

Naidoo, R. (2003) Repositioning higher education as a global commodity: Opportunities for future sociology of education work, British Journal of Sociology of Education, 24, 2, 249–259.

Olssen, M. and Peters, M. A. (2005). Neoliberalism, higher education and the knowledge economy: From the free market to knowledge capitalism. Journal of Education Policy, 20(3), 313–345.

OECD (1996a). The knowledge-based economy. Paris: Author.

OECD (1996b). Measuring what people know: Human capital accounting for the knowledge economy. Paris: Author.

Palmer, C. L. (2001). Work at the boundaries of science: Information and the interdisciplinary research process. Dordrecht: Kluwer.

Pascarella, E. T. (1985). College environmental influences on learning and cognitive development: A critical review and synthesis. In J. C. Smart (Ed.), Higher education: Handbook of theory and research, Vol. 1, (pp. 1–62). New York: Agathon.

Pascarella, E. T. and Terenzini, P. T. (1991). How college affects students: Findings and insights from twenty years of research (1st ed.). San Francisco, CA: Jossey-Bass Publishers.

Pascarella, E. T. and Terenzini, P. T. (2005). How college affects students: A third decade of research. San Francisco, CA: Jossey-Bass.

Rhoades, G. and Slaughter, S. (1997). Academic capitalism, managed professionals, and supply-side higher education. Social Text, 51, 9–38.

Rhoades, R. A. and Rhoades, G. (2005). Graduate employee unionization as a symbol of and challenge to the corporatization of U.S. research universities. The Journal of Higher Education, 76(3), 243–275.

Rhoades, G. and Slaughter, S. (2006). Academic capitalism and the new economy: Privatization as shifting the target of public subsidy in higher education. In R. A. Rhoades and C. A. Torres (Eds.), The university, state, and market: The political economy of globalization in the Americas (pp. 103–140). Stanford, CA: Stanford University Press.

Rhoades, R. A. and Torres, C. A. (Eds.) (2006). The university, state, and market: The political economy of globalization in the Americas. Stanford, CA: Stanford University Press.

Slaughter, S. (2001). Problems in comparative higher education: Political economy, political sociology and postmodernism. Higher Education, 41(4), 389–412.

Slaughter, S. and Leslie, L. L. (1997). Academic capitalism: Politics, policies, and the entrepreneurial university. Baltimore, MD: The Johns Hopkins University Press.

Slaughter, S. and Rhoades, G. (2004). Academic capitalism and the new economy: Markets, states, and higher education. Baltimore, MD: The Johns Hopkins University Press.

Sporn, B. (1999). Adaptive university structures: An analysis adaptation to socioeconomic environments of US and European universities. London: Jessica Kingsley.

Stromquist, N. (2002). Education in a globalized world: The connectivity of economic power, technology, and knowledge. Lanham, MD: Rowman & Littlefield.

Torres, C. A. and Rhoades, R. A. (2006). Introduction: Globalization and higher education in the Americas. In R. A. Rhoades and C. A. Torres (Eds.), The university, state, and market: The political economy of globalization in the Americas (pp. 3–38). Stanford, CA: Stanford University Press.

UNESCO (2012). Global education digest 2012. Paris: UNESCO.

Vaira, M. (2004). Globalization and higher education organizational change: A framework for analysis. Higher Education, 48, 483–510.

Wilson, R. C., Gaff, J. C., Dienst, R. E., Wood, L. and Bavry, J. L. (1975). College professors and their impact on students. New York: Wiley-Interscience.

Wiseman, J. (1998). The global nation: Australia's response to globalization. Melbourne: Cambridge University Press.

3

Beyond 'Enculturation'
Culture, Learning and International Contexts of Higher Education

THUSHARI WELIKALA

This chapter examines how learners who embark on learning sojourns in different cultural contexts make meaning of and respond to the new culture of learning they encounter in their host university. The discussion of this chapter is based on the analysis of empirical data collected from a convenience sample of 30 international postgraduate students in UK higher education. The study presented evidence that the pedagogic encounters within international contexts of higher education do not reflect intellectual or cultural neutral zones. The learners who come from diverse cultures to pursue higher education in the global North bring different cultural scripts for learning (Welikala 2006). These cultural scripts do not neatly reflect the nationalities of the learners. Instead, they reflect different perspectives of learners who have shared beliefs from different cultures of learning and teaching.

The notion of *culture* in this study denotes the 'ensemble of stories we tell ourselves about ourselves' (Geertz 1975: 448). Hence, the culture of learning and teaching reflect the stories we tell about learning and teaching. These stories are shaped by a wide variety of issues such as the beliefs learners hold about learning and teaching; different encounters in life; different (re) configurations of their own identities; and shared values about leaning within the diverse types of groups they belong to: country of origin, social class, ethnicity, religion, gender, age group and dis/ability. The notion of *cultural script* is used to refer to the generalised action knowledge that informs how individuals make meaning of a situation and which also guides their actions in a particular context (Welikala and Watkins 2008).

Internationalisation and the Culture Debate: The UK Research Context

Travelling overseas for higher education is not a new phenomenon in the world. However, the trend for internationalisation within 21st century universities can be seen as a proactive response to the changing social, civic and global issues at both local and global levels. Information overflow, global migrations and interconnectedness between nations and regions have increased the numbers of international students in higher education across the world. Diversity, in terms of the geopolitical locations of student cohorts, their multiple epistemic views and the variety of cultural ways of approaching learning, has now become a common characteristic in most of the universities, in particular in the global North.

Within this context, the nature of cultural differences in learning has been increasingly investigated (Jin and Cortazzi 2011). *Culture* is one of the most problematic and ubiquitous concepts in the world. Kroeber and Kluckhohn identified more than 160 meanings of culture in 1952 (Keating et al. 2002). As Montgomery (2010: 13) holds, even after extensive empirical work, 'culture remains difficult to capture'. As such, the complication of defining culture has been 'overcome' by the majority of literature on internationalisation relating culture to nationality or ethnicity. However, Baumann (1996: 1) notes that the dominant discourse that relates culture to ethnicity reflects 'ethnic reductionism' while Holliday (1999) points out that national labels are a social imaginary constructed through certain political discourses.

The project of conceptualising culture as nationality within international higher education literature shows a move from the celebratory conceptualisation of culture (Hofstede 1980) to culture as a resource (Carroll and Ryan 2005) and, currently, culture as negotiable (Parris-Kidd and Barnett 2011).The celebratory conceptualisation of culture refers to international students as a homogeneous group of national cultures and highlights the need for assimilating them in to host university pedagogic cultures. The conceptualisation of culture as a resource reflects international students as representatives of their national cultures and encourages acculturation into the host university learning culture. In recent years, the notion of culture as nationality has been criticised as polarising, irrelevant within cosmopolitan pedagogic environments, consequently leading to asymmetrical power dynamics and dualistic discourse, between 'international' and 'home' students (Rizvi 2007).This inevitably creates an ontological and hence an epistemic difference or a gap between the two categories of students, home and international. Such divisions normally lead to remedial pedagogies that are assumed to bridge the polarisation between international students' deficit pedagogic approaches and home students' appropriate pedagogic approaches. The emphasis is to provide support for international students to catch up to home students (Marginson and Sawir 2011). Hence, such pedagogies are remedial.

Culture is increasingly identified as a socio-culturally and geopolitically embedded fluid phenomenon that embodies gender, identity, history and politics and resembles the ensemble of the things that people do rather than what is done to people by ethnicities or nationalities (Kristeva 1991; Dunlop 1999). The research discussed in this chapter therefore employs a socially constructed notion of culture that transcends narrow references to nationality and encompasses a socio-politically embedded, liquid meaning.

The Paradox: Internationalisation and the Promotion of National Brand

Arguably, internationalisation is one of the major pre-occupations of the 21st century higher education (Welikala 2011). Intercultural learning is increasingly cited as a desired outcome of the process of internationalisation (Ippolito 2007). However, the project of internationalisation of curricula and pedagogy that is supposed to bring about intercultural learning seems problematic, if not impossible, within the policy framework of marketing higher education to promote the national in the global knowledge economy. This policy framework encourages the imagination that the alternative epistemic views and pedagogic approaches that are not appreciated within the host university lack intellectual depth. For instance, keeping silent during teaching and learning sessions are normally related with passive or received learning in the West. However, some cultures engage in reflective listening and consider frequent verbal interactions as a disruption to active learning (Trahar 2011; Welikala 2006). The actual complexities of creating inclusive pedagogies that address, respect and include different epistemic views have been reduced to the process of supporting international students to follow the 'Western' of higher education. Hence, internationalisation, as it exists today, seems a problematic process since it is based on national values of educational growth and revenue making rather than on developing pedagogic interconnections among diverse ways of creating knowledge (Kehm and Teichler 2007).

This chapter therefore focuses on some salient issues that are inadequately addressed and under-researched in relation to the learning experiences of international students. It addresses the emerging nature of UK higher education pedagogies as encounters of different cultural scripts for knowing; it problematises the feasibility of categorising learners and pedagogic approaches according to geopolitical borders; and considers the possibilities of negotiating between different cultural scripts for knowing to address the emerging inter-perspective pedagogies in international higher education.

The Research

The research discussed in this chapter is based on a narrative study conducted during 2002–2006. The well-reputed UK university in which the study was carried out has a large proportion of international postgraduate students who represent a wide variety of cultures of learning. The sample in the study mainly comprised mature learners who were following doctoral degrees and Masters' degrees in the field of education. The sample comprised students who came from 30 different countries and were experienced professionals in their home countries. A vast majority of them were either secondary school teachers or university teachers. A few of those who were reading for their doctoral degrees have gained their Masters' degrees from the same host university in the UK. More than half of the doctoral students interviewed for this study were in their third year of studies while a few of them were in their fifth or sixth year of study. None of the students in the sample was unemployed by the time the interviews were conducted for this study but they were either on scholarships with paid leave or on unpaid study leave. They represented plurality in terms of their previous experience, age, gender, discipline, socio-economic and geopolitical as well as religious backgrounds.

The study was based on 30 active interviews with international students to co-construct stories about their learning experience in British higher education (Holstein and Gubrium 1995). While the active interviewing process had specific aims and objectives, the interview conversations were considered as encounters within which meanings were co-constructed as active negotiations between the actions and meanings as well as the relationship between the researcher and the participants (Mishler 1986). The meaning-making process was based on a constructivist grounded theory approach (Charmaz 1995).

Why the Narrative Approach?

The study used a narrative approach that was informed by the social constructivist view of knowledge making (Berger and Luckmann 1966). Within the context of this research, a narrative approach helped retrospective meaning-making as a primary form by which human experience is made meaningful (Polkinghorne 1988). The process of using a narrative approach exposed the researcher to multiple issues of politics and culture as they are actually storied by participants as accounts of their own experience (Bruner 1985; Mishler 1986). The analysis of data in the study was a cyclical process going back and forth: collecting data, making meaning of stories and going back to the field to construct more stories until the data were saturated.

In the study findings it emerged that learners who come from different cultures bring different cultural scripts for learning. The emergent themes of the analysis of the students' stories depicted that there are different cultural scripts for (a) different activities for reading, writing and talking for learning and (b) relationships for learning, including peer-interaction, the teacher's role and status, and participation in sessions. While the study revealed that cultural scripts influence learning, it also evidenced that cultural scripts can be encountered across cultures as well as within cultures. The data reflected that cultural scripts respond to pedagogic contexts in varying ways: reshaping and reconstructing actions and meanings related to the process of learning. Cultural scripts thus emerged as fluid rather than rigid, static determinants of culture's influence on learning. Figure 3.1 shows the emergent cultural scripts for learning within the study.

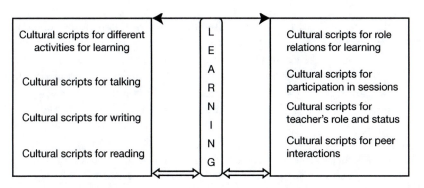

Figure 3.1 Cultural scripts for learning

The experience of embarking on a new culture of learning is complex and brings multiple discomforts to the learners (Gu 2011; OECD 2011). There is ample evidence across universities in the English-speaking North that focus on multiple 'learning problems' experienced by international students due to their undue reliance on rote learning approaches, low level of verbal contributions during sessions and lack of capacity in critical thinking (Prichard and Skinner 2002). However, the study discussed here revealed that while learning is influenced by learners' cultural scripts they are capable of being reformed and reforming knowledge within the host pedagogy. It uncovered that meanings and practices associated with 'rote learning', 'keeping silent' and 'traditional approaches to learning' vary across cultures. What follows is a discussion of cultural scripts that students bring to international pedagogies and how they inform the process of learning and unlearning in a critically reflexive manner.

Learning to Talk Critically: What About Articulate Silences?

The study evidenced that the process of learning as a social act was continuously reshaped and reformed by the life worlds of learners. It emerged that learners do not make sense of pedagogic moments as culture-neutral. Instead, their multiple histories (social, personal, economic, political) and their present identities (which are being reconstructed within the new learning environment) constituted the reforming of their cultural scripts for learning. They often interpreted the host pedagogic practices in terms of their own cultural scripts for learning. For instance, talk for learning, as it was practiced in their host university, was not seen as a positive practice by some learners.

> Believe me, the first day I was shocked to find how the classroom works here. My God! ... Where is the lecture? Why are the students shouting

this much? Why the teacher is listening to students while it should be the other way? ... how can I learn for a MA degree in this manner?

... Back home learning is a big competition. You know ... we have so many ... [mentions a particular nationality] people in Indonesia and they all want their kids to do Science and Math, get the best results, go to university and then do Science ... So, we have no time to waste like this.

(Interview Student [IS] 27)

The data demonstrated that cultural scripts are not simple phenomena only related to learning but are embedded in the learners' personal histories, current experiences and future desires. For instance, verbal arguments that are characteristic of 'critical engagement' within the Western pedagogy were repeatedly referred to as 'shouting' by several participants in this study:

... Even if the course is in Chinese, we would be quiet ... it is the way we do.

(IS 14)

Pedagogies that help learners find, develop and construct voices are called critical pedagogies in the UK. One of the major concerns in UK higher education is that pedagogic moments should promote criticality. Such critical pedagogies may indeed help learners to move away from the contemplative relation with the world. However, criticality does not reflect a singular meaning across cultures:

English people are arguing critically. They talk as if they are writing an assignment. Be critical. Be critical ... not used to this ... the teachers ... think ... you talk; you know everything ... We are self-critical and ... do not ... criticize others openly.

In Japan, if you talk to me nicely, I listen and say 'OK', 'OK'. If you get aggressive and starts shouting at me still I listen and say 'OK', 'OK'. We do not like to confront people.

(IS 2)

Language is embedded in many meanings of the way that people in particular socio-cultural contexts go about living (Bourdieu 1992). 'Languaging' therefore involves much more subtlety than adhering to certain linguistic rules when communicating in a different cultural context. The data from this study illustrated that, in some cultures, talking is not the exact opposite of silence. As Minh-Ha (1989) points out there can be *articulate silences* that are more powerful than verbal articulations. Hence some cultural scripts for talking encouraged learners to critically reflect on the teacher's verbal presentations rather than contributing to it through critical arguments. They were happy to engage in further arguments after the session or during tutorial sessions rather than during formal teaching sessions.

Writing to Know or Knowing to Write?

The lack of English language skills among international students is often highlighted as a barrier to succeed within international higher education (Schmitt 2005; Sawir 2005). However, the data revealed that the host university's academic writing tradition was not embraced by all the students as compulsory. Some students mentioned that their host university academic writing practices were different from their own practices and questioned the need to change their writing style merely because they have embarked on a learning sojourn. For example, IS 14, who was a teacher in a university in her own country, held that using too many citations within the text disturbs reading.

> ... Every statement is been referred to, and even when you read something you get disturbed [by references in the text]. Definitely tooo much. Back home we express things in a better way ... any reader can understand. Here, whatever you write you need to refer it to the writer. Otherwise they call it something. Pagaa ... ism? [plagiarism] I was very angry about this.
>
> Now see, whatever I write is my own and not my own ... my writing is influenced by what I read, listen to and talk with other people ... these individualistic ... societies ... every single thing has an owner. Very different from us.
>
> (IS 4)

Such views about plagiarism imply that different cultures hold different perceptions about 'valuable knowledge' and how valuable knowledge is being created in diverse cultural contexts. The comment above evidences that the process of learning in the student's own culture transcends the institutional meaning of learning that requires the learner to follow a particular set code of conduct, in this case referring to the rules related to the use of citations. Instead, the student's meaning of learning envelops a wide variety of activities and experiences. The student further draws relationships between the meanings of plagiarism to particular characteristics of individualistic societies. This implies that some learners consider the act of writing as a socio-historically embedded process rather than a set of rules to follow. Such views challenge the idea of writing the 'valuable' knowledge using 'right English language' (see Welikala 2008).

Often the 'scientific' ways of knowing the world is supposed to be articulated in a distant, impersonal way (House 1991). Some learners, however, seemed to have alternative views about using language to create 'scientific' knowledge:

... back home what is more important is what you know ... The meaning of what we write – not the linking words or commas or ... In the end of the course, I have learnt how to write in English and nothing else. I did not feel that I learnt anything else.

(IS 10)

Back home, we write adjectives, vivid, emotional language ... We use language to feel. Before I came here, I knew English. A ... h Jee ... sus, since I started writing, I am asking myself 'so, do I really know English?' ... here, it is just blank and flat. No flavour in the language ... Their academic writing is just like their food ... no flavour ... And I am still thinking, so, what is wrong with the English I use?

(IS 20)

I had no idea of writing on our own as they do it here. We always reproduced what the teacher dictated to us. Writing was never developed this way back home ... we were trained to do essays after memorizing certain things ... I want to learn this way of writing and it is a big challenge to me.

(IS 5)

Cultural scripts for writing that students bring help them to identify writing as a part of a macro script for living. Such views reflect the 'alternative academic literacies' perspectives that consider writing as socially situated meaning-making as opposed to skills applicable across contexts without complications (Lea and Street 1998). As such, learners in the study questioned and when possible resisted the asymmetrical power issues related with academic writing that contributed to construct a particular kind of knowledge and created a desire to obtain this knowledge (Appadurai 1996; Koehne 2006). The data demonstrated that academic writing is a process in which students' identities and voices were in constant struggle in an attempt to negotiate between different ways of articulating knowledge (Lea 2004). Being mature students with professional experience in their home countries, the sample of student participants here seemed to have enough confidence to voice their views about academic writing practices in their host university in the UK.

Reading the Text Means Reading the Author

The study showed some evidence that learners bring diverse scripts for reading practices that are not necessarily appreciated within their new learning environment. Reading for information was the main purpose of reading for some students:

In reading ... we do differently ... They [the teachers who have taught her in the past] want us to read for information. I am used to read just what is there in the text. No arguments with the text.

(IS 27)

Asked whether reading for information is sufficient to successfully face the requirements of their course some mentioned that they sometimes find it difficult. However, they did not show any intention of an urgent need to change their skills of reading:

We read what is there in the text. What else?

(IS 8)

Reading for us means to read the whole story. I do not know how we can just read a chapter or two and get what is there in the book. What is this scaaa ... nning or something?

(IS 9)

The data evidenced that there are multiple meanings surrounding the purpose of reading for academic purposes as well as the role of the author and the reader in constructing meaning out of a text. Some believed that the role of the author is to provide the reader with 'the whole truth' about a particular area of knowledge, while the main task of the reader is to understand this single truth. This shows that some cultures believe that texts themselves carry meaning. Hence, critical engagement with the text to reconstruct meaning is considered unnecessary. These quotes also suggest that there are certain cultural values and beliefs that will not be abandoned by learners for the sake of 'adjusting' themselves into a new culture of learning.

Interestingly, cultural scripts for reading did not show any patterns or associations to particular types of countries or cultural groups. For instance, the cultural script for 'reading only for information' was shared by different cultural groups: students who come from European, African and Asian countries; students who were middle-aged and young; and male and female students.

Cultural Scripts for Role Relations

Alongside the activities for learning, and the meanings these activities hold, are the relations that any learner encounters. Most significant amongst these are the relations with teachers and interactions with peer learners within pedagogic contexts (Welikala and Watkins 2008).

The Multiple Versions of the Role of the Teacher

Bernstein stated that in terms of management of classroom knowledge, teachers appropriate a higher position than the students in the hierarchical division of labour. He described that such positions constitute power relations, recreate boundaries, and result in producing dislocations in social space (1990). Participants in this study talked about different kinds of power relationships within pedagogic moments across cultures and how the kind of teacher–learner relationship created varying types of power and authority. There was no single meaning for 'authority' of the teacher across cultures. Even though the unequal power relationship between learner–teacher appeared as a common theme, the meaning of 'power' varied depending on the different ways of responding to authority. The data evidenced that the asymmetrical relationship between the learners and teachers did not necessarily reflect a negative aspect of power or a social issue that should be resisted. For instance:

> Teachers ... are the authorities in our culture ... have the power to change things for the future. More responsible regarding the future of the students ... we listen to the students ... understand their problems, and be moral guides to them ... not as friends ... like to keep my distance as the teacher.
>
> (IS 16)

> We have to respect them. They are our Gurus.
>
> (IS 3)

> Teachers in our society ... are superior to us, have higher positions ... I think that they are experts and have to be respected and listen to.
>
> (IS 23)

> We meet the teacher on the road, in the market place ... call them, 'Hi sir, how are you?' ... We have that bond with the teacher. It is not just teaching something and vanishing. He is there, in the community living with you.
>
> (IS 7)

Figure 3.2 shows how the multiple ways of interpreting 'authority' of teachers reflect on the kind of teacher–student relationship and the assumed status of teachers in different cultures.

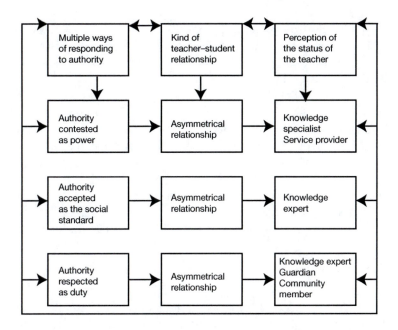

Figure 3.2 Multiple meanings of authority reflecting teacher–student relationship and status of the teacher across cultures

Different Meanings of Peer Interactions

Research on internationalisation highlights various aspects of interactions between home and international students (Kashima and Loh 2006; Harrison and Peacock 2007). The majority of the research, however, does not focus on different perceptions of peer interactions among learners. The study discussed in this chapter showed that learners from different cultures hold multiple views about interactions for learning: peer interactions hinder the learning process; lead to loss of face; provide emotional support; and enhance academic experience. For example:

> No talking about learning in groups. It is all about competing with the other, to get the best results.
>
> (IS 27)

> I know that there are two girls from my culture and they have lot of problems with language. They know very well that I am a lecturer in English. But never talk about such problems with me. We never discuss our learning difficulties with friends ... Kind of losing face.
>
> (IS 11)

In my culture, if you ask for help, someone will stop his work and help you. It is always good to discuss and learn with your friends. Most of the evenings, we get together … talk about our assignments, reading … very helpful and interesting.

(IS 17)

My friend … in another university … has no friends. So, she comes here sometimes, join our discussions … we need that emotional support.

(IS 14)

The insights from the study evidenced that learners from diverse cultures have different values and practices related to interactions for learning. Such values are embedded in their socio-cultural values for living as well as learning.

Cultural Scripts: A Fluid Notion

The multiple cultural scripts that emerged in the study portray subtle shadows of the socio-political histories of learners and the ways in which such histories inform and continuously reshape their process of learning and living. The learners showed ability to consciously and critically engage with the new pedagogic approaches and pedagogic relationships while at the same time being emotionally reflexive of their learning experience in a culturally embedded manner. Rather than being static determinants directing student learning, cultural scripts seemed to enhance their process of learning, providing diverse insights into the ways of negotiating between the new learning environment and their previous culture of learning.

The emergent themes of the study evidenced that learning never emerged as a neutral process of adjusting into the host pedagogic cultures. Instead, the sojourners experience learning as a complex process of negotiation between rational, emotional and socio-culturally as well as geopolitically embodied minds. The data portrayed that learners reflected their awareness of a cultural kind of dislocation between memories of post-colonial histories and current encounters of Euro-centric values of knowing. Within this encounter, the 'value' of the host university pedagogic approaches were acknowledged, challenged and resisted rather than being absorbed into without critique (Grant and Manathunga 2011).

The learners in this study responded to the host culture of learning in multiple ways: they showed willingness to accommodate new pedagogic and epistemic views when they found that they are useful in their future endeavours of learning and living; they tried to resist unfamiliar and different ways of knowing when they identified that those would not contribute to enhance their journey of knowing; and they enacted agency when they were able to challenge the existing and accepted epistemic views and pedagogic methods of the new learning culture by engaging in alternative ways of learning. Hence, the insights from this study did not show any particular patterns or trajectories of learning (Ward 2004) that specifically reflected their national or regional cultures. Some research has identified Asian students having specific problems and 'learning difficulties' in adjusting themselves to their host university's pedagogic approaches (Sawir 2005). None of the stories comprised themes of cross-cultural adjustment that can neatly be divided under cognitive, behavioural and affective aspects of adjustment. Rather, learning appeared as a complex process of negotiation between different scripts for knowing and different encounters of pedagogic moments. As such, the insights of this study critically complicate the existing stereotypical constructions of the deficit model of the international student who is interpreted as a passive being from a fixed national culture (Bochner 1986).

As Church (1982) cautions, a single, comprehensive, universally applicable theory of sojourner adjustment is unlikely to be found. The emergent themes in this narrative study did not provide universally applicable knowledge and understanding about the nature of the mediation of culture in learning within international higher education across contexts. However, this study has explored some salient issues that have so far been inadequately addressed in relation to the encounter of diverse cultures of learning within international higher education contexts. Even though there is a rich growth of literature and research on the mediation of culture within international pedagogic encounters, they often limit the opportunities of looking at international students as agents who can transform or influence the host culture of learning. Instead, the international student is constructed as the cultural 'Other' who is determined to adjust and follow the host culture of learning (Marginson and Sawir 2011).

The Pedagogy of the Other

Often, research on internationalisation tends to construct culture and its role in the process of learning in a rather instrumental manner: depicting culture as nationality and constructing culture as a barrier to succeed in learning. Such research mainly focuses on creating models of cultural differences in learning among international students, the 'problems' created by different cultures of learning (Sawir 2005) and strategies of overcoming such differences to help learners to adjust into the host culture of knowing (Furnham and Bochner 1986). The immediate consequence of this approach was the beginning of polarised identification of two main ways of learning between those who are called 'home students' and the so-called 'international students'. Within the global North, the term international student, 'lumps together individuals with a huge diversity of prior experiences, skills and expectations' (Haigh 2002: 52). Hugh (2008) in Montgomery (2010) points out that the research literature constructs essentialist views of inter-national students as constituting a 'homogenous group'. Devos (2003) found that the media constructs a particular identity for international students and uses dichotomous discourse to differentiate between international students as the 'Other', a construct that only exists in contrast to another construct, namely 'home students'.

According to Leonard et al. (2004) it is surprising to find the aspects of liter-ature that focus on the learning 'problems' of international students and the need to 'help' them to acquire the host university strategies of learning. Asian students in mainland English speaking universities are often identified as 'relentless rote learners, surface learners, and syllabus dependent, passive and lacking in initiative and independence (Gatfield and Gatfield in Ramburuth 2001: 2). 'Adjustment' within international contexts of higher education is often a one-sided attempt; the host country supports the students to change and students have to change. The process of adjusting and assimilating inter-national students into the pedagogy of host universities is called 'intercultural education'. Concepts and practices that are related to such models embed asymmetrical power and involve the risk of normalising particular epistemic views that are appreciated within the host university culture. They tradition-alise and devalue alternative forms of knowing (Yang 2002). This discussion, therefore, will provide insights to academics, researchers, higher education policy makers, as well as students about the complex ways by which culture mediates in knowing and unknowing within the encounter of different peda-gogic approaches and epistemic views.

Conclusion: Culture's Mediation in Learning

This chapter has sought to stimulate discussion relating to the mediation of culture and cultural scripts in the process of learning within interna-tional higher education contexts. It has argued that how learners go about multiple activities related to learning, and different relationships that influ-ence learning, reflect complex cultural scripts that transcend the national categories of learners. By so doing, the chapter problematises the practice of compartmentalising learners and their processes of learning according to nationalities of the learners. The study discussed in this chapter uncovered that learners who cross geopolitical boundaries for higher education bring different cultural scripts for learning. While cultural scripts greatly inform their learning journeys in multiple ways, such scripts do not stay fixed. Instead, cultural scripts change taking different forms over the years responding to new pedagogic encounters in complex manners. The analysis of data also revealed that learners are not prepared to embrace the host pedagogic cultures and completely give up their own cultural scripts for learning. Instead, they critically and self-consciously engage in reading and reacting to multiple aspects of the new pedagogic environment. Such engagements involve accommodating to new ways of knowing, resisting the unfamiliar and inappropriate and enacting agency when there is opportunity for that.

By arguing that cultural scripts are fluid and that learners respond to their new pedagogic environment in a critically reflexive manner, I propose that the commonly constructed image of international student as passive followers of the 'rules of the game' warrants debate. The data in this study showed that constructing particular identities for 'international' students is problematic and inherently flawed. The literature on internationalisation evidences that host universities consider 'helping' international students to adjust and become like home students as their main responsibility. However, the students question the 'support' discourse and their constructed identities as 'passive' and 'traditional' 'surface learners'. The data postulated that rather than experiencing a particular learning trajectory, starting with cultural shock, undergoing a series of surprises and disappointments and finally getting immersed in the host learning culture, learners are in a continuous struggle of re-engaging with their multiple learner identities.

The articulations of their understanding about being a particular learner from a certain culture of learning and how that awareness informs the way they expect to become someone else involves layers of subtle negotiations. The data showed that the learners in this study rejected social or collective identity, or self-definition through 'membership of, or identification with a particular group or groups'; instead their identities are 'actively, on-going, and, dynamically constituted' (Benwell and Stokoe 2006: 17) within different pedagogic moments and relationships. By establishing empirical evidence on such negotiations between learner identities and pedagogic moments, it is suggested that learner identities are not fixed phenomena that can be discovered by the researchers without complications.

The study also uncovered that the current practice of romanticising cultural differences within international contexts of learning is not appreciated by learners. The data suggested that highlighting the role of cultures in learning contributes to marginalising particular ways of creating knowledge. There were references in the data that learners identify themselves as learners rather than cultural 'Others'. The data evidenced that learners are aware of some of the elements of cultural politics and power issues involved in the epistemic practices of their host university. However, there were scant references to being self-imposed victims of such politics. Rather, learners problematised the idea of cultural imperialism in terms of their relationship with the university as customers who bring rich revenue to the host university.

The continuous practice of homogenising learners as international and home create imagined learner communities. Such practices overshadow the complexity of the epistemic encounter of diverse cultures that reflect multiple cultural scripts for learning, different perspectives about knowing and varying ways of responding to pedagogic relationships. They encourage universities to construct intercultural pedagogies and curricula that are assumed to bring synergy among different national cultures. However, making such synergies warrant debate, firstly because universities mainly operate within national value systems to achieve national education targets, even though their mission statements may be global; secondly, learners' nationalities do not necessarily harmonise with their cultures of learning. Throughout the data, there were references to the host university teachers' misreading of the international students. The learners critically commented on certain practices of their host institution that do not adequately address the complexities of knowledge creation within a radically unknowable, pedagogic encounter. The multiple perspectives learners bring into international contexts of learning problematises the concept of intercultural pedagogies since mere meeting of different cultures would not contribute to illuminating learning experiences.

The emergent themes of the study brought into light that achieving inclusive international higher education for all the students is a highly complex process that demands a considerable rethinking and re-planning of the university curriculum, pedagogy, assessment and management systems. Attempts to develop intercultural curricula do not guarantee the emergence of intercultural pedagogies. As the data in this study evidenced, the meaning and practices associated with interculturality themselves are problematic. While culture mediates learning, it does so in diverse ways depending on the particular discipline, pedagogic relationship and the pedagogic context as well as the individual's idiosyncratic scripts for learning. The learning process emerged as a rich struggle for developing new cultural scripts and unlearning some old scripts that students found either disturbing or of less use in succeeding in the new culture of learning at the same time. Within this struggle, the learner identities, their socio-economic and geopolitical histories, different disciplinary ways of going about leaning, multiple social locations and cultural politics of the learning contexts represented a variegated world of clashing ideas and norms about knowing. It emerged that the encounters of different cultures of learning contributed to encounters of diverse perspectives about life and learning. But at the same time, their sojourn of learning showed the possibilities of the existence of different people with different perspectives bound by a simple nexus of common values and humanity. Rather than vague intercultural spaces, such encounters evidenced the emergence of a third culture, a third space (Bhaba 1994) in-between the interfaces of the epistemic encounters.

What is necessary therefore is to create pedagogic spaces in which both learners and teachers with diverse perspectives of knowing the world can radically question their multiple epistemic views. By helping the learners to critically engage in the epistemic insecurity, universities can help the emergence of inter-perspective pedagogies that recognise infinite ways of knowing and unknowing the uncertain world. Such pedagogies can include all the students and academics and their changing understandings and scripts for learning and teaching.

International higher education contexts provide rich encounters of diverse perspectives, complex values and learning behaviours. Such complex encounters cannot be related to nationalities. As such, it would be useful for the practitioners, policy makers and researchers to rethink the feasibility of homogenising particular groups of learners using cultural determinism.

In the meantime, this study was conducted within a particular higher education context and the respondents were mainly mature students reading for their postgraduate degrees. Multiple other scripts for learning might have emerged if the research context and the methodologies were different. Further research therefore is needed to enrich the concept of cultural scripts for learning in higher education.

References

Appadurai, A. (1996) *Modernity at large: cultural dimensions of globalization.* Minneapolis, MN: University of Minnesota Press.

Baumann, G. (1996) *Contesting culture: discourses of identity in multi-ethnic London.* Cambridge: Cambridge University Press.

Benwell, B. and Stokoe, E. (2006) *Discourse and identity.* Edinburgh: Edinburgh University Press.

Berger, P. L. and Luckmann, T. (1966) *The social construction of reality: a treatise in the sociology of knowledge.* Harmondsworth, Middlesex: Penguin Education.

Bernstein, B. (1990) *The structuring of pedagogic discourse, Volume 1V: class, code and control.* London: Routledge.

Bhaba, H. (1994) *The location of culture.* London: Routledge.

Bochner, S. (1986) Coping with unfamiliar cultures: adjustment or culture learning? *Australian Journal of Psychology,* 38 (3), 347–358.

Bourdieu, P. (1992) *Language and symbolic power.* Cambridge: Polity Press.

Bruner, J. S. (1985) Narrative and paradigmatic modes of thought. In E. Eisner (Ed.), *Learning and teaching the ways of knowing,* Chicago, IL: University of Chicago Press, pp. 97–115.

Caroll, J. and Ryan, J. (2005) *Teaching international students: improving learning for all.* Abingdon: Routledge.

Charmaz, K. (1995) Between positivism and postmodernism: implications for methods. *Studies in Symbolic Interaction,* 17, 43–72.

Church, A. (1982) Sojourner adjustment. *Psychological Bulletin,* 91 (3), 540–572.

Devos, A. (2003) Academic standards, internationalisation, and the discursive construction of 'the international student'. *Higher Education Research and Development,* 22 (2), 155–166.

Dunlop, R. (1999) Beyond dualism: towards a dialogic negotiation of difference. *Canadian Journal of Education,* 24 (1), 57–69.

Furnham, A. and Bochner, S. (1986) *Culture shock: psychological reactions to unfamiliar environments.* London, New York: Routledge.

Geertz, C. (1975) *The interpretation of cultures.* New York: Basic Books.

Grant, B. and Manathunga, C. (2011) Supervision and cultural difference: rethinking institutional pedagogies, *Innovations in Education and Teaching International,* 48 (4), 351–354.

Gu, Q. (2011) An emotional journey of change: the case of Chinese students in UK higher education. In L. Jin and M. Cortazzi (Eds.), *Researching Chinese learners: skills, perceptions and intercultural adaptations,* Basingstoke: Palgrave Macmillan, pp. 212–232.

Haigh, M. (2002) Internationalization of curriculum: designing inclusive education for a small world. *Journal of Geography in Higher Education,* 26, (1), 49–66.

Harrison, N. and Peacock, N. (2007) Understanding the UK student response to internationalisation. *UKCISA World Views,* Summer, 23, 4–6.

Hofstede, G. (1980) *Culture consequence: international differences in work related values.* Beverly Hills, CA, and London: Sage.

Holliday, A. (1999). Small cultures. *Applied Linguistics,* 20 (2), 237–264.

Holstein, J. A. and Gubrium, J. F. (1995).*The active interview.* Qualitative Research Methods Series. No.37. London: Sage.

House, E. R. (1991) Realism in research. *Educational Researcher,* 20 (6), 2–25.

Ippolito, K. (2007) Promoting intercultural learning in a multicultural university: ideals and realities. *Teaching in Higher Education,* 12 (6), 749–763.

Jin, L. and Cortazzi, M. (Eds.), (2011) *Researching Chinese learners: skills, perceptions and intercultural adaptations.* Basingstoke: Palgrave Macmillan, pp. 212–232.

Kashima, E. and Loh, E. (2006) International students' acculturation: effects of international, conational and local ties and need for closure. *International Journal of Intercultural Relations,* 30, 471–485.

Keating, M., Martin, G. S. and Szabo, E. (2002) Do managers and students share the same perceptions of societal culture? *International Journal of Intercultural Relations,* 26 (6), 633–652.

Kehm, B. M. and Teichler, U. (2007) Research on internationalisation in higher education. *Journal of Studies in International Education,* 11 (3/4), 260–273.

Koehne, N. (2006) (Be)Coming, (be)longing: ways in which international students talk about themselves. *Discourse: Studies in the Cultural Politics of Education,* 27 (2), 241–257.

Kristeva, J. (1991) Strangers to ourselves. Translated by L. S. Roudiez. Herefordshire: Harvester Wheatsheaf.

Lea, M. (2004). Academic literacies: pedagogy for course design. *Studies in Higher Education,* 29 (6), 740–756.

Lea, M. and Street, B. (1998) Student writing in higher education: an academic literacies approach. *Studies in Higher Education,* 23 (2), 157–172.

Leonard, D., Pelletier, C. and Morely, L. (2004). *The experiences of international students in UK higher education: a review of unpublished material.* London: UKCOSA.

Marginson, S. and Sawir, E. (2011) *Ideas for intercultural education.* New York: Palgrave Macmillan.

Mishler, E. G. (1986) *Research interviewing: context and narrative.* Cambridge: Harvard University Press.

Montgomery, C. (2010) *Understanding the international student experience.* Universities into the 21st century series. Basingstoke: Palgrave Macmillan.

OECD (2011) *Education at a glance,* OECD indicators. Paris: OECD.

Parris-Kidd, H. and Barnett, J. (2011) Cultures of learning and student participation: Chinese learners in multicultural English class in Australia. In L. Jin and M. Cortazzi (Eds.), *Researching Chinese learners: skills, perceptions and intercultural adaptations*, Basingstoke: Palgrave Macmillan, pp. 169–187.

Polkinghorne, D. E. (1988) *Narrative knowing and the human science.* Albany, NY: State University of New York Press.

Pritchard, R. and Skinner, B. (2002) Cross-cultural partnership between home and international students. *Journal of Studies in International Education*, 6 (4), 323–354.

Ramburuth, P. (2001) Cross cultural learning behaviour in higher education: perceptions versus practice, *ultiBase Articles*, May edition, http://citeseerx.ist.psu.edu/viewdoc/download?doi=10.1.1.202.446&rep=rep1&type=pdf.

Rizvi, F. (2007) Internationalisation of curriculum: a critical perspective. In M. Heyden, J. Levy and J. Thompson (Eds.), *The Sage handbook on research in international education*, London: Sage, pp. 390–403.

Sawir, E. (2005) Language difficulties of international students in Australia: the effects of prior learning experience. *International Education Journal*, 6 (5), 567–580.

Schmitt, D. (2005) Writing in the international classroom. In J. Carroll and J. Ryan (Eds.), *Teaching international students: improving learning for all*, Oxon: Routledge, pp. 63–74.

Trahar, S (2011) *Developing cultural capability in international higher education: a narrative inquiry,* Oxon: Routledge.

Trinh, T. Minh-Ha (1997) Not you/like you: postcolonial women and the interlocking questions of identity and difference, In A. McClintock, A. Mufti and E. Shohat (Eds.), *Dangerous Liaisons: Gender, Nation, and Postcolonial Perspectives*, Minneapolis: University of Minnesota Press, pp: 415–419.

Ward, C. (2004) Psychological theories of culture contact and their implications for intercultural training and interventions. In D. Landis, J. M. Bennet and M. J. Bennet (Eds.), *Handbook of intercultural training.* (3rd ed.) Thousand Oaks, CA: Sage.

Welikala, T. C. (2006) Cultural scripts for learning in an intercultural higher education context: a narrative approach. Unpublished PhD thesis. Institute of Education. University of London.

Welikala, T. C. (2008) Disempowering and dislocating: how learners from diverse cultures read the role of the English language. *London Review of Education*, 6 (2), 159–171.

Welikala, T. C. (2011) *Rethinking the internationalisation of the curriculum in higher education: mapping the research landscape.* A position paper commissioned by Universitas 21, the network for international higher education.

Welikala, T. and Watkins, C. (2008). *Improving intercultural learning experiences in higher education: responding to cultural scripts for learning.* London: Institute of Education Publishers.

Yang, R. (2002) University internationalization: its meanings, rationale and implications. *Intercultural Education*, 13, 81–95.

4
The Virtual Student
A Distant, Global, Connected Learner

GRÁINNE CONOLE AND GABRIEL B. REEDY

The growth in the numbers of global students in many ways has paralleled the emergence of technology as a viable and useful educational tool. Globalisation has encouraged students and institutions to take a more global perspective, and to cross national boundaries more willingly than before. However, globalisation as a phenomenon could not have arisen without the corresponding growth and popularisation of technology. From relatively cheap air travel, enabling both students and academics to easily roam far from home, to the ubiquity of the personal computer and the global connectivity of the Internet, technology has enabled a kind of internationalisation very different to what was experienced even a generation ago.

Today's learners operate in a complex digitally enhanced learning context, in which they have access to a global network of peers and a plethora of free tools and resources to support their learning. They have multiple ways in which they can organise and represent content and ways of communicating and collaborating with others. Jenkins (2009) argues that learners need a particular set of digital literacies in order to be part of what he refers to as today's 'participatory culture' (i.e. the notion that social and participatory media enable users to interact more and to publish rather than just consume content), defined by Jenkins et al. as:

> … a culture with relatively low barriers to artistic expression and civic engagement, strong support for creating and sharing one's creations, and some type of informal mentorship whereby what is known by the most experienced is passed along to novices. A participatory culture is also one in which members believe their contributions matter, and feel some degree of social connection with one another (at the least they care what other people think about what they have created).
>
> (2006: 3)

Today's learners have grown up in a digital landscape; they cannot conceive of a world without computers, iPads and Google. Nonetheless it is far from true that they are competent at harnessing the power of technologies for academic purposes. Many lack the necessary skills to make effective judgements about whether or not a particular resource is relevant for their learning. Many lack the skills needed to organise and use effectively the mix of technologies that make up their Personal Learning Environment (PLE).

In order for practitioners to make informed choices about how to use technologies to support learning, we need a better understanding of how students are using technologies and what their perceptions of technologies are. However, the student experience of e-learning is less studied than it should be (Conole et al. 2006; Sharpe and Benfield 2005). While the literature is dominated by studies pitting technology against traditional teaching, or by 'optimist rhetoric" detailing the virtues of technology (Reynolds, Treharne and Tripp 2003), much empirical and theoretical work on the use of e-learning technologies is from the perspective of the teacher (or, as technology adoption in higher education is often an expensive, strategic project, from the perspective of managers and administrators). The perspective of students has, it seems, taken a back seat to the rather functional approach that dominates the use of technology in higher education. If student perspectives on e-learning are thin on the ground, even rarer are studies on global online students. In many ways, then, the goals of this chapter are difficult ones to attempt: what might we have to say about a subject that has little presence in the literature and that is only now emerging?

However, the large body of research on educational technology, which in turn has begun to give rise to a literature base on how students use, value and participate in e-learning, can help us explore the global student experience in a meaningful, theoretically grounded way. When viewed through the lens of the growing literature on the international student experience and on comparative and international higher education, of which this volume is a part, we hope this chapter clarifies some of the issues at play. This chapter draws on research on learner experiences of using technologies that has been undertaken in recent years (Sharpe et al. 2010). It summarises the range of social and participatory media that have emerged in the last half of the first decade of the 21st century, discusses their characteristics, and provides examples of how they can be used to support different types of pedagogies (Borgman et al. 2008; Conole and Alevizou 2010).

How Do E-Learning Technologies Help Support the Student Learning Experience?

In recent years there has been an emergence of literature exploring learners' use and perceptions of technologies. Some, such as Oblinger and Oblinger (2005) and Prensky (2001), argue that today's learners are different, that they are technologically immersed and see technologies as important learning tools.

They talk about the notion of digital natives to describe these learners. Others are more nuanced, arguing that it is more complicated than that (Jones 2011; Kennedy, Judd et al. 2008; Sharpe, Beetham and de Freitas 2010). What is evident though is that today's students are technologically immersed and see technologies as part of their core learning toolset. Some students are able to appropriate and personalise technologies to support their learning; however, other students often struggle, unable to harness the potential of technologies effectively – not understanding that surfing Google for three hours does not equate to three hours of effective learning. Many are unable to prioritise and unable to make effective judgements about whether or not a resource is relevant in a particular context.

Existing literature on e-learning has explored in some detail, and has argued from various theoretical perspectives, the ways in which technology supports student learning (Conole and Oliver 2007). Various kinds of e-learning technologies, and increasingly mobile devices, can allow for and encourage different kinds of student learning (Conole 2010). It is these affordances, how the inherent and designed properties of technologies allow various kinds of learning activities and interactions to take place (Conole and Dyke 2004), which can help us to understand more about the learner experience of technology. More recent studies of how students perceive technology to enhance their learning (Gilbert et al. 2007; Sharpe and Benfield 2005) provide a good method of triangulating this perspective: in many cases, the design features and affordances of the technologies are exactly the things that students perceive to be advantageous or efficacious in their learning, such as mechanisms to promote reflective or dialogic learning and means of collaborating with peers.

Availability of the Learning Environment

One major benefit of technology to the student experience is that students can access the learning environment whenever and wherever they need to. As Virtual Learning Environments (VLEs) or Learning Management Systems (LMSs) are based on web technologies, they are designed to be accessed from any Internet-connected device with a web browser, and students can effectively engage in study wherever and whenever they choose. Although this is clearly a benefit for all students, especially as modes of study have evolved and changed and as more students are blurring the lines between full-time study and part-time work, it is even more beneficial for international students. In studies of the student experience of e-learning, this feature consistently emerges as a central one (see Sharpe et al. [2010] for a summary of research on learner experience). They note that students appreciate the ability to access learning material and to communicate with each other at a time and place of their choosing.

Working with learning groups across time zones, as is common among an internationalised student cohort, can be particularly challenging, but the asynchronous nature of many computer-mediated communication technologies (online forums, for instance), minimises some of the issues associated with temporal and physical distance. Students can interact with each other at whatever times are good for them, rather than being required to be present for a single time or co-located in the same physical space.

Mobile learning technologies take the potential for the availability of the learning environment even further. Though traditional VLE and LMS environments are built with the desktop computer in mind, students often bypass these altogether and use mobile technologies to communicate with each other and to find information (Conole et al. 2006). The ubiquity of mobile Internet connectivity in many countries makes it possible to use these mobile devices for learning regardless of location – the notion of learning anywhere, anytime is now a reality; mobile devices provide attractive interfaces for presenting learning materials. New smart phones and tablets provide rich environments for students to learn on the go and enable materials to be presented in a variety of rich multimedia representations. Mobile learning, as a result, is becoming an increasingly important means of enabling learners to learn anywhere and anytime.

Ability to Allow for Collaborative Learning

As Stahl et al. (2006) point out, two decades of research on computer-mediated communication tools as used in online environments show that they both allow for, and in many cases produce, a meaningful and collaborative learning environment for students. From the student experience perspective, learning in this way is much less about the passive receipt of knowledge from a more experienced teacher. Rather, learning becomes something that happens between and among the learning community, of which both students and teachers are part. In reality, many VLEs are used as content repositories; however, social and participatory media provide a rich variety of ways in which learners can communicate and collaborate with peers and with tutors. This collaboration, which can consist of students 'expressing their questions, pursuing lines of inquiry together, teaching each other and seeing how others are learning" (Stahl et al. 2006: 410), nonetheless is difficult to engender, and both requires and is afforded by online technologies. The power of collaborative learning is significant, and the emerging theory of group cognition argues that it is by engaging in collaborative learning activities that both group and individual learning occurs. Such collaborative learning challenges existing ways of engaging with teaching and learning, and indeed is a drastic move away from how many VLEs and LMSs are frequently used – as repositories for learning materials.

Synchronous Engagement

Especially within the VLE and LMS context, most e-learning activities occur using asynchronous technologies – tools like online forums that allow students and teachers to interact with each other without having to be online at the same time. However, the growing availability of more synchronous technologies has converged with ubiquitous and mobile Internet connectivity to allow virtual 'face-to-face' meeting opportunities. Indeed, technology now allows a geographically dispersed community of learners to converge electronically, creating the potential for meeting each other in online space but at the same time. This trend, which like many, began in commercial contexts with webinars (through platforms such as WebEx), and is used extensively in a globalised economy where frequent travel has become prohibitively expensive. Earlier student experience work (Conole et al. 2006) shows evidence that synchronous text-based technologies, such as instant messaging tools, are especially valuable to students and can create significant learning experiences. Stahl's (2010a) Virtual Math Teams Project showed that simple, text-based chat rooms were the centre of an emerging form of collaborative meaning-making and knowledge building, or what his research group called 'group cognition', and that engaging in structured learning experiences in these chat rooms produced a profound shift in the nature of students' learning (Stahl 2010b, 2010c).

The availability of video and audio technologies that connect people in real time over the Internet has meant that software like Skype, MSN and iChat is now available on almost every Internet-capable device. These tools make it easy for students to connect personally with each other or with their teachers across distances while retaining some of the feeling of face-to-face interaction. Educators have also begun to use more robust and fully featured synchronous teaching software, in many cases developed in parallel with meeting software for use by distributed working teams in commercial contexts. These tools allow for shared synchronous experiences, group and one-to-one text chat, shared artefacts like whiteboards, and video and audio conferencing in one system. From the student perspective, synchronous engagement can eliminate some of the physical distance between and among a distributed cohort, allowing students and teachers to engage in a personal way.

Reflection and Its Role in the Learning Process

Reflection is a core facet of learning, i.e. the ability for learners to step back and think about their learning, to internalise it and appropriate it to their own context. One of the benefits of online learning technologies, especially asynchronous ones, argue Conole and Dyke (2004), is that they specifically allow students to engage with ideas on their own terms: in their own time, in a location and using learning approaches that make sense for the learner.

This contrasts with in-person and face-to-face learning activities, which force students to engage within real and limited time constraints.

Online learning can provide the international student with opportunities to consider, reflect upon and engage with learning materials and discussion in ways that are not possible in face-to-face environments. When participating in an online discussion, for instance, students can read a message thread multiple times, use reference materials if necessary to query both disciplinary or language concerns, and carefully consider and compose a response. In a face-to-face classroom based in a Western academic tradition, where student engagement is characterised by students actively participating in classroom discussions, and where a discursive environment is often considered a normal part of the learning experience, international students can be left feeling unable to follow and contribute to classroom discussion.

A significant portion of student learning at university already occurs outside the classroom, a research finding (Kuh 1995) that is also reflected in higher education practice and policy. Higher education bodies in the US and the UK, for example, expect students to spend anywhere from three to five times as much time in personal study as they do in classroom-based activities. In the case of international students, this out-of-class activity is even more important, as frequently students are learning in a second or even third language and engage in social meaning-making activities with colleagues in order to understand the activities. The use of podcasts, with transcripts of the audio, is a valuable way of presenting information, particularly for international students. They can augment this by communicating with peers to co-construct understanding.

In an e-learning setting, having the ability to work outside the context of the classroom means that students can take time and space to consider and reflect on the tasks at hand. Additionally, e-learning material represents a further set of artefacts upon which this reflection can be based; students no longer have only a textbook and their own notes to pour over, but potentially also the reflective postings of colleagues, the recording of a previous lecture or practical demonstration, or any number of other artefacts that they consult during their study. Whether doing so in an attempt to enhance the meaning they are making from the learning experience or in an attempt to clarify a linguistic point, the ability to use these disparate artefacts to reflect upon their own thinking can only enhance the learning experience for students.

Currency and Appropriateness of Learning Materials

In the context of traditional face-to-face learning experiences, students often use textbooks and printed materials that have been produced months or years before. Because online learning environments can be continually updated, however, there is the potential for immediate and meaningful learning opportunities to be integrated into the learning environment at a moment's notice. Although some fields and disciplines are more dynamic than others, there is an almost universal proliferation of new knowledge. In addition, there are now numerous tools to enable learners to create their own learning materials, which they can share with others, as well as wikis for collaborative activities, blogs for reflection and social bookmarking tools to amass resources. New learning technologies allow this distributed knowledge to be aggregated and allow for participative and collaborative knowledge building. The compressed timescales associated with online publishing (indeed, the immediacy of web publishing in some academic contexts) mean that new knowledge is accessible by academics and learners much more quickly than in the past. In so doing, these tools allow knowledge to be harnessed for the benefit of students rather more immediately than is possible in traditional academic environments.

Traditionally, academic notions of the universality of knowledge – that knowledge and ideas generated in one context can be applied unproblematically in any other context – have meant that academic knowledge flowed from the Northern and Western hemispheres to other parts of the world (UNESCO 2005). However, learning technologies allow a globalised learning community to contribute locally relevant knowledge to the learning experience. For example, a learning community that includes learners from many different geographical and cultural contexts has the benefit of exposing all the members of that community to a diversity of approaches and experience. A university business course that includes managers from a European manufacturing company as well as entrepreneurs from a developing economy, for example, can result in a unique exchange of both ideas and working practices between and among those contexts. In this way, ideas and examples of theory-in-action that are relevant across multiple contexts can, in turn, encourage more persistent and meaningful learning experiences for students.

Learner Control and Participation In Learning

Didactic approaches to classroom teaching, which dominated the university experience for centuries, put the educator in control and placed students in a position of knowledge recipient. Although progressive pedagogical approaches are challenging this in face-to-face environments, the choices that students have when making decisions about their own learning are often limited: they can choose whether to attend class, to what extent they attend to lectures or participate in activities, and so forth. They cannot, however, make decisions about how and when they learn, how and when they engage, and in what order they learn. Technology-enhanced learning environments take a step further in this direction, by providing the ability for students to take a more active and engaged approach in their own learning and make these choices for themselves. Indeed, some educators are talking about the notion of the flipped classroom, in which interactions with technologies now means that the traditional roles of teacher and student are blurring or even reversing; thus putting the student at the centre of the learning process (Bergmann and Sams 2012).

What are Students Learning, and What Is Their Learning Experience Like?

There has been a shift in the last ten years or so away from didactic and individualised approaches to learning towards more constructivist and socially situated pedagogies (Conole 2010; Mayes and de Freitas 2004). In addition, Siemens (2005) argues that networked technologies enable a form of distributed connectivist learning. Siemens developed connectivism as an approach that emphasises the connected and networked nature within which modern learning occurs (2005). This includes a learning ecology model that considers the elements involved in the learning process and how they can be facilitated within a networked ecology. It emphasises the networking affordances of technologies. New technologies, and in particular social and participatory media, provide a rich range of ways in which these pedagogies can be instantiated.

Increasingly, learning is just-in-time, collaborative and participatory. In today's complex societal context learners need to move beyond simple knowledge recall to become lifelong learners. Most will have more than one career and will need to constantly update their skills base. New models of informal learning are emerging which foster connectivism, for example informal learning spaces in social and participatory media. In addition, we have seen the emergence in recent years of Massive Open Online Courses (MOOCs), where both the course resources and the expertise are free. Students can choose to work through the course in whatever way they want, creating their own individualised learning pathway. There is little in the way of teacher-facilitated support; more emphasis is placed on peer support and facilitation. At the end of the course, students can choose whether or not they want to be formally accredited for their learning. The sheer scale of these courses (the Stanford Artificial Intelligence course had more than 90,000 participants in 2011) means that the affordances of social and participatory media (openness, peer critiquing, distributed cognition, collective aggregation, etc.) are possible, resulting in an approach that is very much routed in connectivism.

Daniel (2012) argues that to meet the needs of tomorrow's learners we would need to be opening a new bricks and mortar university every week, and indeed something of this nature is happening in China. However, in reality this is not sustainable worldwide; hence e-learning provides a solution to meet these anticipated needs. Furthermore, the traditional 18-year-old, full-time, campus-based student is becoming a minority. More and more learners combine their studies with work and hence need flexible educational offerings.

The role of traditional institutions must change to be more flexible and must shift from a role as content providers to providing pedagogically effective learning pathways, support and guidance and accreditation routes.

The Growth of Learning Platforms, and Their Use To Broaden and Globalise the Student Base

While much has changed about university life in the last 20 years, many of the most salient features of the experience have remained the same. In universities and colleges around the world, undergraduate students gather together in lecture halls and seminar rooms at the appointed hour to hear lectures and participate in seminars or tutorials given by highly trained academics (and, increasingly, by their postgraduate students). Students then go off from these sessions to do their assigned reading, lab work and other independent study, perhaps complaining about one aspect or other of the workload. But one only needs to hear the first few words of many of these lectures or seminars, or to see any of those students open their laptops to begin working on their homework, to recognise that something significant has changed about the way that students experience university education in the early 21st century. The VLE or LMS platform has become central to the student experience of higher education.

Most institutions now have an institutional VLE or LMS and increasingly students are expecting to be able to access course content and administrative details online. A 2011 project at the University of Leicester, a traditional research university in the UK, conducted a major review of how the university's VLE, BlackBoard, was used across all four colleges. The resulting data provided a rich insight into how the VLE is being used, what other tools are being used and any support issues. Disappointingly, much of the use of the VLE/LMS was as a content repository, although there were some pockets of innovation. These include the use of podcasts and interactive videos in the sciences, and the use of online social networking to promote communities of practice across the university. The university was able to use the data from the project to develop a series of pedagogical templates in the VLE, along with examples of good practice from across the colleges, which can be shared with practitioners and used as inspiration and guidance on how to instantiate different pedagogies. Four templates were developed: a calendar/unit based template, a topic-based template, a project/case-based template and a problem-based learning template. Similar processes are underway at many universities as institutions became increasingly dissatisfied with the ways in which their virtual learning platforms were being used and supported.

Some of the findings from this project to date include the fact that, unsurprisingly, there remains a tension between teaching and research, even when teaching uses innovative technologies. The majority of academics in the

Leicester project reported being reluctant to try out innovative approaches to teaching, perhaps because of an inherent conservatism in the academy. Why spend a few hours creating new teaching materials when the same time spent on a research application or a paper will count towards a potential promotion? In addition, many are put off by what they describe as the clunky and non-intuitive interface of the VLE or LMS. Typically, only one or two people in any department are significant users of the VLE or LMS, while the majority simply use it as a content repository for lecture notes. This raises issues in terms of the equity of the student experience across the university.

Nonetheless, a range of exemplars of good practice are emerging from the project. Chemistry, for example, reported examples of using a problem-based learning approach within the VLE, and the use of screencasts. Engineering reported the development of an extensive range of podcasts, called 'profcasts'. These are particularly valuable for international students where English is not their first language, as the podcasts include a script to accompany the audio. This means that students can read the text and pause and rewind as much as they like. They are also useful for revision purposes. Mathematics reported developing a range of mini-maths videos to explain difficult concepts. Psychology, meanwhile, reported using Google Docs in conjunction with the VLE to enable student collaboration, and education reported using the freely available tool, VoiceThreads, to promote collaborative discourse.

As VLEs have proliferated, they have begun to create a new interface between academics, university and students. In their literature review of student experiences with e-learning, for instance, Sharpe and Benfield (2005) highlighted the VLE or LMS as a major interface between the university and the student, and student expectations of their learning experience are now mediated by their online experiences. To the extent that the materials and activities that students need for their learning are easily accessible and available online, students are relatively pleased with their interaction (Sharpe and Benfield 2005). Indeed, when VLEs and LMSs function as 'virtual repositories' of information to enhance face-to-face learning, as is the case with many institutions, students can perceive the VLE or LMS as the one-stop shop for everything that is necessary for their learning. In the context of the global and distance student, however, this expectation can quickly outstrip the ability of institutional infrastructures to deliver.

In institutions like Leicester, as this 'virtual repository' notion continues to be challenged with pockets of innovative practice, the VLE or LMS is beginning to realise some of the potential that the technology affords, providing the unique and necessary benefits for a distributed, global student community. In particular, the VLE or LMS e-learning platform is beginning to develop as more of a web-based learning hub, and a host platform that helps to mediate interaction between student and teacher and among students. As such, the e-learning platform is starting to reshape the notion of 'contact' in an educational sense. While traditionally learning was conceptualised as the amount of time students spend in a classroom or in a tutorial, e-learning platforms allow a new notion of the student learning experience to come to the fore. In the new globalised online student experience, there is less focus on interaction between student and teacher, and much more of a focus on interaction between the student and learning artefacts; between student and fellow student; and between student and the discipline or subject of enquiry.

In many ways, the development of VLE and LMS platforms has paralleled the development of distance learning. As VLEs and LMSs have developed, distance learning has moved from being an online repository for information that supported other means of learning (sometimes blended with face-to-face contact, such as at The Open University in the UK) to supporting what is now the norm in many distance learning settings: completely virtual learning. This has changed the student experience dramatically, especially for international and global students, and has enabled students to engage with programmes and institutions far removed from their own geographies. The Open University in the UK, for example, regularly recruits approximately 10 per cent of its students from outside the UK; these students engage almost exclusively with the learning experience using the university's VLE.

In a sense, then, it could be argued that the VLE and LMS has led to the emergence of a type of completely virtual and international mode of study, where the respective locations of student and teacher, and of students to each other, is less important than it has ever been. The ability to interact and learn in virtual space is much more important than is the ability to gather in the same time and place. Around the world, this is not just important for studying across cultural and geographical contexts, but also within them: some universities (e.g. UNISA, the University of South Africa) serve populations that cannot easily travel beyond their local contexts, so are moving directly from a correspondence-tuition model to a VLE-based online learning experience where formerly isolated students now connect to each other and their teachers in online learning environments. In many localities, UNISA has established local study centres or contracted with local internet cafes, where students can work on Internet-enabled computers that they might not have access to at home.

However, there is a tension between institutional e-learning platforms and the use of freely available tools and resources. On the one hand, the VLE or LMS provides a standardised environment, which is controllable and can provide a common look and feel for the students. Also such platforms provide monitoring tools to enable academics to see what learners are doing. Free tools and resources provide additional functionality, but cannot be controlled and there may be issues in terms of how they are integrated with the platform. Nonetheless, learners are increasingly making use of these technologies. Many have their own email accounts, and may already use Google Docs, blogging tools, and other freely available tools, and may prefer to use these instead of institutional tools.

Open Educational Resources, MOOCs and the International Student Experience

Open Educational Resources (OER) are freely available educational materials that can be reused and repurposed by anyone for educational purposes. These resources, normally (but not always) digital materials, are often produced by individual educators and institutions and distributed through online repositories that provide insight into the resources' provenance and potential uses. It has now been a decade since UNESCO introduced the term Open Educational Resources, and even longer than that since the Massachusetts Institute of Technology (MIT) introduced its Open Courseware initiative to make all of its teaching material freely available online. The Open Courseware project, which allows people anywhere to freely access the teaching materials of one of the premier computer science, technology and engineering universities in the world, has since offered more than 2000 courses online. The stated aim of the project is to provide course material for educators to reuse and repurpose for their own teaching, but the project also acknowledges that learners can use the material for self-study (MIT 2012).

Perhaps not surprisingly, a concise definition of OER has yet to be agreed upon. The movement was, in many ways, based on a development model that intended to make educational materials available globally, and to promote the diffusion of knowledge from universities to learners who did not have the opportunities to access a university education. Since then there has been a phenomenal growth in the OER movement worldwide. Significant sums of money have been spent on developing vast repositories of OER, and the movement is beginning to shift its focus from the development of resources to their reuse. OER are increasingly having an impact on traditional educational institutions, which seek to find ways of integrating them into teaching and learning activities; indeed, in 2011, a survey showed that over 57 per cent of university leaders believed that OER were valuable to their university's teaching and learning efforts (Allen and Seaman 2011). Within this context, new business models are emerging. For example, the OER University is an international consortium of institutions where learners can work through any OER they want to and then choose to be accredited through one of the partner institutions. The Peer-to-Peer University enables peers to get 'badges' on particular skills. In the context of the globalised student, OER can allow students to interact with the university in an educationally meaningful way without engaging in a particular course of study. However, they are increasingly being seen by universities as 'tasters' of the kind of learning experiences that might await them as they become fully fledged, enrolled students.

Similarly, in recent years we have seen the emergence of MOOCs (Downes 2012; Educause 2011). In a sense, MOOCs seek to use technology to radically open formal educational courses to vast numbers of students, potentially spread around the world. Learners can register for free and can choose to be assessed and accredited or not.

What Is the Future of Online Learning?

Future projections, especially where technology is concerned, are usually folly: as Nobel prize-winning economist Paul Krugman asked in 2009, 'where are the flying cars?' However, there is some benefit to exploring how current trends that have been discussed in this chapter may continue to develop over time, and exploring how those trends might play out in the learner experience.

For a start, the many benefits that have emerged from technology-enhanced learning until the present will not recede: it will most likely not, for instance, become more difficult to collaborate online, or to publish learning material easily and quickly online, or to meet virtually, synchronously, using technology. Indeed, as technology continues apace, the overwhelming sense is that these emergent benefits will rather continue to become more refined and more beneficial to learners and teachers alike. Personalisation of the learning environment, which learning research has shown to be valuable for students in primary and secondary education, will continue its move to the fore in higher education and lifelong learning also. Artificial intelligence, though still in its infancy, will undoubtedly play a role in the development of new ways to access and process knowledge in the future; and, thus, will play a role in how we teach and learn. In a sense, then, the future of online learning is as limitless as the potential for the technologies that are currently in development and that will continue to be developed. This notion is solidly backed by US university leaders' opinions about the importance of technology, and of online learning in particular, to their own institutions' future success: over 65 per cent said that 'online learning is critical to the long-term strategy of my educational institution', up from fewer than 50 per cent less than a decade ago (Allen and Seaman 2011: 4).

As technology continues to become pervasive in peoples' lives, the modes of technology-enhanced learning will likely develop as well. Social media, which emerged through the first decade of the 21st century, have in a very short period of time become central to many peoples' lives: almost a billion people, or nearly one sixth of the world's population, use the social networking website Facebook at least once every month (Facebook 2012). Educators are desperate to harness these technologies for their own purposes, yet remain stymied by learners' unwillingness to let their social spaces be taken over by educators. The challenge of how to develop social media for learning will continue to drive educational decisions into the next decade.

Similarly, although mobile devices have been slow to be integrated into institutional approaches in the higher education sector, there is some emerging evidence that mobile phones, tablets, and other mobile and personal electronic devices can become central to the student learning experience – if thoughtfully and carefully integrated into the pedagogical approach.

Pedagogies themselves continue to develop also, building on the new technologies to argue for new theoretical frameworks within which to consider teaching and learning. Connectivism, for instance, builds on the ideas of constructivist pedagogy but places it within the context of the constantly and multiply connected environments that students and institutions find themselves in (Siemens 2005). In doing so, it positions the very connectedness of the system as being capable of learning and enabling a new kind of learning to occur.

For higher education institutions, it seems that the next logical step in the progression of institutional technology platforms (VLEs and LMSs) is their use in developing and opening up markets across geographies. Open and distance learning universities, like The Open University in the UK and UNISA in South Africa, have made clear that their aspirations are to serve their respective continents rather than just their home countries. They anticipate doing this by continuing their current trends of opening up distance-learning courses to international students.

And, the reasoning goes, if the learning experience works well with very little or no face-to-face contact, then students anywhere can tap into the benefits of a traditional university – the name, the institutional legitimacy, the other perceived benefits of the institution – no matter where in the world they are. MOOCs may indeed become more and more viable, as institutions seek to open markets with no respect to traditional geopolitical borders. The benefits for institutions, especially cash-strapped public universities funded by a continually shrinking public funding stream, are obvious.

Business schools were among the first to 'go global' in this sense, perhaps seeing the trends of globalisation happening in industry. Several universities in Europe and North America now have virtual business schools in East Asia, involving limited face-to-face contact and extended virtual engagement. Latterly, other fields and disciplines are beginning to see the benefits of a global reach. One university in the UK has, for instance, managed to bring a struggling programme in Early Childhood Education back into rude health by creating an online version of the course for students from all over the world. The course now has hundreds of students, including a particularly large cohort from India, but is taught and administered from a small office in north London.

Within this context, the international student experience continues to evolve and change, and over time the relationships between student, teacher, institution, physical presence and learning context will continue to become more fluid. Regional, national and international borders will become less important to students, who are now beginning to study outside local geographic catchment areas and expand their choices of international study beyond ones that they may have previously considered. For some of these students, technology and the changing landscape of higher education means that educational migration can be digital rather than physical; they can join a group of colleagues from around the world while remaining in their local family contexts. In some cases, international universities and branches of long-established universities being established around the world allow an international experience but with a relatively local flavour. To whom the benefits of this fluidity in the higher education landscape will accrue remains an open question; however, it is inevitable that technology has begun to open educational experiences to students around the world in ways never before imagined.

References

Allen, I.E., and Seaman, J. (2011).Going the distance: online education in the United States, 2011. Babson College: Babson Survey Research Group. http://www.online-learningsurvey.com/reports/goingthedistance.pdf

Bergmann, J. and Sams, A. (2012). *Flip Your Classroom: Reach Every Student, in Every Classroom, Every Day*. Washington, DC: ISTE (International Society for Technology in Education).

Borgman, C.L. et al. (2008). Fostering learning in the networked world: the cyberlearning opportunity and challenge. Report of the NSF Task Force on Cyberlearning. http://www.nsf.gov/pubs/2008/nsf08204/nsf08204.pdf

Conole, G. (2010) Review of pedagogical frameworks and models and their use in e-learning. http://cloudworks.ac.uk/cloud/view/2982/

Conole, G. and Dyke, M. (2004). What are the affordances of information and communication technologies? *ALT-J: Research in Learning Technology*, 12(2), 113–124.

Conole, G. and Oliver, M. (2007). *Contemporary Perspectives in E-learning Research: Themes, Methods and Impact on Practice*. London, RoutledgeFalmer.

Conole, G. and Alevizou, J. (2010). A literature review of the use of Web 2.0 tools in Higher Education. A report commissioned by the Higher Education Academy. www.heacademy.ac.uk/assets/EvidenceNet/Conole_Alevizou_2010.pdf (accessed 16 November 2011).

Conole, G., de Laat, M., Darby, J. and Dillon, T. (2006) An in-depth case study of students' experiences of e-learning – how is learning changing? Final report of the JISC-funded LXP Learning Experiences Study project, Milton Keynes: Open University.

Daniel, J. (2012). Dual-mode universities: way station or final destination? *Open Learning: The Journal of Open and Distance Learning*, 27(1), 89–95.

Downes, S. (2012). Connectivism and connective knowledge: essays on meaning and learning networks. http://www.downes.ca/files/Connective_Knowledge-19May2012.pdf

Educause (2011). Seven things you should know about MOOCs. http://net.educause.edu/ir/library/pdf/ELI7078.pdf

Facebook (2012) Facebook Newsroom. http://newsroom.fb.com/ (accessed 1 June 2012).

Gilbert, J., Morton, S. and Rowley, J. (2007). E-learning: the student experience. *British Journal of Educational Technology*, 38(4), 560–573.

Jenkins, H. (2009). Confronting the challenges of participatory culture: media education for the 21st century. The John D. and Catherine T. MacArthur Foundation Reports on Digital Media and Learning. Cambridge, MA: MIT Press. http://digitallearning.macfound.org/atf/cf/%7B7E45C7E0-A3E0-4B89-AC9C-E807E1B0AE4E%7D/JENKINS_WHITE_PAPER.PDF

Jenkins, H., Clinton, K. et al. (2006). *Confronting the Challenges of Participatory Culture: Media Education for the 21st Century*. Chicago, IL: The MacArthur foundation.

Jones, C. (2011). Students, the net generation and digital natives: accounting for educational change. In M. Thomas (ed.), *Deconstructing Digital Natives: Young People, Technology, and the New Literacies*. Abingdon, UK: Routledge, pp. 30–48.

Kennedy, G., Judd, T.S. et al. (2008). First year students' experiences with technology, are they really digital natives? *AJET*, 24(1), 108–122.

Krugman, P. (2009) Interview between Paul Krugman and Charlie Stross, 6 August 2009. Transcript: http://www.steussy.com/blog/2009/08/krugman-and-stross-transcript/ Audio: http://cluebytwelve.net/anticipation/Stross-Krugman%202009-08-06-24.mp3

Kuh, G.D. (1995). The other curriculum: out-of-class experiences associated with student learning and personal development. *Journal of Higher Education*, 66, 123–125.

Mayes, T. and De Freitas, S. (2004). Review of e-learning frameworks, models and theories, JISC e-learning models desk study. JISC Report. http://www.jisc.ac.uk/uploaded_documents/Stage%202%20Learning%20Models%20%28Version%201%29.pdf

MIT Open Courseware (2012). http://ocw.mit.edu.

Oblinger, D.G. and Oblinger, J. (2005). *Educating the Net Generation*, Educause. http://net.educause.edu/ir/library/pdf/pub7101.pdf

Prensky, M. (2001). Digital natives, digital immigrants. *On the Horizon*, 9(5).

Reynolds, D., Treharne, D. et al. (2003). ICT – the hopes and the reality. *British Journal of Educational Technology* 34(2), 151–167.

Sharpe, R. and Benfield, G. (2005). The student experience of e-learning in higher education : a review of the literature. *Brookes e-Journal of Learning and Teaching*, 1(3), September 2005. http://www.brookes.ac.uk/publications/bejlt/volume1issue3/academic/sharpe_benfield.html

Sharpe, R., Beetham, H. and de Freitas, S. (2010). *Rethinking Learning for the Digital Age: How Learnes Shape Their Own Experiences*. London: Routledge.

Siemens, G. (2005). Connectivism: a learning theory for the digital age. *International journal of instructional technology and distance learning*, 2(1), 3–10.

Stahl, G. (2010a). The Virtual Math Teams (VMT) Project. http://gerrystahl.net/vmt/

Stahl, G. (2010b). Group cognition as a foundation for the new science of learning. In M.S. Khine & I.M. Saleh (eds.), *New Science of Learning: Cognition, Computers And Collaboration in Education*. New York: Springer, pp. 23–44.

Stahl, G. (2010c). Group-cognition factors in sociotechnical systems. *Human Factors. Special issue on Collaboration, Coordination, and Adaptation in Complex Sociotechnical Systems*, 52(2), 340–343.

Stahl, G., Koschmann, T. and Suthers, D. (2006). Computer-supported collaborative learning: an historical perspective. In R.K. Sawyer (ed.), *Cambridge Handbook of the Learning Sciences*. Cambridge, UK: Cambridge University Press, pp. 409–426.

UNESCO (2005). Towards knowledge societies. Paris: United Nations Educational, Scientific and Cultural Organization (UNESCO). http://unesdoc.unesco.org/images/0014/001418/141843e.pdf

5

Academic Literacy and Language Development

ARLYS VAN WYK AND NAN YELD

Increasing numbers of students from other countries, especially sub-Saharan African countries, are choosing to register at universities in post-apartheid South Africa. The need to understand how student access and success is influenced by language and medium of instruction and, in turn, how institutions view and provide educational responses to student needs, is therefore growing in importance. Adding to the challenges faced and posed by the increase in international students, however, is the fact that in Africa generally, the language of instruction in education is not the mother tongue of students. This means that universities face a significant challenge – that of providing effective and meaningful language learning and development opportunities for the great majority of their students, and not only for a relatively small number of international students.

International students come to South African universities for a variety of reasons. Amongst these two stand out: deteriorating conditions in higher education in many African countries, and a desire to gain internationally recognised qualifications. For students from sub-Saharan Africa, the fact that they pay local fees – in recognition of the role that several sub-Saharan countries played in supporting the anti-apartheid movement during struggle for independence – is an added attraction. Interviews with a group of international, first-year students registered at the University of the Free State elicited the following comments:

> I had a friend who learned here so he told about it and I did my research and found out that the fees were a bit low as compared to other universities. I visited the main campus before I applied and I liked the environment and the quality lecture rooms. Bloemfontein also is a quiet town and I liked the notion of learning in a quiet town that way I could concentrate more on my studies without major disturbance.
>
> (Zimbabwe)

> It offers a degree I wanted to pursue and is close to home.
>
> (Maseru- Lesotho)

Close to home and good quality education.

(Lesotho)

Many students receive government grants or bursaries from their home countries and are directed to specific universities to study in professional areas where skills are needed in the home country.

It wasn't really up to me, but don't regret the experience.

(Botswana)

As a result of political and social upheaval in their countries, many people from elsewhere in Africa have flocked to South Africa (Steyn 2007:16). It is estimated (no official statistics exist) that since 1994, between eight and nine million people from other African countries have entered South Africa (de Wet and Wolhuter 2009: 371). As would be expected, such upheavals have also impacted on the quality and provision of higher education opportunities, and students come to South Africa in pursuit of internationally recognised qualifications. Illustrations of the kinds of challenges experienced by many universities in Africa are discussed in such reports as the African Union / New Partnership for Africa's Development Workshop 'Renewal of higher education in Africa' (NEPAD 2005) and include such issues as the impact of the brain drain of highly educated Africans to developed countries, rapidly rising student numbers, political interference and information and communications technology challenges.

Africa has been through much turmoil historically as a result of colonialism, post-colonial wars and finally independence from colonial powers, but the yoke of language division that also embodies divisions of power has proved highly resistant to change (Alidou 2004). In many African countries colonial languages 'have generally come to be used for high-level purposes in each African country south of the Sahara' (Heugh 2009:105). Language in education policies in many sub-Saharan countries follow an early exit from mother tongue. In countries such as South Africa, Zimbabwe, Zambia, Lesotho and Swaziland many learners at school exit into English at a very early age before the process of 'learning to read' has been achieved. In South Africa this transition takes place at the age of nine years. What follows is a subtracted kind of bilingualism in the classroom as teachers – who are themselves frequently not proficient in cognitive academic language proficiency (CALP)-type language proficiency competencies – grapple with introducing academic concepts that are 'new' to learners in a language that is foreign to teachers and learners alike, viz. English. According to Cummins (2009) CALP is the kind of linguistic proficiency needed in learning contexts. This kind of proficiency allows learners to read and produce increasingly complex texts as they progress through the grades. This concept is discussed in more detail below. In multilingual situations, students' mother tongues are important and valuable resources for language and content acquisition (Cummins 1996: 60).

There is overwhelming evidence (Janks 2010; Alidou, Aliou, Brock-Utne, Diallo, Heugh, and Wolff 2006; Alexander 2005; Heugh 2000) that militates against a monolingual approach to language in education in multilingual countries. In general, the research concludes that monolingual approaches to language in education have hampered student access and chances of success. Alexander (1999: 6) articulates the serious implications of such approaches for education:

> The disastrous fact that in most African countries, after two or three years of mother tongue or home language medium, there is an automatic switch to one or other foreign language as the main medium of primary-school education, is the single most destructive datum on the continent of Africa.

Maintaining a colonial language as the medium of instruction, it is argued, leads to students' inability to comprehend or participate in classroom activities to the extent where they are learning and progressing. This inability to access learning is the main cause of the low academic achievement of many African students at all levels of education (Alidou et al. 2006: 6; Alidou 2004: 195; Bokamba 1984: 4). Despite all the evidence of the harmful effects of an early switch to a foreign language as the medium of instruction, the hegemony of colonial languages still characterises education policy making and negatively impacts on the CALP essential to students' success in higher education. The useful distinction drawn by Cummins (2009) between basic interpersonal communicative skills and CALP is discussed in more detail below.

This monolingual approach to language in education in the face of so much research to the contrary is perplexing. However, the question here is: How do we in higher education deal with local and international students who have been disadvantaged as a result of this reductionist approach? In responding to this question, this chapter draws on data from two main sources: focus group interviews with international students at a South African university, and national performance data of applicants to higher education, both international and local, on academic literacy tests. A mixed method approach was taken for purposes of this study, viz. quantitative and qualitative methods. Quantitative data were gathered from the results of first-year students' performance on the National Benchmark testing as discussed below and qualitative data were gathered from two focus group interviews with fourteen first-year international students from countries bordering South Africa. The students were registered for a variety of undergraduate programmes. The article outlines the role of language in education and then addresses the challenges, opportunities and differences of language and literacy in higher education.

The article concludes with a brief look at current international issues and what can be drawn from other experiences.

The Role of Language Development and Academic Literacy within the Student Experience

A major, stock-taking research project on mother-tongue education and bilingual education in sub-Saharan Africa has contributed to our overall understanding of the role of language in African education and the negative effects of monolingual approaches to educational planning in multilingual countries (Alidou et al. 2006). The need for research on the use of African languages in education arose from a biennial meeting in 2003 of the Association of the Development of Education in Africa (ADEA). The document ensuing from this research was intended to inform educators and policy makers. Based on this extensive project, it seems that educational planners and economists have a sketchy understanding of several key relationships that are central to language development in the education triangle. Wolff (2006: 6) observes that

> the connection between (a) development and language use is largely ignored, the connection between (b) language and education is little understood outside expert circles and the connection between (c) development and education is widely accepted on a priori grounds, but with little understanding of the exact nature of the relationship.

As summarised by Wolff in the stock-taking document: 'Language is not everything in education but without language, everything is nothing in education' (2006: 50).

Many international students, also, come to South African universities from countries that follow an early transition model for language in education. This means that students are exposed to a foreign language as the medium of instruction at an early age. This policy denies African learners the opportunity of acquiring the academic language proficiency needed to ensure epistemological access (Morrow 1994) at university level. The process of acquiring CALP takes a period of six to eight years of successful learning in the content areas through the mother tongue at school level (Cummins 1984). The gradual development of CALP from grade to grade 'requires expansion of vocabulary, grammatical and discourse knowledge far beyond what is required for social communication' (Cummins 2009: 22). Alidou et al. (2006: 15) summarise: 'The development of the type of literacy necessary for reading and writing about science, history and geography, or understanding problems in mathematics, becomes increasingly complex and difficult from the fourth year of school onwards.' The type of literacy needed in higher education is incrementally developed from Grade 4 onwards. Students who enter higher education without a thorough grounding in CALP are set up for a struggle to access content, rhetorical knowledge and linguistic knowledge at university.

Cummins (2009: 24) points out that it becomes more difficult as each year passes for what he terms, in this context, the linguistic minority student to 'catch-up' with a 'moving target'. The student studying in the mother tongue makes considerable CALP gains with each passing school year, thus widening the gap between those studying in their mother tongues and those who are not. The destructive role that this gap plays in students' success at university is far-reaching as students need a good grounding in CALP to enable them to acquire the academic literacy required in higher education. All assessment in higher education occurs in English and Afrikaans in South Africa, which gives the second-language speaker of English, in particular, from the above educational background where CALP was not developed sufficiently, much diminished opportunities to demonstrate educational achievements. Students study in the medium of English and, in addition, they are faced with acquiring a 'new' discourse, viz. that of academic literacy.

Academic Literacy and Its Impact on Learning

Once students join the university, they are at once members of a very elite group: the academic community. They have to acquire a 'new' discourse, which as Bourdieu and Passeron (1990: 115) point out, is nobody's mother tongue. They have to acquire a new way of 'saying (writing) – doing – being – valuing – believing combinations' (Gee 1996: 127). Pennycook (1999: 330) calls this 'new' academic discourse a 'secret language'. According to Gee (1990: 1):

> You learn the Discourse by becoming a member of the group: you start as a 'beginner', watch what's done, go along with the group as if you know what you are doing when you don't, and eventually you can do it on your own.

Gee (1990: 159) calls this phenomenon 'mushfaking'. Students are apprenticed into this new discourse when they enter university. Access is exacerbated if students are acquiring this new discourse in a language that is not their mother tongue and they lack the necessary CALP skills to acquire the new discourse.

If students come from a schooling system where they have mastered the required CALP skills, then this transition or 'mushfaking' period should not be an arduous transition. For those students, such as many of our international students, however, who come from schooling contexts where a colonial language is the language of instruction, access becomes a mammoth, daunting process. There are the lucky ones who were schooled in their mother tongues for long enough to acquire the necessary CALP, like the student Lihle from Zimbabwe. Her mother tongue is Ndebele. She experiences little difficulty with the academic reading and writing tasks and her results demonstrate this. She had seven years of mother tongue instruction, and is the exception – a fact of which she is very well aware, as witness her observation that:

> I perform very well better than those girls from South Africa.

Why is this so? Why do 'those girls from South Africa' perform more poorly? The short answer to this lies in South Africa's apartheid legacy of impoverished schooling for black South Africans. While the advent of democracy has begun to improve matters, the conditions of schooling for the majority of South Africans remain very poor and disadvantaging. Two examples of relevance to this paper serve to illustrate the severity of the problem.

Table 5.1 illustrates literacy test data (Isaacs 2012) from the Western Cape Education Department (the province with the highest level of educational attainment in South Africa) and shows alarming differences in the performance of students from different types of school. The tests were administered to all Western Cape Grade 6 students, in the medium of instruction of the school, and are aimed to assess how many students are performing at the expected grade level.

It can be seen that less than one quarter of the students whose mother tongue is not the language of instruction are performing at the expected grade level in English literacy. The consequences of this, as has been pointed out above, for the acquisition of CALP skills and future academic performance, are devastating. The contrast in performance with students whose mother tongue is English is striking – 86.4 per cent (in 2009) of these students are performing at expected levels. These differentials in performance persist into higher education – called the 'durable injustice' (Green 1971) – and present one of the major challenges facing higher education in South Africa.

The second example draws on data from the National Benchmark Tests (NBTs). This initiative was established by Higher Education South Africa, in

Table 5.1 Literacy test data and language background: Western Cape Education Department

School type	Language background of students	2005	2007	2009
Historically disadvantaged	100% English second or additional language	4.7	14.1	24.2
Historically advantaged	Predominantly MT speakers of English	86.9	83.8	86.4

response to concerns about the very high failure rates in higher education. The tests, based in three core areas that underlie future academic performance (academic literacy, quantitative literacy and mathematics), were introduced in 2009. They are designed to deliver diagnostic information about student preparedness in these areas, and therefore about the kinds of educational support that institutions need to provide if students are to have a reasonable chance of succeeding with higher education study. Descriptions of the inferences to be drawn from the three categories of performance are shown in Table 5.2, along with broad recommendations about the levels of educational interventions needed.

Figure 5.1 depicts the performance, in these benchmark categories, of the students writing the NBT academic literacy test prior to entry to higher education for the 2012 year (n=49,281). As the data show, there is considerable cause for concern: 24 per cent of the writers were deemed to need 'extensive and long-term' support, and nearly half to need some level of support if they were to have any reasonable chance of success in their studies. Only 28 per cent were judged to be proficient in academic literacy – that is, not to need academic literacy support to progress satisfactorily.

The data reflected in Figure 5.1 includes all NBT writers for the 2012 entry cycle. A somewhat different picture is gained when all English mother tongue speakers are removed from the analysis.

Differences, Challenges and Opportunities for International and Home Students

Figure 5.2 includes only English second language speakers, and further categorises these test writers into two groups, international (n=194) and South African (n=3,076). The analysis reveals important differences between these

Table 5.2 High-level benchmark descriptors

Category of performance	Descriptor
Proficient (≥65%)	Performance in this domain (academic literacy) suggests that academic progress in higher education will not be adversely affected.
Intermediate (42–64%)	Challenges have been identified in this domain such that it is predicted that academic progress will be affected. If admitted, students' educational needs should be met in a way deemed appropriate by the institution (for example by extended or augmented programmes and special skills provision).
Basic (≤41%)	Serious learning challenges have been identified: it is predicted that students performing at this level will not cope with degree-level study without extensive and long term support, perhaps best provided through pre-university programmes.

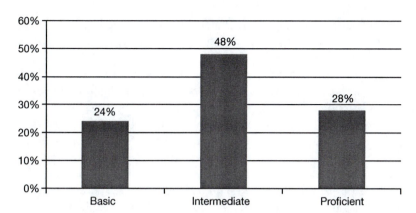

Figure 5.1 NBT: academic literacy test writers in 2011 for entry to higher education in 2012

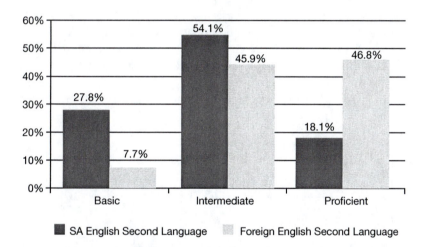

Figure 5.2 NBT: academic literacy performance of international and South African English second language speakers

two groups in terms of overall academic literacy proficiency. Figure 5.1 shows that 28 per cent of the writers fell into the proficient category. Figure 5.2 reveals, however, that 46 per cent of the international students, despite speaking English as a second language, perform at the proficient benchmark level, compared to only 18 per cent of their South African counterparts.

It can be seen that the levels of support needed for the South African group are far more significant that those of the international group. Over a quarter of the South African students fall into the basic category, whereas only about 8 per cent of the international group manifest a need for this very extensive level of support. In summary, over 80 per cent of the South African group need some level of educational intervention, compared to just over half of the international group.

It could be expected that the language needs for these two groups would be similar. However, as Figure 5.3 shows, they differ in some important respects – both in severity and type. Figure 5.3 illustrates performance in the skills clusters covered by one particular NBT: the academic literacy test, written in August 2011. It should be noted that whereas Table 5.1 shows the percentages of South African and international applicants who sat an equivalent academic literacy test in one of various sittings in the 2012 admissions cycle, the data in Figure 5.3 are based on the writers for one test version only. This was necessary to enable reporting on performance on clusters of items, based on the kinds of language skill or knowledge tapped. The numbers tested were, respectively, South African English second language speakers (n=3,076) and international English second language speakers (n=194).

Several observations can be made about the performance of these two groups. First, the most challenging area for all groups of students is that of separating the essential from the non-essential ('essential/non-essential' in Figure 5.3). More specifically, this cluster area focuses on the kinds of knowledge and ability involved in separating main ideas from supporting details, statements from examples, facts from opinions, propositions from their arguments, and classifying and categorising information in text. It is of concern

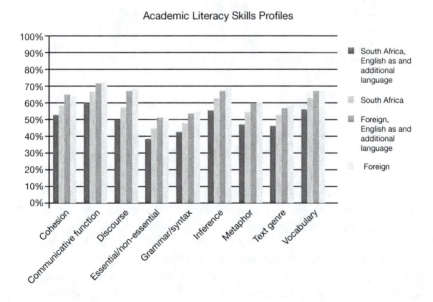

Figure 5.3 NBT: academic literacy performance of international and South African applicants, August 2011

that this absolutely fundamental type of academic competence is so challenging for students: on average, South African English second language speaking applicants achieved only 38 per cent on the items in this cluster. This implies that these applicants are not able to use English as an effective tool in the higher education learning environment, and further that universities admitting such students would need to provide the kinds of support that enable students to develop these core CALP skills. The international English second language group fares better, but still performs at a marginal level.

Serious challenges are also evident in relation to student performance on the cluster dealing with the syntactical basis of the English language. The highly multilingual nature of the South African educational context has led to a more sympathetic view of grammatical issues; however, since the focus of the NBT academic literacy test is on the relevance of language and language-related skills to academic performance, poor performance in this cluster suggests that students will find it difficult to use the structural basis of the English language as a learning resource.

In terms of the greatest differentials in performance, the discourse cluster stands out. This relates primarily to the ability to understand relations between parts of text and/or text extracts by recognising indicators in discourse (especially for: introducing, developing, transition and conclusion of ideas), and signalling relations between phenomena. A possible reason for the, relatively, much weaker performance of the South African group here is the widely reported scarcity of opportunities provided by schooling for students to work with and produce extended texts, and the generally low levels of competence of teachers in English, although it is the official medium of instruction in virtually all English as an Additional Language schools.

Overall, however, it can be seen that international speakers of English as an additional language perform considerably better in this test than the South African English as an additional language applicant pool. This accords with the scores gained on international tests such as Trends in International Mathematics and Science Study (TIMMS) and Programme for International Student Assessment (PISA), where South Africa comes last even when countries with lower gross domestic products are included, such as Zambia or Ghana. This is hardly a surprise, since CALP (academic literacy) skills focus on the kinds of language use and knowledge that are most systematically acquired through formal education – and for the majority of South Africans, the quality of learning opportunities is very low. Reasons for this are many (cf. Jansen 2004). While it is not the task of this paper to discuss this issue, the fact remains: in South African higher education, the most serious language-related needs are those experienced by South African English as an additional language students, not international students.

For the universities, this has far-reaching implications. Long and hard experience has shown that offering a stand-alone language course, for example an

'English for Academic Purposes' course, is effective really only for students who are borderline proficient. For students with more serious language-related needs, what is needed is ongoing language support that is embedded in curricula. Examples of the kinds of language support that might address student needs include the design of language-intensive tasks with careful scaffolding and opportunities for students to receive detailed feedback on drafts in core courses such as economics in commerce, sociology in humanities, and zoology in science, and focused attention in course assignments given to language issues in addition to 'content', and reading circles and groups on core texts. Such support requires additional curriculum space and time and so courses that are augmented in this way usually require the extension of the degree programme by at least a year. They also require highly collaborative teaching approaches, with language specialists working alongside their discipline-based colleagues.

One of the opportunities afforded language practitioners in higher education in Africa is that they are in a position to draw widely on international research and praxis. Due to globalisation, many countries are faced with similar linguistic and educational concerns. Weber (2007: 280) uses the abstraction 'glocalisation' to describe the above dialectic between the global and the local when referring to social change. How, then, can we 'glocally' transform praxis in higher education when it comes to meeting the educational needs of international students enrolled in our universities?

An important step in the process of transforming pedagogy to meet the needs of students is the process of critical awareness-raising. Pennycook (1999: 332) contends that critical awareness is generated by research that attempts to explain complex contexts, collaborative research across contexts and descriptions of specific contexts. Thus, texts such as this one go a long way to raise awareness about the needs and experiences of the international student in higher education.

Most universities in South Africa have a policy of open access with various entry options. Unfortunately, access often does not translate into epistemological access for many international students who come from schooling systems that have not optimally equipped them with the linguistic means of coping in higher education. In other words, creating open access in higher education does not necessarily translate into effective learning and knowledge acquisition in the academy. Engstrom and Tinto (2008: 46) declare that 'Access without support is not opportunity.' Thus, the most important challenge is the linguistic support provided to students.

The challenge remains to provide meaningful scaffolding to academic learning for students (local and international) who need it. Ovando, Collier and Combs (2003: 345) define scaffolding as 'providing contextual support for meaning through the use of simplified language, teacher modelling, visuals and graphics, cooperative learning and hands-on learning'. Thus, content-based courses that provide scaffolding into content that is relevant, authentic and meaningful to the students are required. Current thinking in second-language teaching and learning (Crandall and Kaufman 2002) is that language should be taught through content that is authentic and meaningful to the student, if the goal is to improve academic access. Thus, the goals of language are achieved through teaching concepts in content such as psychology, science, law and other subject areas (Ovando et al. 2003: 310).

International Issues and Comparisons

For many university entrants globally, higher education is an alien world where they are expected to socialise in their study areas in ways that may be foreign to them. Every time they are expected to respond to an academic prompt or read a text to extract meaning for a task or assignment, they are 'inventing the university for the occasion' (Bartholomae 2003: 623). Regardless of the country or the context, students all have to 'try on the peculiar ways of knowing, selecting, evaluating, reporting, concluding and arguing that define the discourse of our community' (Bartholomae 2003: 623). For students who have difficulty accessing this discourse, completion of their studies is often not achievable.

Studies (Ozga and Sukhnandan 1998: 316) in student retention identify preparedness (in this case linguistic preparedness) as a major factor in students' non-completion in higher education. Students who were not afforded the opportunity to gain proficiency in the required medium of instruction in the home, the school or the community have only a slim chance of gaining epistemological access. In many former colonies, the language of the coloniser has become the main language in education, resulting in lack of cognitive growth for many students in multilingual situations. Students in many of these situations resort to coping mechanisms like copying, plagiarism and rote learning, which all militate against a process of making meaning and deep learning. In post-colonial countries, language policies for higher education differ according to various political and sociopolitical agendas.

In many sub-Saharan countries English is viewed as means of progress and a valuable commodity at 'national, subnational and supranational levels' (Tsu and Tollefson 2004: 6) and therefore many international students study in English when they attend South African universities. In South Africa there are only two languages of instruction at higher education level: English and Afrikaans, with English being the medium of choice for most speakers of indigenous African languages and international students. The sad fact is that the implementation of successful language policies for education still remains a dream for many post-colonial countries in Africa (Alidou 2004: 195). There are, however, examples in Africa where mother tongue as the medium of instruction is slowly gaining ground at school level, such as Ethiopia.

Except for a short occupation by Italy, Ethiopia did not endure colonisation by another power, but English was selected as the language of formal education in the 20th century until 1955 when Amharic was designated as the medium of instruction at primary school level (Heugh 2009: 108). Political change in 1994 brought about the inclusion of other Ethiopian languages as media of instruction in schools. This is accompanied by an additive bilingual approach where English is taught alongside the mother tongue medium and the switch to English is made much later in secondary education. Ethiopia undertakes regular assessment of the achievement of their learners. The data demonstrates that 'the longer students have MTM [mother tongue medium], the better their overall academic achievement' (Heugh 2009: 113). It could reasonably be deduced that students whose conceptual knowledge has been firmly established through the mother tongue are more prepared for higher education than their counterparts who learn in a language that is not their mother tongue.

There is evidence that when the switch is made to the recognition of other languages besides English at school level, this transition is more easily made in higher education. Malaysia offers such an example (Gill 2004: 139). Although English is an official language, it was decided in 1958 to transition to Bahasa Malaysia as a medium of instruction at primary school level. In 1983 Bahasa Malaysia was implemented as a language of instruction at university level. Unless the indigenous languages are given what Alexander (2005: 13) terms 'market value', there is little hope of liberation from the hegemony of English and other colonial languages.

Unfortunately, the converse is also true: in countries where English is the dominant language of instruction in higher education, the demand for English at school level is increased, such as is the case in the Philippines (Nical, Smolicz and Secombe 2004: 153) and parts of India (Annamalai 2004: 184). Annamalai (2004: 188) sums up the problem of access through a colonial language: 'The advantage of English medium in higher education and employment is a mirage for those students whose command of English is poor at the end.' Without real epistemological access at school level, the colonial language does not benefit the student in the long run in higher education. South Africa and other sub-Saharan African countries would do well to draw on the positive approaches to language in education as practised by countries such as Ethiopia and Malaysia.

Conclusion

As this paper has argued, the 'language issue' in higher education in South Africa – indeed, in all levels of education – is a very complex one. It is unlike the situation in most developed countries, in that it is the great majority of students, and not only foreign language speakers, who face serious educational challenges related to their proficiency in the use of the medium of instruction as a learning vehicle. Moreover, it is the local students who face the more serious challenge, in many regards.

In multilingual settings, language in education policies need to take a multilingual approach to teaching and learning and not opt for the convenience of a monolingual approach. As suggested above, diversity needs to be acknowledged and what the student brings to the classroom should be valued and harnessed in the learning situation.

Addressing the language-related needs of students therefore needs to be a systemic undertaking. In South Africa, serious consideration is currently being given to recognising that the great majority of the 50 per cent of students who qualify at all in the country's universities take at least one extra year to complete their studies (Yeld 2006). The proposal, broadly speaking, is that an extra year be added to current curriculum structures, and that this extra time be used to address students' educational needs more thoroughly and consistently than is currently possible. This would allow language-related needs to be met where they are encountered – that is, in 'mainstream' curricula. This is not to say that separate courses focusing on specific aspects on language use have no place; rather, that CALP knowledge and skills are more effectively developed over time and in authentic contexts.

It should be acknowledged that some students, and in particular those from Francophone or Lusophone African countries, have some language-related needs that are distinct from those of English second-language students that have been the focus of much of this chapter. For this reason, it is clear that a variety of approaches need to be followed, encompassing workshops and courses dealing with particular challenge areas, expansion of Writing Centres to provide detailed and supporting feedback and guidance, and such initiatives as Writers' Circles, which encourage the creation of networks and opportunities to speak and share challenges in a supportive setting.

References

Alexander, N. (1999). An African renaissance without African languages. *Social Dynamics.* 25(1), 1–12.

Alexander, N. (2005). *After apartheid: the language question.* http://www.pclt.cis.yale.educ

Alidou, H. (2004). Medium of instruction in post-colonial Africa. In J.W. Tollefson and A.B.M. Tsui (Eds.), *Medium of instruction policies: Which agenda? Whose agenda?* (pp. 195–216). London: Lawrence Erlbaum Associates Publishers.

Alidou, H., Aliou, B., Brock-Utne, B., Diallo, Y.S., Heugh, K. and Wolff, E. (2006). *Optimizing learning and education in Africa – the language factor. A stock-taking research on mother tongue and bilingual education in sub-Saharan Africa.* Paris: Association for the Development of Education in Africa (ADEA). http://www.adeanet.org/biennial–2006/doc/document/B3_1MTBLE_en.pdf.

Annamalai, E. (2004). Medium of power: The question of English in education in India. In J.W. Tollefson and A.B.M. Tsui (Eds.), *Medium of instruction policies: Which agenda? Whose agenda?* (pp. 177–194) .London: Lawrence Erlbaum Associates Publishers.

Bartholomae, D. (2003). Inventing the university. In V. Villanueva (Ed.), *Cross-talk in comp theory: A reader* (2nd ed., pp. 623–653). Urbana, IL: National Council of Teachers of English.

Bokamba, E. (1984). French colonial language policies and its legacies. *Studies in linguistic Sciences*, 14, 1–34.

Bourdieu, P. and Passeron, J.C. (1990). *Reproduction in education, society and culture.* Newbury Park: Sage Publications.

Crandall, J. and Kaufman, D. (2002) *Content-based instruction in Higher Education setting.* Virginia: Teachers of English to Speakers of Other Languages, Inc.

Cummins, J. (1984*) Bilingualism and special education: issues in assessment and pedagogy.* Clevedon, England: Multilingual Matters.

Cummins, J. (1996). *Negotiating identities: education for empowerment in a diverse society.* Ontario, California: California Association for Bilingual Education.

Cummins, J. (2009). Fundamental psychological and sociological principles underlying educational success for linguistic minority students. In T. Skutnabb-Kangas, R. Phillipson, A.K. Mohanty and M. Panda (Eds.), *Social justice through multilingual education* (pp. 19–35). Bristol: Multilingual Matters.

De Wet, C. and Wolhuter, C. (2009). A transitiological study of some South African educational issues. *South African Journal of Education*, 29(3), 359–376.

Engstrom, C. and Tinto, V. (2008). Access without support is not opportunity. *Change.* Jan/Feb. 46–50.

Gee, J.P. (1990). *Social linguistics and literacies: ideology in discourses.* London: Falmer Press.

Gee, J.P. (1996). *Social linguistics and literacies: ideology in discourses* (2nd ed.). London: Taylor and Francis.

Gill, S.K. (2004). Medium-of-instruction policy in higher education in Malaysia: nationalism versus internationalization. In J.W. Tollefson and A.B.M. Tsui (Eds.), *Medium of instruction policies: Which agenda? Whose agenda?* (pp. 135–152). London: Lawrence Erlbaum Associates Publishers.

Green, J. (1971). (cited in Coombs, J.R. (1994)). Equal access to education: the ideal and the issues. *Journal of Curriculum Studies* 26(3), 281–295.

Heugh, K. (2000). The case against bilingual and multilingual education in South Africa. *PRAESA Occasional Papers* No. 6. Cape Town: University of Cape Town.

Heugh, K. (2009). Literacy and bi/multilingual education in Africa: recovering collective memory and expertise. In T. Skutnabb-Kangas, R. Phillipson, A.K. Mohanty and M. Panda (Eds.), *Social justice through multilingual education.* Bristol: Multilingual Matters.

Isaacs, D. (2012). Highlighting the factors leading to learner achievement in basic education. Paper presented at the 'Transformation and Governance in Basic Education Summit 2012', 18–20 April, Johannesburg South Africa.

Janks, H. (2010). *Literacy and power.* London: Routledge.

Jansen, J. (2004). An open letter to the Minister of Education. http://www.chet.org.za/papers/open-letter-new-minister-education

Morrow, W. (1994). Entitlement and achievement in education. *Studies in Philosophy and Education*, 13, 33–47.

NEPAD. (2005). Renewal of higher education in Africa. Report of AU/NEPAD Workshop, Johannesburg, 20 November 2005. http://www.chet.org.za/papers/renewal-higher-education-africa

Nical, I., Smolicz, J.J. and Secombe, M.J. (2004). Rural students and the bilingual education program on the island of Leyte. In J.W. Tollefson and A.B.M. Tsui (Eds.). *Medium of instruction policies: Which agenda? Whose agenda?* (pp. 153–176). London: Lawrence Erlbaum Associates Publishers.

Ovando, C.J., Collier, V.P. and Combs, M.C. (2003). *Bilingual and ESL classrooms: teaching in multicultural contexts.* Boston, MA: Addison-Wesley/Longman.

Ozga, J. and Sukhnandan, L. (1998). Undergraduate non-completion: developing an explanatory model. *Higher Education* Quarterly, 52(3), 316–333.

Pennycook, A. (1999). Introduction: critical approaches to TESOL. *TESOL Quarterly*, 33(3), 329–348.

Steyn, J. (2007). Taal kan weens syfers 'verdwyn': Universiteite se beleide bedreig Afrikaans nog verder. *Beeld*, 12 April. 16.

Tsu, A.B.M. and Tollefson, W.F. (2004). The centrality of medium-of-instruction policy in sociopolitical processes. In J.W. Tollefson and A.B.M. Tsui (Eds.), *Medium of instruction policies: Which agenda? Whose agenda?* (pp. 1–20). London: Lawrence Erlbaum Associates Publishers.

Weber, E. (2007). Globalization, 'glocal' development and teachers work: a research agenda. *Review of Educational Research*, 77(3), 279–309.

Wolff, E. (2006). Background and history – language politics and planning in Africa. In H. Alidou, B. Aliou, B. Brock-Utne, Y.S Diallo, K. Heugh and E. Wolff (Eds.), *Optimizing learning and education in Africa – the language factor. A stock-taking research on mother tongue and bilingual education in sub-Saharan Africa* (pp. 26–55). Paris: Association for the Development of Education in Africa (ADEA). http://www.adeanet.org/biennial–2006/doc/document/B3_1MTBLE_en.pdf.

Yeld, N. (2006). Academic literacy. In H. Griesel (Ed.), *Access and entry level benchmarks: the National Benchmark Tests Project.* Pretoria: Higher Education South Africa.

6

Employability, Key Skills and Graduate Attributes

HEIKE BEHLE AND GABY ATFIELD

As higher education (HE) has expanded, there has been increased emphasis on the skills students learn during their time in HE. These skills are not confined to subject-specific knowledge and expertise (Mason, Williams and Cranmer 2006), but incorporate softer, more generic, 'employability' skills, such as the ability to communicate well, manage time and work in a team. In this chapter, the case study of the UK highlights the intricacies of the supply and demand relationship that exists between higher education institutions (HEIs), students and employers in relation to employability skills, and the further complexities faced by international students studying in the UK. The UK has one of the most international student populations within the Organisation for Economic Co-operation and Development (OECD). In 2009, 15.3 per cent of all students in tertiary education in the UK were international students, which is about twice as much as the OECD average (6.37 per cent) (OECD 2011). As the cost of HE participation continues to increase in the UK, questions about the role of HEIs in providing students with the kind of skills that are valuable in the competitive graduate labour market have become ever more prevalent.

In the global competition for international students, it is increasingly important that HE sectors are able to highlight what students can gain by choosing to study in their country. For the UK, the subject of this chapter, there is considerable debate about the variable fees for home and European students introduced in 2012, and the higher fees paid by international students from non-European countries. As 'the most established Anglophone higher education (HE) system in the world' (Behle and Purcell 2012), continuing to maintain a competitive advantage through demonstrating that expected skills gains are translated into positive labour market outcomes is essential. While subject-specific competencies may be indicated by the degree class achieved by a student, there is an issue about how more generic employability skills may be measured to adequately determine the benefits students derive from their participation in tertiary education. However, little empirical research exists on the relationship between students' experiences of studying outside their home nation and their subsequent employability as graduates. It is important to bear in mind that skill acquisition does not start with HE, and previous cultural and social experiences need to be taken into account (Findlay et al. 2012).

Firstly in this chapter, the concepts of 'employability' and 'employability skills' and the ways in which the aspirations and attitudes of international students differ from UK home students are discussed. The different types of of employability skills that may be developed through study in a different country are outlined, and possible barriers to this type of skill acquisition are explored.

Second, data from a longitudinal study of 2005/6 HE applicants (Futuretrack[1]) is used to examine how far international students studying in the UK have been able to develop the employability skills they consider necessary for achieving their aspirations vis-à-vis the graduate labour market. The Futuretrack survey is a longitudinal survey of the Universities and Colleges Admissions Service (UCAS 2012a) applicants who applied to enter full-time undergraduate education in the UK in 2005/6. Respondents were first surveyed in spring and summer 2006 prior to HE entry, again a little over a year later, and in the spring and summer as they approached the end of their three or four year undergraduate programmes, in 2009 or 2010. They were surveyed for a fourth and final sweep of the survey in autumn and winter 2011/12. The sample is weighted by gender and tariff score, to take account of under-representation of certain groups relative to their known proportions in the population of accepted students who applied to enter HE through UCAS in 2005/6.

This focus on the development of skills-for-employment, rather than simply on employment rates themselves – a measure that has been widely criticised (see, for example Harvey 2001: 97) – allows us to present a more nuanced picture of how different groups of international students become 'employable' in a variety of contexts. The extent to which students perceive that their skills have been developed while they have been in HE is outlined, along with their knowledge of the skills employers are seeking, and their views about the graduate labour market and their own employment prospects.

The Concept of Employability and Key Skills

A plethora of different definitions of employability exist (see Hind and Moss 2011; Belt, Drake and Chapman, 2010; McQuaid and Lindsay 2006; Harvey 2001). For the purpose of this chapter, employability is defined not only as 'having the skills and abilities to find employment', but also 'having the skills to remain in employment and progress within the workplace' (see Belt et al. 2010; Hillage and Pollard 1998). In this chapter, we concentrate on these individual factors, i.e. individual possession of skills, attributes and knowledge, although it must be noted that external labour market factors and personal circumstances and preferences also play an important role in determining the success of an individual's labour market transitions (McQuaid and Lindsay 2006).

Increases in an individual's employability skills may not yield returns in the labour market if that labour market has no suitable employment that calls upon those skills. This is particularly important when the economic downturn and recession in the UK and many countries around the world has resulted in fewer openings for graduates (Coward, 2011).Various authors and UK government agencies have attempted to produce a list of the key skills for employability. Briefly, these lists tend to include skills such as: written and spoken communication; numeracy and information technology skills at an appropriate level; problem solving; the ability to work as part of a team; and a range of skills related to self-management such as organisation, time-keeping, self-motivation, the ability to work hard and commitment (see UK Commission for Employment and Skills [UKCES] 2009; National Committee of Inquiry into Higher Education [NCIHE] 1997 for different lists of key skills). Some commentators, such as the Confederation of British Industry (CBI) (2007) include business or entrepreneurial skills as essential for employability.

Employability Skills and HE

While both graduates and employers see primary responsibility for gaining and retaining employability with the individual (McQuaid and Lindsay 2006), there has been an increasing onus put upon HEIs in the UK to ensure that their graduates have the opportunities to develop the key employability skills necessary to find work of an appropriate level. In 2008 the Department for Innovation, Universities and Skills (DIUS) issued a statement saying, 'We want to see all universities treating student employability as a core part of their mission. So we believe it is reasonable to expect universities to take responsibility for how their students are prepared for the world of work' (DIUS 2008: 6). This theme was repeated in an announcement by the UK Secretary of State for Business, Innovation and Skills in 2010 that, in the face of financial constraints imposed by the recession: 'The truth is that we need to rethink the case for our universities from the beginning. We need to rethink how we fund them, and what we expect them to deliver for the public support they receive' (Cable 2010: 1).

How HEIs can play a role in the development of a student's key employability skills has been somewhat less clear (Teichler 2007). While the labour market outcomes of graduates has been measured by the Higher Education Funding Council for England (HEFCE) since 2001, the mechanisms for delivering employability skills learning have varied considerably across HEIs and different subjects within them, from stand-alone modules to full embedding into existing courses, as well as work placements and experiential learning (Atfield and Purcell 2010). The success of these different methods depends, in part, on the relevance of the skills gained to a student's proposed career. It is also recognised that the acquisition of key employability skills neither starts nor finishes with a student's time in HE (Campbell 2009; Harvey 2001).

International Students' Acquisition of Employability Skills

International students have moved to a different country than their own to study (Kelo, Teichler and Waechter 2006) and live in a different cultural environment, mixing with other students who have had a different educational upbringing (Benzie 2010). This means they often start at a different point to home students in their prior acquisition of employability skills, as well as the skills they perceive they need to develop in order to become employable in the labour market. Experiences and skills gained while studying in a foreign country can provide them with a head start in competing for graduate jobs, which may put them in a position to offer more than the home student, giving them 'an employability advantage' (Crossman and Clarke 2010: 603) over other applicants. However, questions about the transferability of employability skills to different labour market contexts are a key issue. What is considered to be a key employability skill by employers in the UK may be somewhat different to employers in a student's home country or international employers (Dietrich and Olson 2010). Especially for non-Western students returning to their home countries, it is unclear whether some skills and attributes defined by Western society are relevant or even compatible with not only the skills demanded by employers in the student's home country, but also with previously acquired and culturally identified generic skills.

> Most generic skills are developed within the context of the home country environment, where parents, significant adult role-models and the values of the local community have a major role in shaping the specific generic skills and attributes that are valued in the specific socio-cultural context.
> (Campbell 2009: 494)

Selected Key Competencies: (English) Language Proficiency,
Cultural Awareness, Global Competences

The European Parliament and Council identified key competencies that must be furthered in education (The European Parliament and the Council of the European Union 2006). These key competencies are very similar to those identified by UK employers and policy makers, but include communication in a foreign language and social and civic competence, which are the two areas where much previous research on students' experiences of studying abroad has concentrated (Halász and Michel 2011), along with broader cultural competencies such as cultural awareness and expression at the individual, country and global level. As has been noted, in the acquisition of the first of these competencies, communication in a foreign language, many students who study outside their home country will have an advantage; however, what constitutes social and civic competence and how this may be demonstrated is more culturally specific.

Language learning, especially the learning of the English language as the 'lingua franca' of the business world (Bryant et al. 2006; Chan and Dimmock 2008), has been identified by many authors (e.g. Bosch 2009; Bretag 2007; Crossman and Clarke 2010; Davesne and Cummins 2009; OECD 2011; Taillefer 2005; Teichler and Janson 2007; West et al. 2000) as one of the key skills that can be acquired by studying in the UK. Ideally, graduates or students with foreign language skills should be able to communicate in a range of settings for a variety of purposes and develop skills in each of the four modalities: speaking (productive), listening (receptive), reading (receptive) and writing (productive) (Dietrich and Olsen 2010). It is important to bear in mind, however, that the level of English language skills differ among international students. Some international students are native speakers and come from English-speaking countries whilst others have grown up bilingual, because English is one of the official languages of their country of origin, because of family circumstances or because of prior language education. Some students become confident speakers of English as children and might have attended English-speaking international schools, whilst others have only become confident speakers as adults. This is an important distinction as it avoids the form of 'othering' described by Benzie (2010), whereby all non-native speakers are treated as having low English levels, while, conversely, all local students are assumed to experience no difficulty with English language.

Cultural awareness and expression has been identified by many authors (e.g. Anderson et al. 2006; Behrnd and Porzelt 2011; Davesne and Cummins 2009; Leask 2009; Pedersen 2010; Teichler and Janson, 2007) as a benefit of studying in a different country. The term can be further divided in the following components: internationally oriented substantive knowledge; empathy or intercultural competence, which describes the ability of an individual to put her- or himself into another person's shoes; and approval in terms of favourable attitudes or valuations of things abroad (Lambert 1994). This enables a graduate to see that 'his or her culture is one of many diverse cultures and that alternate perceptions and behaviors may be based in cultural differences' (Dietrich and Olson 2010: 148) and demonstrate that they can use 'knowledge, diverse cultural frames of reference, and alternate perspectives to think critically and solve problems; ... [and] accepts cultural differences and tolerates cultural ambiguity' (ibid.). Cultural awareness can enhance graduates' skills to argue and negotiate, especially in an international context (Bosch 2009), and is increasingly considered as an important skill by employers (Crossman and Clarke 2010).

Global competences and perspectives relate to the development of substantive knowledge, perceptual understanding, capacity for personal growth, ability to develop international interpersonal relationships, the ability to act as a cultural mediator, cross-cultural awareness, perspective consciousness, state-of-the-planet awareness, knowledge of global dynamics and awareness of human choices (Hanvey 1976). Global competences deriving from studying in a foreign country are especially relevant for jobs in international companies where a global point of view is needed to relate to a 'highly interconnected world' (Bosch 2009: 284).

In addition, international experience is also connected with developments in soft skills such as 'the ability to develop different skills and acquire different knowledge relevant to unfamiliar contexts. This facilitates the successful transfer of existing self-confidence to unfamiliar academic and cultural contexts' (Campbell 2009: 494). Students have been reported to gain maturity, competiveness and management skills, which are being developed by staying at a differently organised university (Bosch 2009).

Very few studies evaluate the labour market performance of returning foreign-educated graduates, and those that do highlight that graduates returning to their home country to seek employment appear to face barriers in achieving returns on their international experience. Lianos, Asteriou and Agiomigianakis (2004), in their study of Greek students returning home, report serious losses of human capital and misallocation of resources in terms of the time necessary for job search and the mismatch between level of study and subject and the role filled, while a survey of Norwegian graduates found that students with a foreign degree, who also held higher performance scores from upper secondary schools, faced a more challenging transition between HE and labour market (Wiers-Jenssen 2011).

Differences, Challenges and Opportunities for International and Home Students

Given that the transition of indigenous UK students from UK secondary schools to HE is often difficult (e.g. Briggs, Clark and Hall 2012), it is not surprising that international students may face additional challenges. These include: incompatibility with expectations of previous skills development and knowledge; the country-specific focus of some courses, either in terms of subject matter or preparation for entry into a particular labour market; and language competency issues.

Variations in the educational and cultural background of students mean that they usually have different subject-specific knowledge upon entering HE in the UK as well as having 'acquired different skills, and varied levels of skills. Some may be independent learners, some may be very structured and methodical in their approach ... and some may need more guidance' (Bosch 2009: 293; see also Benzie 2010). While this pattern may be seen across different groups of home country students, it is also a key issue for international students, especially when courses are developed with UK students in mind. One creative arts and design student from France in the Futuretrack survey commented on this:

> Being an international student I already came in with a broad mind and I think the universities should have more knowledge in international matters. The course is orientated on the UK only.

This can be further complicated by the variability in entry requirements for international students wanting to study in the UK. It has been suggested by Bretag (2007) that students may be accepted on to courses without having the necessary skills to succeed because of the fees they are willing to pay, and, furthermore, students may be allowed to pass courses despite their work not being up to standards. The new variable tuition fees that will be introduced in English HEIs in September 2012 may change this distinction, as home and European students will be paying almost as much as international students.

International students are required to have a qualification in English or to take a special test in English, but the standard of written and spoken English required for entry into HE differs by course and the HEI. However, Bretag (2007) has found that there is evidence that some students are not equipped with the English language skills they need to successfully complete the work required and that they do not receive the support required to develop their skills to an appropriate level. Failure to master the necessary English language skills, even with increased time spent in an English-speaking environment, can hinder a student's expression and threaten their self-esteem (Halic, Greenberg and Paulus 2009).

A further issue faced by international students is in acquiring labour market information about their home countries. This can result in mismatches between the types or level at which subjects are studied and the occupation the student wishes to enter upon graduation (Lianos et al., 2004), and in graduates being under or over qualified for the occupation they hope to enter. This difficulty in developing knowledge about the country's labour market they wish to enter can be compounded by a lack of clarity about which country the student wishes to work in, either in the short or long term. The likelihood that a graduate will return to their country of origin depends upon their perceptions of the labour market in the host and home countries, as well as the individual graduate's adjustment process and family and other personal ties and commitments (Baruch, Budhwar and Khatri 2007). The information on the relationship between HE and the world of work is still far from satisfactory (Teichler 2007) for students studying in their home country, let alone for international students.

The Role of Employability within the Student Experience

Respondents to the Futuretrack survey were asked a series of questions about the skills and attributes they believe they have, whether they have developed these through their HEI course or through other means. They were also asked what kinds of skills and attributes they think employers were looking for when recruiting for graduate jobs and whether they believed they had the skills necessary for finding the kind of employment they aspired to, both immediately post-graduation and in the long term. Students self-perception can vary from the perception of potential employers; however, using self-perceived employability (Rothwell and Arnold 2007) allows us to focus on the individual acquisition of skills, as well as differentiating between different types of employability skills, in a way that using other measures of employability, such as institutional employment rates (Harvey 2001) or students' job offers (Gokuladas 2010) does not.

In the analysis, we divide student respondents into three groups: those who were born in the UK; those who were born in non-UK European countries, including students from the European Economic Area (EEA) and Swiss nationals (referred to as European students in this chapter for ease of labelling); and other international students (referred to as international students).

UK students make up 94 per cent of the Futuretrack sample of final year undergraduate students, with European students comprising 1.9 per cent and other international students 4.1 per cent. The proportion of international students in the sample is somewhat lower than the figures reported by the OECD, which estimated that international students comprised 14 per cent of enrolments in tertiary education in the UK in 2006 (OECD 2008).

International students are less likely to enter HE in the UK at the age of 18 (the typical age of entry for UK students). More than half (52 per cent) of the UK final year students entered HE at the age of 18 or younger, while this figure was 43 per cent for European students and 35 per cent for other international students. This largely reflects the different secondary education systems in the different countries of origin. Almost a quarter (24 per cent) of students from other overseas countries were aged 26 or over on entering UK HE. These students are likely to have significant experience of employment prior to starting their courses in the UK, which will have an impact on the types of skills and labour market awareness they possess. The proportion of male students was slightly higher amongst the other international students (45 per cent) than amongst the UK (42 per cent) and other European groups (41 per cent). Students from other overseas countries are more likely than UK students to be studying some subjects[2] that are traditionally male-dominated, such as mathematical and computer sciences, and engineering and technologies, and less likely to be studying subjects that are traditionally female-dominated, such as creative arts and design, and historical and philosophical studies. The five most common subject groups studied by students in each group are shown in Table 6.1.

In the sample of final year students, as would be expected amongst the European countries, larger countries, such as Germany and France, and those with a significant non-student community in the UK, such as Poland, are the most commonly represented countries of birth. The most common countries

Table 6.1 Five most common subject groups, by group

Ranking	Uk students	European students	International students
1	Interdisciplinary subjects, eg maths and economics; history and french (14.8%)	Interdisciplinary subjects (15.8%)	Interdisciplinary subjects (15.8%)
2	Bioliogy, veterinary science, agriculture and related (11.7%)	Social studies (13.1%)	Subjects allied to medicine (12.9%)
3	Subjects allied to medicine (10.5%)	Creative arts and design (9.1%)	Social studies (10.4%)
4	Creative arts and design (9%)	Bioliogy, veterinary science, agriculture and related (8.4%)	Business and administration studies (10%)
5	Social studies (7.7%)	Subjects allied to medicine (8.4%)	Bioliogy, veterinary science, agriculture and related (9.3%)

Source: Futuretrack 2006 combined data set: final year students on three and four year courses, weighted.

of origin of other international students in the sample are those that have a historic connection with the UK and/or are English speaking: Hong Kong, South Africa, USA, Nigeria, Australia, Zimbabwe and Pakistan.

As has been noted, students enter HE with different base level of skills. Figure 6.1 shows the proportion of international students who rated their spoken communication skills as excellent or very good when they entered HE and in their final year. A similar distribution can be seen when the students rated their written communication skills. It should be noted that the question refers to communication skills rather than English language skills. The students were grouped by the time at which they acquired English language skills in order to take different language skills into account.

As would be expected, all groups have shown an increase in their communication skills during their time in HE (see previous research by Sasaki 2007). Students who said that they became competent speakers of English as a teenager or adult, the group with a notably lower proportion of students rating their written and spoken communication as excellent or very good on entry, show the biggest gains. By the students' final year, the proportion of students in this group rating their written and spoken communication skills as excellent or very good is roughly comparable to the other groups. Students who are bilingual in English and another language were more likely to rate their written and spoken communication skills highly than those for whom English is their first or only language, which may reflect their ability to communicate fluently in multiple languages.

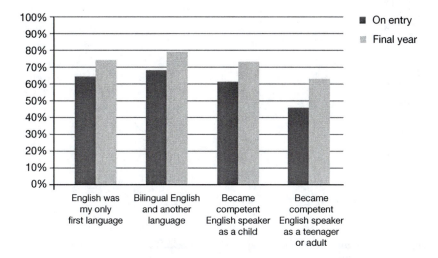

Figure 6.1 Students with excellent or very good spoken communication skills on entry to HE and in their final year, by time they learned English

Source: Futuretrack 2006 combined data set: final year students on three and four year courses, weighted.

Figure 6.2 shows the proportion of students who report that in their final year of study they have excellent or very good numeracy skills, computer literacy and self-confidence. In the case of numeracy and self-confidence, both groups of international students were more likely than home students to rate their skills highly, and the proportion of students from the other international group was the highest in all three cases.

The higher proportion of other international students reporting excellent or very high numeracy skills can be attributed to the subject choice of many students in this group. As seen before, students from Asia and Africa are particularly likely to study numerical subjects in the UK, especially engineering and technology subjects. Students from non-UK European countries show a more diverse mix in the subjects they study, with interdisciplinary courses, business and administration studies, and social sciences accounting for the highest proportions of students from this group (Purcell et al. 2009: 136).

The higher proportion of international students who rate their self-confidence highly is likely to be related to the decision to study in a foreign country, which in itself requires a degree of self-confidence, as well as the previous educational successes of these students, who are often high achievers in their pre-university education. Students who decide to study abroad are a self-selecting group and often show higher levels of independence, self-motivation and achievement than students who remain in their home country (Chirkov

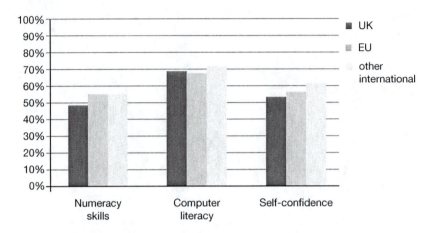

Figure 6.2 Proportion of students rating other key skills as excellent or very good, by group

Source: Futuretrack 2006 combined data set: final year students on three and four year courses, weighted.

et al. 2007; Waters 2009; Wiers-Jenssen 2011). For this reason, it is important to assess not just an individual's skill level, but also the extent to which it has been developed in determining the role played by HE in international student employability.

When looking at the skills students believe their course has enabled them to develop very much or quite a lot, the skills were broadly similar across the three groups. Over 80 per cent of students in each group believe that their course enabled them to develop research skills, specialist knowledge, the ability to apply knowledge, critical analysis skills and the ability to think logically either very much or quite a lot. The pattern is somewhat different when looking at the skills students were least likely to believe their courses enabled them to develop very much or quite a lot, with the international students being considerably more likely to believe they had developed numerical and entrepreneurial skills.

Figure 6.3 shows the skills where there was a clear difference between the responses of the three different groups. The first set of skills are those that both European and international students are more likely than their UK counterparts to believe they developed very much or quite a lot on their course, while the second set of skills are those the international students are again the most likely to believe they had developed, but the European students are the least likely. Overall, international students are more likely than other groups to believe their courses enabled them to develop a number of skills very much or quite a lot, while European students are less likely, and, in some cases, the proportion of European students falls below that of the UK students. However, the differences between the European students and UK students show no clear pattern and the differences are small. This may be because the UK and European students study similar subjects and perhaps also enter HE with similar skills and knowledge.

The higher proportions of international students who say their courses have enabled them to develop numerical and business-related skills and computer literacy reflects the types of subjects studied by other international students. These skills tend to be highly valued by some employers, and it would be expected that the other international student group would experience greater employability as a result of their skills development in these areas, a point discussed further below.

For all groups, it is a concern that some attributes that were mentioned at the beginning of this chapter as being key employability skills, and which students believe employers look for, appear not to be developed to a great extent on

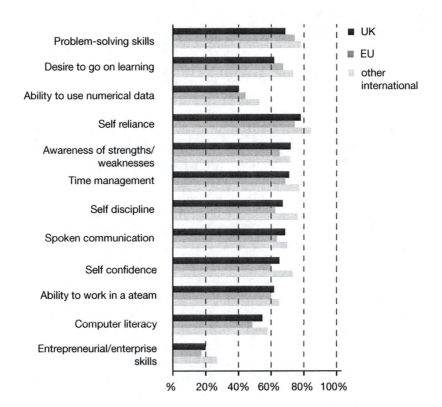

Figure 6.3 Selected skills developed very much or quite a lot on HE courses, by group

Source: Futuretrack 2006 combined data set: final year students on three and four year courses, weighted.

students' courses, regardless of their national background. This is particularly the case for spoken communication and team-working skills. However, it must be noted that students tend to rate their spoken communication highly, and, as Figure 6.1 showed, it is clear that international students believe they have developed this skill while in HE, so it may be the case that there is less need for students to develop this skill as part of their course because there are other avenues for doing so while a student is in HE. A similar case may be made for team-working, where engagement in extracurricular activities, such as playing sports or joining a club, may allow a student to adequately develop these skills as long as they understand the need to do so.

As well as developing skills in the classroom, students may also undertake periods of work experience as part of their course. This enables them both to develop skills and to gain a greater understanding of the kinds of skills they need to develop. In our sample of final year students, 40 per cent of European students and 36 per cent of other international students reported that they had done some kind of work placement or year abroad, a proportion that is similar to UK students (39 per cent). Students can also gain work-related skills and knowledge by undertaking paid work outside their studies, although the extent to which this enables them to gain the kinds of skills necessary to find graduate employment is somewhat debated, with authors such as Mason et al. (2006), Stewart and Knowles (2000) and Brown and Hesketh (2004) suggesting that work experience that is unrelated to a student's career ambitions, particularly if it is relatively unskilled work, does not necessarily develop the skills and attributes employers look for. Crossman and Clarke (2010: 605) point out that international employers or employers in the home country value international experience according to how relevant it is to their own activities, as well as the type of work undertaken and the reputation of the employer it is undertaken with.

As has been noted, international students may be at a disadvantage in understanding the skills and attributes employers value, especially in their home countries. Inevitably, there are some attributes that are intrinsic to the recruitment process, such a gender, physical appearance and social background (Allen and van der Velden 2001) that are a combination what Comte (1854) called 'natural inequalities' and Bourdieu and Passeron (1977) 'cultural capital', which are immutable. However, these were rarely mentioned by the Futuretrack respondents.

Table 6.2 shows selected responses to the question 'What do you consider to be the three most important skills or attributes that employers are looking for in recruiting graduates?' with the skills and attributes cited grouped into broader categories.

As Table 6.2 shows, in general, the list produced by the respondents bears a very close resemblance to the lists produced by employers and policy makers provided at the start of this chapter. The small proportions of students who

Table 6.2 'What are the kind of skills employers look for?', by group

Skills employers look for	UK students	European students	International students
Good work ethic	32.1	30.0	29.6
Communication skills	29.0	22.6	33.8
Team work skills	24.5	26.6	29.4
Ability/competence	18.3	24.7	18.3
Self motivation	19.6	23.5	13.0
Analytical skills	7.1	3.7	10.3
Numeracy	1.4	1.4	1.8
Commercial awareness	1.2	1.4	0.9

Source: Futuretrack 2006 combined data set: final year students on three and four year courses, weighted.

mention numeracy and commercial awareness as amongst the most important skills employers look for has been noted by many employers as a key concern, and they suggest that these skills are undervalued and underdeveloped by their graduate recruits.

When looking at similarities and divergence between the groups of UK students and students from European countries or other overseas countries, it is notable that the most frequently mentioned types of skills are very similar. Notable differences occur when looking at the proportion of each group who mentioned communication skills, ability, self-motivation and analytical skills as being amongst the three most important skills employers were looking for. Students from other overseas countries were more likely than students from the other two groups to mention communication skills, and there is a particularly notable difference between students from other overseas countries and European countries that suggests that this difference cannot be solely attributed to differing English language skills.

Students from European countries were much more likely than other groups to have given ability or competence-related skills and self-motivation as important skills employers look for, while self-motivation was much less likely to be mentioned by international students. These differences are likely to reflect broad differences in the types of employability skills sought by employers in different countries. The higher proportion of students from overseas countries stating that analytical skills are important, conversely, is likely to reflect the types of subjects studied by students in this group and consequently the types of work they are looking for, which, as has been noted, is more likely to be in areas such as engineering and technology where analytical skills are particularly highly sought. It is somewhat surprising that numerical skills were not more frequently mentioned by this group.

Having established the kinds of skills students have developed on their courses and the kinds of skills they believe employers look for, the question can be asked whether students believe they will be able to get the kind of job they want when they graduate (see Figure 6.4).

As Figure 6.4 shows, students from other overseas countries were much more likely to agree that it will be easy for them to find the kind of job they want when they graduate. These students are more likely to be studying subjects that tend to have good graduate employment rates. The lower proportions of European students who agree, and the similarity between their responses and those of the UK students, suggests that it may be this factor, together with factors that are intrinsic to the labour markets where they hope to find work, that explains this difference, rather than any specific value that may be attached to the experience of being an international student.

It has been suggested that studying abroad is one reaction of better-off students to the expansion of the HE systems in their countries of origin, and it is also seen by increasing numbers of students as a way to get a head start in the competition for graduate jobs (Behle and Purcell 2012). However, Waters (2009) argues that the overseas degree has become subject to credential inflation in certain countries due to increasing student mobility. The presented findings suggest that students from other European countries expect no easier transition from HE to the graduate labour market than UK students, although the picture is slightly different for other international students.

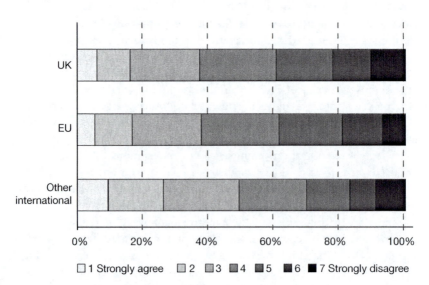

Figure 6.4 'It will be easy for me to get the kind of job I want when I graduate', by group

Source: Futuretrack 2006 combined data set: final year students on three and four year courses, weighted. EU refers to students from other European countries.

One increasingly common way of attempting to make finding graduate employment more likely, as well as delaying transition into the labour market until such time as it becomes more conducive to finding suitable employment, is undertaking a postgraduate degree. Waters (2009) has found that undertaking a postgraduate degree is seen by some international students as a way to separate themselves from others who have studied overseas. Amongst the Futuretrack respondents, this is particularly seen amongst the European students. More than a quarter (27 per cent) of European students planned to undertake a full-time postgraduate course after graduating, compared to 18 per cent of UK students and 19 per cent of other international students. This reflects the different tradition of HE in European countries. In non-UK European countries, many employers are not familiar with the Bachelor's degree as it exists in the UK, and are even less aware of the skills they can expect a graduate to possess. In other words, the UK Bachelor's degree and the skills it develops are not yet completely compatible with other labour market system in these countries.

International Issues and Comparisons of Employability

The findings suggest that students from all groups make definite skills gains as a result of their participation in HE in the UK. In some areas, and for some groups of students, these skills gains are very significant. We have also shown that students have a good awareness of the skills employers look for, but that, in this, international students face some notable problems. Difficulties in gaining an understanding of the skills employers may be looking for in their home country have been highlighted, as have areas of incompatibility between the skills students have learnt and the skills students believe that employers are looking for. There has been an increased onus on the UK HE system to equip students not just with the subject-specific skills they need to get a job but also the generic employability skills employers are seeking. However, the UK HE system is inevitably orientated to providing UK students with the skills they need to find employment in the UK labour market.

While HEIs may, to a greater or lesser extent, take account of the particular situation of international students, certain incompatibilities exist between the skills developed on UK HE courses and the skills that would enable a smooth labour market transition for students returning to their home countries to seek employment. This means that students may not reap the returns that might be expected from not just their skills development in HE, but the very specific skills and attitudes that result from studying abroad, which it may be expected employers would value highly amongst graduate recruits. More research is required to determine how students who study abroad can derive the greatest benefits from their experience, as well as on the different types of employers who value this experience more or less highly.

These findings are problematic to contrast with UK migrant students. First of all, the UK is a destination country for many international students, and the number of UK students going abroad to study is very small. The main destination for UK students is North America (Waters and Brooks 2010), and it is debatable whether employers' expectations in these countries differ noticeably from UK-based employers.

It is hard to predict the future of student migration towards the UK after the introduction of variable fees in 2012. The number of UK and European applicants has decreased (UCAS 2012b) but we do not know how UK eligible students to HE who decided against application to HE plan to substitute tertiary education: whether they will enrol into different kinds of education (further education, apprenticeships) within the UK or migrate to another country to study. The number of applicants from international non-European countries, on the other hand, has increased; however, it is not known if HEIs plan to admit more international students to make up the numbers. If this should be the case, the already discussed conflict between the fees international students are willing to pay and the standard of HE needs to be closely observed.

Another interesting point of research aims at mobile European students. The decreased numbers of applications suggest that many will choose a different country to study or decide to remain in their home countries. Finally, the similarities between UK indigenous students and students from other European countries are remarkable, especially in comparison with students from other overseas countries. It is unclear, however, if this can be seen as one indicator of success in creating a joined European Higher Education Area, as promoted in the Bologna Process (European Ministers of Education 1999).

Notes

1   More information on the Futuretrack project is available on the website http://go.warwick.ac.uk/futuretrack
2   The subjects were coded according to the Joint Academic Coding System (JACS) http://www.hesa.ac.uk/dox/jacs/JACS_complete.pdf (accessed 4 July 2012).

References

Allen, J. and van der Velden, R. (2001) Educational mismatches versus skill mismatches: Effects on wages, job satisfaction and on-the-job search. *Oxford Economic Papers* 3(2001): 434–452.

Anderson, P. H., Lawton L., Rexeisen, R.J. and Hubbard, A. C. (2006). Short-term study abroad and intercultural sensitivity: A pilot study. *International Journal of Intercultural Relations* 30(4): 457–469.

Atfield, G. and Purcell. K. (2010) *Graduate labour market supply and demand: Final year students' perceptions of the skills they have to offer and the skills employers seek.* Working Paper 4. http://www2.warwick.ac.uk/fac/soc/ier/futuretrack/findings/ft3.1_wp4_skills.pdf (accessed 31 January 2012).

Baruch, Y., Budhwar, P. S. and Khatri, N. (2007) Brain drain: Inclination to stay abroad after studies. *Journal of World Business* 42(1): 99–112.

Behle, H. and Purcell, K. (2012) Why have German and Indian students chosen to study on full-time undergraduate courses in the UK? Paper currently under review.

Behrnd, V. and Porzelt, S. (2011) Intercultural competence and training outcomes of students with experiences abroad. *International Journal of Intercultural Relations* 36(2): 213–223.

Belt V., Drake, P. and Chapman, K. (2010) *Employability skills: A research and policy briefing*, UK Commission for Employment and Skills.

Benzie, H. J. (2010) Graduating as a 'native speaker': International students and English language proficiency in higher education. *Higher Education Research and Development* 29(4): 447–459.

Bosch, G. (2009) The 'internationalisation' of law degrees and enhancement of graduate employability: European dual qualification degrees in law. *The Law Teacher* 43(3): 284–296.

Bourdieu, P. and Passeron, J.-C. (1977) *Reproduction in education, society and culture*, translated by R. Nice. London: Sage Publications Ltd.

Bretag, T. (2007) The emperor's new clothes. Yes, there is a link between English language competence and academic standards. *People and Place* 15(1): 13–21.

Briggs, A. R. J., Clark, J. and Hall, I. (2012) Building bridges: Understanding student transition to university. *Quality in Higher Education* 18(1): 1–19.

Brown, P. and Hesketh, A. (2004) *The mismanagement of talent – Employability and jobs in the knowledge economy*. Oxford: Oxford University Press.

Bryant, M., Metz, K., Sheehan, D. and Vigier, M. (2006) Improving students' communicative language skills. One French business school's experience. *Journal of Language for International Business* 17(2): 60–71.

Cable, V. (2010) Higher education. Speech given in his capacity as Secretary of State for Business and Skills, 15 July. http://www.bis.gov.uk/news/speeches/vince-cable-higher-education (accessed 30 July 2010).

Campbell, A. (2009) Developing generic skills and attributes of international students: The (ir)relevance of the Australian university experience. *Journal of Higher Education Policy and Management* 32(5): 487–497.

Chan, W.,and Dimmock, C. (2008) The internationalisation of universities. Globalist, internationalist and translocalist models. *Journal of Research in International Education* 7(2), 184–204.

Chirkov, V., Vansteenkiste, M., Tao, R. and Lynch, M. (2007) The role of self-determined motivation and goals for study abroad in the adaptation of international students. *International Journal of Intercultural Relations* 31(2): 199–222.

Comte, A. (1854) *The positive philosophy* (translated and condensed by Harriet Martineau). New York: D. Appleton & Co.

Confederation of British Industry (CBI) (2007) *Shaping up for the future – The business vision for education and skills*. London: CBI.

Coward, R. (2011) However much universities improve on employability issues, it won't magic up jobs where none exist. http://www.guardian.co.uk/commentisfree/2011/jul/19/graduates-generation-abandoned (accessed 4 July 2012).

Crossman, J. and Clarke, M. (2010) International experience and graduate employability: Stakeholder perceptions on the connection. *Higher Education* 59(5): 599–613.

Davesne, C. and Cummins, P. W. (2009) European language policy and quality assurance tools for management education. *International Journal of Management in Education* 3(3–4): 388–401.

Department for Innovation, Universities and Skills (DIUS) (2008) *Higher education at work: High skills, high value.* http://www.bis.gov.uk/Consultations/higher-education-at-work-high-skills-high-value (accessed 1 March 2012).

Dietrich, J. W. and Olson, C. (2010) In quest of meaningful assessment of international learning: The development and implementation of a student survey and eportfolio approach. *JGE: The Journal of General Education* 59(3): 143–158.

European Ministers of Education (1999) *Bologna Declaration: Joint declaration of the European Ministers of Education,* Bologna: http://ec.europa.eu/education/policies/educ/bologna/bologna.pdf (accessed 4 July 2012).

Findlay, A. M., King, R., Smith, F.M., Geddes, A. and Skeldon, R. (2012) World class? An investigation of globalisation, difference and international student mobility. *Transactions of the Institute of British Geographers* 37: 118–131.

Gokuladas, V. K. (2010) Technical and non-technical education and the employability of engineering graduates: An Indian case study. *International Journal of Training and Development* 14(2): 130–143.

Halász, G. and Michel, A. (2011) Key competences in Europe: Interpretation, policy formulation and implementation. *European Journal of Education* 46(3): 289–306.

Halic, O., Greenberg, K. and Paulus, T. (2009) Language and academic identity: A study of the experiences of non-native English speaking international students. *International Education* 38(2): 73–93.

Hanvey, R. G. (1976, reprint 2004) *An attainable global perspective.* New York: Centre for Global Perspectives in Education; reprint available: http://www.globaled.org/an_att_glob_persp_04_11_29.pdf – (accessed 30 January 2012).

Harvey L. (2001) Defining and measuring employability. *Quality in Higher Education* 7(2): 97–109.

Hillage, J. and Pollard, E. (1998) *Employability: Developing a framework for policy analysis.* London: Department for Education and Employment.

Hind, D. and Moss, S. (2011) *Employability skills.* 2nd edition. Sunderland: Business Education Publishers

Kelo, M., Teichler, U. and Waechter, B. (2006) Toward improved data on student mobility in Europe. Findings and concepts of the Eurodata Study. *Journal of Studies in International Education* 10: 194–223.

Lambert, R. (1994) Parsing the concept of global competence. In R. Lambert (Ed.), *Educational exchange and global competence* (pp. 11–23). New York: Council on International Educational Exchange Publications.

Leask, B. (2009) Using formal and informal curricula to improve interactions between home and international students. *Journal of Studies in International Education* 13(2): 205–221.

Lianos, T. P., Asteriou, D. and Agiomigianakis, G. M. (2004) Foreign university graduates in the Greek labour market: Employment, salaries and overeducation. *International Journal of Finance & Economics* 9(2): 151–164.

Mason, G., Williams, G. and Cranmer, S. (2006) *Employability skills initiatives in higher education: What effects do they have on graduate labour market outcomes?* London: National Institute of Economic and Social Research. http://www.niesr.ac.uk/pdf/061006_91251.pdf (accessed 4 July 2012).

McQuaid, R. W. and Lindsay, C. (2006) The concept of employability. In R.W. McQuaid, A. Green and M. Danson (eds.) *Employability and local labour market policy* (pp. 6–28). Abingdon: Routledge.

National Committee of Inquiry into Higher Education (NCIHE) (1997) *Higher education in the learning society, report of the national committee of inquiry into higher education.* London: HM Treasury.

Organisation for Economic Co-operation and Development (OECD) (2008) Education at a glance 2008: OECD indicators. www.oecd.org/edu/eag2008 (accessed 2 November 2012).

Organisation for Economic Co-operation and Development (OECD) (2011) Education at a glance 2011: OECD indicators. www.oecd.org/edu/eag2011 (accessed 2 November 2012).

Pedersen, P. J. (2010) Assessing intercultural effectiveness outcomes in a year-long study abroad program. *International Journal of Intercultural Relations* 34(1): 70–80.

Purcell, K. Elias, P., Atfield, G. and Behle, H. (2009) *Plans, aspirations and realities: Taking stock of higher education and career choices one year on*, Manchester: HECSU (November).

Rothwell, A. and Arnold, J. (2007) Self-perceived employability development and validation of a scale. *Personnel Review* 36(1): 23–41.

Sasaki, M. (2007) Effects of study-abroad experiences on EFL writers: A multiple-data analysis. *The Modern Language Journal* 91(4): 602–620.

Stewart, J. and Knowles, V. (2000) Graduate recruitment and selection: Implications for HE, graduates and small business recruiters. *Career Development International* 5(2): 65–80.

Taillefer, G. F. (2005) Foreign language reading and study abroad: Cross-cultural and cross-linguistic questions. *The Modern Language Journal* 89(4): 503–528.

Teichler, U. (2007) Does higher education matter? Lessons from a comparative graduate survey. *European Journal of Education* 42(1), 11–34.

Teichler, U. and Janson, K. (2007) The professional value of temporary study in another European country. Employment and work of former ERASMUS students. *Journal of Studies in International Education* 11: 486–495.

The European Parliament and the Council of the European Union (2006) *Recommendations of the European Parliament and of the Council of 18 December 2006 on Key Competences for Lifelong Learning (2006/962/EC)*. Official Journal of the European Union, 30 December.

UCAS (2012a) English language proficiency. http://www.ucas.com/students/whereto-start/nonukstudents/englangprof (accessed 30 January 2012).

UCAS (2012b) Applicant figures. http://www.ucas.com/about_us/media_enquiries/media_releases/2012/20120531 (accessed 4 July 2012).

UK Commission for Employment and Skills (UKCES) (2009) *The employability challenge.* http://www.ukces.org.uk/publications/employability-challenge-full-report (accessed 4 July 2012).

Waters, J. and Brooks, R. (2010) Accidental achievers. International higher education, class reproduction and privilege in the experiences of UK students overseas. *British Journal of Sociology of Education* 31(2): 217–228

Waters, J. L. (2009) In pursuit of scarcity: Transnational students, 'employability', and the MBA. *Environment and Planning A* 41(8): 1865–1883.

West, A., Dimitropoulos, A., Hind, A., and Wilkes, J. (2000) Reasons for studying abroad. A survey of EU students studying in the UK. Paper presented at the European Conference on Educational Research, Edinburgh, 20–23 September.

Wiers-Jenssen, J. (2011) Background and employability of mobile vs. non-mobile students. *Tertiary Education and Management* 17(2): 79–100

7

Assessment and the Student Experience

ROSALIND DUHS

This chapter explores the complexities of the international student experience of assessment. According to the International Student Barometer (ISB), 86.5 per cent of students in the 24 countries surveyed were satisfied with their overall experience of assessment in 2011 (Barrett 2012, slide 12). Conversely, if 13.5 per cent of the some 3.7 million (Olds 2011) international students globally are not satisfied with their experience of assessment, that amounts to approximately half a million students. Potentially problematic areas of assessment for international students are therefore highlighted here. Suggestions are made for the design of assessment systems that minimise the risk of problems arising and offer all students opportunities to learn from their diverse peers in the global setting of the 21st century university.

An overview of competition for international students and the economic gains they bring to host nations is provided as a backdrop for a discussion on the impact of international students on assessment. Aspects of the international student experience are foregrounded including emotional and ethical issues. Diverse influences on assessment – global, national and local – are explored through the concept of 'glonacal' higher education. The centrality of assessment to the student is highlighted and approaches to a balanced blend of summative, formative and diagnostic assessment are presented. The advantages of designing assessment regimes that enhance learning are outlined, emphasising feedback to students on their learning.

These points are illustrated and analysed through examples of issues raised by students: feedback, comparability and fairness of grading, alignment, validity and skills development are discussed and potential problems with writing skills, referencing and plagiarism are debated. The chapter includes suggestions of solutions that enhance international (and other) students' learning, such as details of a dialogic feedback system and proposals for innovative assessment tasks. The concluding prognosis recommends a more active student role in assessment.

Methods

This discursive chapter draws on a wide range of literature on international students and assessment. The author's extensive international personal experience of developing assessment has also been exploited. Fresh qualitative data has been gathered using three methods: primary documentary sources, a focus group interview and an interview with a member of staff who works with international students. Those interviewed were volunteers at a Russell Group (research-intensive) university in the United Kingdom (UK). Statistical data was also accessed online.

Documentary sources were found online using a range of search terms such as 'international students', 'assessment', 'feedback' and 'grading'. Primary sources are both governmental (for example the British Council, the European Union, the UK Quality Assurance Agency [QAA], the United States [US Department of State]) and derived from social media (student blogs). A semi-structured focus group discussion on assessment and feedback with five randomly selected international students at a Russell Group university who had volunteered to participate and provided written consent also provided illustrative data. The discussion was recorded and transcribed as was the interview with the staff member. The texts were analysed through close reading to identify themes that informed the focus of the chapter. This approach to data gathering was selected as it facilitated the collection of a wide spectrum of material suitable for a diverse readership.

International Students: Economic Gain, Competition and Impact

There is a strong temptation to rejoice at 'Going Global' (British Council 2012), as the financial rewards for universities are considerable. International students generally pay higher fees than home students; their contribution to national economies is significant. In the UK, 'export earnings from international students totalled £8 billion ($12 billion) in 2009 and could grow to £17 billion by 2025' (The Economist, 2012) and in the US 'international students contribute more than $21 billion to the U.S. economy' (US Department of State 2011).

Competition for international students is stiff, as indicated by a discourse of 'market', 'market share' and 'customer' in English-speaking countries, for example: 'the creation and the delivery of superior customer value become important in creating a sustainable advantage in the highly competitive international education market' (Arambewela and Hall 2009, 555). It would therefore appear to be advisable to consider the assessment requirements of international students on economic grounds, but always with the proviso that assessment tasks are 'objective, valid, fair ... ' and that assessment designers use 'best practices to design valid and reliable test questions' (Hill and Zinsmeister 2012,129).

The Impact of International Students on Assessment

The impact of international students on tertiary education is strong, particularly in relation to assessment. Students who choose to study abroad select their destination primarily because of perceptions of teaching quality (around 94 per cent), then for the reputation of the qualification and institution (around 92 per cent) (Barrett 2012, slide 18). International students accounted for 16.1 per cent of UK higher education (HE) student enrolments 2009/10 and 23.8 per cent in Australia (Institute of International Education 2011). Adjustments to their needs are important and have the potential to benefit all students (Duhs 2010). There have, however, been fears that some UK assessment systems have become less robust in response to the challenges faced by international students and even that 'postgraduate degrees are awarded to students lacking in the most basic language skills' (Coughlan 2008). Pelletier points out that 'the extent to which UK institutions should ... adapt assessment procedures to meet the needs of overseas students is a contentious issue' (2003, 10).

Tensions may arise between the need to create conditions for a positive experience of assessment for international students and the maintenance of quality. The UK QAA expects that: 'Higher education providers ensure the assessment of students is robust, valid and reliable and that the award of qualifications and credit are based on the achievement of the intended learning outcomes' (QAA 2011, 1). In essence, assessment is valid if it assesses what it is meant to assess and what is taught. Inter-scorer reliability is achieved when two markers award the same grade for a piece of work. The maintenance of robust (trustworthy and fair) assessment may be more challenging when the student body is diverse, but the significant enrichment of university learning afforded by the participation of students from a range of diverse cultures with varied perspectives is of great benefit to all concerned (Volet and Ang 2012). When home and international students work together on assessment tasks, they become better at intercultural communication. They are involved in careful listening, negotiating meaning and adapting their approaches so that they are acceptable and comprehensible to peers with disparate world views. Students' ability to work in international groups can be specified as a learning outcome and assessed.

Emotional and Ethical Issues

The importance of foregrounding ethical issues, such as the promotion of lecturers doing the best they can for all their students, including international students, emerged from data gathered for this chapter. High ethical standards are particularly relevant in assessment: 'ethical teaching includes attention to avoiding actions or inactions that may cause students educational or emotional harm' (Hill and Zinsmeister 2012, 125).

Emotional harm caused by negative assessment outcomes such as low marks or discouraging feedback can occur more easily among students who are far from home and family support. International students frequently suffer from culture shock (Hofstede 2001), financial problems, (Brown 2009), difficulties with language (Mori 2000; Yeh and Inose 2003; Huang 2007), discrimination (McAlpine and Turner 2012) and even racism (Yeh and Inose 2003). It would be wrong to over-emphasise these challenges, as the student experience of assessment is generally satisfactory after initial adaptation. Nevertheless, a postgraduate US student in the UK with relatively minor cultural differences to contend with wrote:

> I also had my first in-class essay exam. I'm a bit nervous to find out my grade. I've never had an exam like that before, even in my undergrad. I will just be glad to see how my professor marks his papers so I will know how to improve my writing.
>
> (Collom 2011)

This and other international student blogs (see for example http://blog.internationalstudent.com/) reveal that more information to students, such as examples of good work, assessment criteria and how they are applied, and opportunities for feedback on drafts, would be appreciated. They would also enhance learning (Mentowski and Associates 2000; Rust et al. 2003). More solutions to shortcomings in the international student experience of assessment and proposals for lessening student anxiety follow.

In considering the setting in which international students negotiate their way into new assessment systems, Marginson and Rhoades' (2002) concept of 'glonacal' higher education is useful (see Figure 7.1). It is helpful to recognise that global, national and local influences on higher education interact. This interaction creates 'glonacality', the mix of a variety of influences. These blend to form a dynamic, rich cocktail, resulting in the distinct identity of individual higher education institutions across the world.

Universities are not global in terms of losing their national base. Approaches may vary locally from institution to institution, but UK universities, for instance, still have a UK assessment identity despite the globalisation of higher education. As regards summative assessment in the UK, traditional timed 'unseen' (with no advance information on questions) written examinations are widespread and often account for a significant proportion of marks (Pilcher et al. 2009). International students often find them 'the most challenging and stressful form of assessment' (Kingston and Forland 2008, 215). Multiple choice questions (MCQs) and short answers are often easier for examinees whose first language is not English. Other forms of assessment (such as essays, project reports, laboratory reports) are predominantly written. Extended written texts are common. This is not the case globally. Many national systems

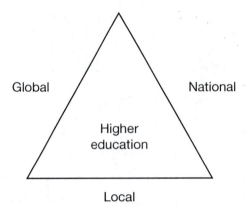

Figure 7.1 Dimensions of higher education (based on Marginson and Rhoades 2002)

foreground oral assessment; international students are often accustomed to very different home assessment regimes (Pilcher et al. 2009, 8).

Students seek globally recognised degrees from today's glonacal universities; top international students' destinations were the US and UK in 2010 (Institute of International Education 2011). In China, for instance, it appears that prestige is attached to the acquisition of a foreign degree: 'a foreign degree simply carries more prestige in China than a local one' (Tom 2011). National systems accredit those degrees, but the universities where international students study are often closely bound up with the civic life of the towns where they are situated, which may affect the subjects on offer and local attitudes to study and assessment.

Assessment and the Student Experience

The aims of university study are multifaceted, but students, whatever their background and wherever they come from, generally hope to leave higher education with a degree. A staff member who works with international students in a UK research-intensive university said:

> I think that international students particularly, they're taken into this [university] … because of the reputation they want to come here, they want to go home with a [name of university] degree … because it helps them to get work and do more things in their country.
>
> (Interview, March 2012)

Many international students make a heavy financial investment in their university education and naturally want a return on that investment. The assessment system that enables them to qualify for a degree is therefore an extremely important part of the 'glonacal' student experience. This has led to the term 'backwash' (see for example Biggs 2003, and illustrated in Dysthe et al. 2007 and Meyers and Nulty 2009). Backwash refers to the overwhelmingly strong influence of assessment on students' approaches to learning; assessment is like a powerful wave that shapes university students' lives, drenching everything in its path.

The centrality of assessment can be daunting, especially if students are unfamiliar with the national and local assessment systems. Familiarisation with assessment is an important part of the transition to university at all levels and stages of study. That transition will be challenging in different ways for every student. International students who are also adapting to a new culture and studying in a second or foreign language are faced with a more complex set of hurdles to negotiate than those in a more familiar setting.

Summative, Formative and Diagnostic Assessment

This chapter focuses on both summative assessment, which contributes to students' final degree classification, and formative assessment, which provides students with feedback on their work. There can be a mistakenly stark division between these two types of assessment. Students naturally benefit from feedback on work that contributes to their final award; in this case, it can be advantageous to combine summative and formative assessment. Students also need 'low stakes' formative assessment tasks so they can check their understanding and do work which is adventurous, not always 'playing safe' for fear of a low grade.

Approaches to summative assessment vary internationally as mentioned above. Synoptic assessment entails examining a whole course or even a whole degree on completion in the form of a set of summative assessment tasks at the end of a period of study. In the UK this type of assessment often takes the form of a series of timed, invigilated, unseen, written examinations sometimes known as 'finals' (for instance at Oxford University in England). These are 'high stakes': students' all-important degree classification depends on them. Continuous assessment (or coursework) during a course of study can also contribute to final course results. A combination of both synoptic and continuous assessment works well for international students as it spreads the assessment burden and provides learners and teachers with valuable information on any areas that need to be developed before it is too late.

Diagnostic assessment is sometimes added as a separate category. It is used to establish how much students know of a subject of study, often at the start of a course. There is no reason why diagnostic assessment should not also be formative and a source of feedback to students.

We have seen that different types of assessment overlap, but the student experience depends on the creation of an assessment diet (a mix of assessment

tasks) that fosters holistic development, including personal and professional development, in addition to the acquisition of skills, knowledge and
understanding. There is evidence that holistic development is appreciated
by international students (see for example Kuznetsov and Kuznetsova 2011).
Authentic modes of assessment that mirror the demands of professional life
promote personal development and enrich the student experience (Mentowski
and Associates 2000). Assessment *for* learning (Black et al. 2003), which is
designed to promote learning, is central to international students. Assessment
of learning acts like a rubber stamp on completed work, offering a paucity of
learning opportunities.

The global student experience can be enhanced if approaches to assessment
balance the summative imperative with a rich range of formative assessment
tasks to enable students to learn from multiple iterations of feedback on their
work. An overly strong focus on assessment for certification or accreditation
(the award of a degree or professional qualification) suggests an instrumental
conception of higher education. This relates to the view of university as a
gateway to individual prosperity rather than a way of helping humankind to
meet the many global challenges, which current university students will face
(see for example McMahon 2009). If, on the other hand, university learning is
regarded as developmental, even transformative (illustrated in Fetherston and
Kelly 2007; Mezirow 1991), then process as well as product is more likely to be
foregrounded.

Effective formative assessment is central to such meaningful learning; feedback fuels learning. Encouragement is vital as it is motivating and increases
engagement with studies; positive feedback enhances learning (Hattie 1987;
Black and Wiliam 1998). Learning processes that embed multiple opportunities for useful feedback to students help the individual learner and potentially
by extension also the societies in which graduates will work. Students can be
supported in their learning through formative assessment so that graduates
emerge from university as discerning, responsible individuals, more able to
play a role in improving society and appreciating the value of democracy (as
suggested in Peters 2010).

Differences, Challenges and Opportunities for International and Home Students

Differences, challenges and opportunities for international students are
complex and potentially enriching. Coping with differences and meeting challenges increases the confidence of international students. In the words of Ann
Stock, US Assistant Secretary of State: 'young people who study abroad gain
the global skills necessary to create solutions to 21st Century challenges. In
turn, international students globalize our campuses and communities' (US
Department of State 2011). This is an unsurprisingly upbeat approach from a

politician. There are many layers to reveal beneath the glossy surface glitz of globalisation.

This section analyses and problematises the assessment experience of international students. The data comes from the literature, social media (student blogs), personal experience, and the themes that emerged from a focus group and interview at a Russell Group (research-intensive) university in the UK. The aim has been to use student voices to illustrate the points made where possible.

The experience of these five students illustrates themes that have emerged from the literature. Students' experiences are influenced by a complex range of factors and a single interview can only create a snapshot. Another focus group might highlight other issues. Five volunteers, four postgraduates and one undergraduate, took part in the focus group interview, which was held in a quiet classroom in the late afternoon. Students were relaxed and keen to air their views. The interview was transcribed. The topics discussed were: background educational experience, feedback on work, the impact of assessment in a language that is not your mother tongue, assessment tasks, assessment criteria, fairness and the role of assessment in promoting learning.

The focus group participants exemplify the diversity of international students today, with students from the US, Singapore, China, Poland and Germany. International students are far from homogenous and often have blurred cross-cultural identities. For example, the US student was ethnically Japanese and had experienced both Japanese and US higher education. There are 16 million international couples in the EU population (European Union 2011). Other students had done 'A' (advanced) Levels, (examinations that qualify students for university) in the UK, so were familiar with the country and speaking and writing in English.

Feedback to Students

Arambelawa and Hall (2009) identified 'valuable feedback from lecturers' as one of the 'most important variables influencing student satisfaction' (561). Satisfaction with feedback varies enormously. Individual tutors and institutional cultures influence the student experience. Expectations also play an important role. One undergraduate Chinese student commented:

> ... it really depends on the seminar tutor you have. Some are quite hard working, they will mark you [sic] and give it back, but some like ... it seems they are quite busy, couldn't give you feedback in time.
>
> (Student C, March 2012)

One tutor had not given sufficient feedback because of lack of time and had even cancelled timetabled sessions because of commitments abroad. In contrast, another student's experience at a US university was extremely positive. She had received detailed, useful feedback on drafts which enabled her to improve:

> with every assignment in the USA the professors would give us about a page worth of feedback, and then we would meet with them if we wanted to talk about it. So it was really helpful.
>
> (Student A, March 2012)

More than half way through the academic year (March), an EU Master's student explained:

> so far I got just one essay assessed so it's really hard to say at this stage, cos [sic] most of my assessments were ... well they're spread throughout the year, so it's quite early to say. So I just got one essay marked and ... well the feedback was pretty short, but it's okay, I knew what was wrong so ... it's fine for me.
>
> (Student D, March 2012)

This student had already experienced study in the UK and considered he could manage on his own. He was aware of the shortcomings in his work and felt he could rectify them. Such self-reliance is far from universal amongst international Master's level students. Their courses are relatively short and concentrated so they have to 'hit the ground running'.

The Student Experience: Satisfaction Levels

The competition for students means that unpalatable truths such as the limited time some academic staff can devote to providing their students with feedback are sidelined. A UK staff member commented:

> ... once they get here I just don't think the support's in place for them. I think that ... they do need extra help. Now regardless of whether you say 'well you should be at a level now to do this', they do have language barriers, they do have cultural barriers, and I think you know they've come to a completely different country to study.
>
> (Staff member A, March 2012)

The ISB investigates a range of aspects of the international student experience. Over one million students at around 1,200 universities are surveyed twice a year in 24 countries. The figures for summer 2011 indicate that 88 per cent of students at the leading UK Russell Group universities were satisfied with their overall experience. However, satisfaction with feedback and marking criteria appears to hover around the 65 per cent mark (Traynor 2011, personal communication).

US

The US is the top destination of choice for thousands of international students (US Department of State 2011). The international student experience of assessment is favourable in the US, contributing to overall satisfaction. The fall 2011 survey indicates that 92 per cent of international students in the US are satisfied with their experience of assessment overall while 87 per cent are satisfied in other countries (Barrett 2012, slide 30). Student satisfaction with marking criteria indicates that assessment systems are well thought through and appear fair to students. In the US, 90 per cent of students are satisfied with marking criteria, while an average of 82 per cent are satisfied elsewhere (Barrett 2012, slide 30). The US also scores well on performance feedback, with 89 per cent of students satisfied, while 83 per cent are satisfied elsewhere (ibid.).

These statistics indicate that, on average, assessment and feedback in the US supports international students in their learning so that their experience is positive. It is impossible to establish how far this is linked to a sense of achievement among students because of grade inflation in the US (Rojstaczer and Healy 2010). US students in Europe are often unaware that grades will be lower. Information on this is essential for the preservation of student self-efficacy, the belief that they have the potential to be successful. A US postgraduate in Spain commented:

> ... I'm not used to the European grading system. In my mind, anything less than 90 per cent means I did something wrong. Over here, I've heard some of my European classmates say 'average' is around a 5 or a 6 on a 10 point scale ...
>
> (Brattin 2008)

UK

As exemplified by the quotes above, students often show tolerance of vagaries in higher education grading systems. This also emerged in the UK. A German postgraduate student said the following regarding summative assessment:

> I think it's never completely fair because that's an unrealistic ... yeah it can't be fair, because it's always people who mark it so ... I think it's fairly okay, like I wouldn't say it's too bad, but yeah to say it's fair is just ... that can't be a question.
>
> (Student E, March 2012)

Moderation of marks and external examiners promote fairness in complex assessment systems, although the literature can be critical of these practices (see Knight 2002; Sadler 2009; Bloxham et al. 2011). The universal adoption of the European Credit Transfer System (ECTS) seven-grade scale throughout the European Higher Education Area (EHEA) would simplify mobility and be more realistic and reliable than attempts at more fine-tuned marking (for instance to percentage points).

Alignment, Validity and Skills

A cornerstone of fairness in assessment, especially for international students who may be adapting to new approaches, is that students are assessed on curriculum content and prepared for assessment tasks. Assessment cannot take place without recourse to a variety of skills. Students have to make their learning visible if it is to be assessed, whether through writing, speaking, practical performance, or perhaps video, audio, calculations or illustrations. There has to be a product that can be assessed. Grades are inevitably influenced by students' ability in the skills needed to create that product, whether it is an examination script or an online portfolio.

Preparation for assessment often fails to include the opportunity to develop and practise the skills that are required for assessment tasks. Students who have never been asked to analyse or think critically will benefit from examples of analytical and critical writing, and taking part in discussions as to what makes for successful analysis or critique. It can be demanding to exercise these skills, especially when time is limited, but students appreciate the opportunity to think for themselves and apply their knowledge rather than repeating what they have learnt. Pilcher et al.'s study illustrates this well. A Spanish student said:

> When you being critical because that's a hard thing they expect from us … how I'm going to erm write the topic and at the same time show my opinion about that and you need time because for me it was like a joy. Really was a precious joy.
>
> (Pilcher et al. 2009, 9)

This quotation shows the stimulus and opportunity for development offered to international students. The challenges of fresh approaches to assessment led to meaningful, perhaps even transformational, learning in this case.

Writing Skills, Referencing Conventions and Plagiarism

Writing is considered to be the most challenging aspect of working in a second or foreign language (Richards and Renandya 2002). Academic writing, with its formal style and conventions, is particularly challenging, but there is often an assumption that although undergraduate students may need to develop their academic writing skills, graduate students can cope. If students, especially international students, do not have the opportunity to practise writing in the required style, problems can arise when they turn in their final high stakes piece of work for summative assessment.

There are several issues that make academic writing difficult. One is referencing conventions and avoiding plagiarism. Correct referencing is naturally difficult for home students, too. However, it has been suggested that international students have 'a lack of cultural awareness as well as lack of full understanding of plagiarism in the western construct' (Juwah et al. 2006). An encounter with a postgraduate student who genuinely did not understand the concept of plagiarism was an eye-opener. It took some time and several meetings to convey the potential gravity of the situation in a comprehensible way. The pain of recognition was acute. The individual concerned was visibly diminished, lost confidence, and abandoned the (optional) module in question. Timely monitoring of drafts would have been invaluable. Ultimately the difficulty was both cultural and linguistic.

There is much evidence of writing difficulties in the literature. 'Patchwriting' is a natural stage in the development of academic writing (Pecorari 2003). Often, students cannot find the words they need to express the complex ideas they have to grapple with at tertiary level, so they 'borrow' text. One student at Master's level had quoted and correctly referenced 50 per cent of the text of her dissertation. She could not be awarded a pass. Early supervision of her work would have been a time- and resource-saver for all concerned.

Practice, Development and Language Difficulties

These extreme examples may not be widespread but they are acute. They are also avoidable. Students need the opportunity to practise summative assessment tasks (writing, speaking, presenting an argument, analysing, referencing, etc.) so they can achieve the required standard. Of course the same applies to home students, but the consequences of failure can be disastrous for international students. Their investment in their education is considerable. Failure is unpalatable and demotivating for all learners, but for students from Confucian heritage cultures where loss of face is particularly shameful, and some other Asian cultures, failure can result in distress, depression and even suicide (Interview, March 2012).

Language is a major issue that is often downplayed in monolingual universities where English, the academic lingua franca (Mauranen et al. 2010), dominates. Students may pass the required International English Language Testing System (IELTS) tests, but this does not mean that they are ready to take on demanding courses requiring large volumes of difficult reading and excellent academic writing for assessment. One of my informants explained that university language centres are extremely adept at teaching to the IELTS test (Interview, March 2012) but that students' academic writing skills are not sufficiently developed. Even home students find the transition from under-graduate to postgraduate study demanding; it is not surprising that students from other cultural and linguistic backgrounds struggle (see for example Muttaqi 2010).

Diagnostic Assessment

Early diagnosis of writing ability is essential if such situations are to be avoided. Practice texts of different lengths need to be written by all students, but such opportunities do not always seem to be offered. Sometimes there is little or no formative assessed work before high stakes summative assessment. One US Master's student in the UK commented: 'there really isn't very much support throughout the first term for anything at all … ' (Student B, March 2012). Shortcomings of this type need to be identified, explored and rectified. It is an ethical issue in the simple sense of beneficence, in this case doing the best for the students who come to global universities, wherever they come from.

Spreading the Feedback Workload and Iterative Feedback Systems

Hard-pressed academic staff do not always have time to provide support and feedback themselves, although some tasks should be compulsory so that progress can be tracked. Practice written texts can be shared online in a virtual learning environment. Initial feedback, including feedback on refer-encing, can be provided by peers. Annotated examples of good writing, with comments explaining why quality is considered high, are helpful. Teaching assistants can also provide extra advice. This is invaluable to all students, not only international students. Developmental writing integrated into courses does not have to be time-consuming. Texts can be written in short sections, gradually working towards full length, highlighting clarity of structure (Kali et al. 2009).

Feedback based on a dialogue with multiple participants and iterations creates repeated opportunities for learning that are much needed by interna-tional students and enrich their learning experience. Figure 7.2 illustrates the process of draft and redraft that mirrors the way academic staff work when they are preparing articles for publication. An essential aspect of the process is the careful study and use of feedback by students. In Figure 7.2, the thick arrow to the left signifies student engagement with feedback so that learning can take place, resulting in steady improvement. Calculations and designs can also be done using the same approach. Students who collaborate and cooperate, discussing and debating their work, do better (Johnson et al. 2007; Sweeney et al. 2008; Kali et al. 2009; Laal and Ghodsi 2012). When these discussions take place across cultures, they enrich all involved, including students who are coping well with their studies (Shimazoe and Aldrich 2010; Volet and Ang 2012). Collaboration needs to be carefully planned. Students need to know how to work together and why it is advantageous to cooperate. Krause (2007) provides an accessible account of practical approaches as do Shimazoe and Aldrich (2010).

Peer Mentoring

Peer mentoring is an underused source of feedback to students; mentors also learn a lot from providing feedback and general guidance to less experienced students (Colvin and Ashman 2010, 128–129). Provided roles are clear, mentoring is a positive experience for mentors and mentees alike and can provide support that is useful at all levels of study; postgraduates have also benefited (McAlpine and Turner 2012). Preparation for undergraduate summative assessment has been successfully run by peers. One US student mentee explained:

> … we had a study group with our mentor, and she went over the test and any questions we had, and I thought that was really good because she took her time to meet with students for the class, to help us prepare for the exam. Not a lot of instructors have time to actually do that with their students.
>
> (Colvin and Ashman 2010, 126)

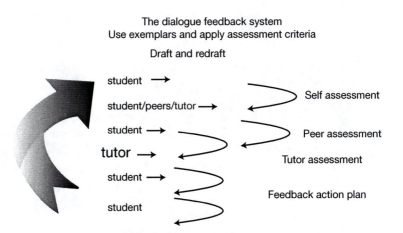

Figure 7.2 The dialogic feedback system
Source: Duhs 2010, 5.

Home student peers are also supportive to international students. When students need help with language, peers often provide it, as there are no language teachers in many university departments. An undergraduate student from China said:

> ... because English is my second language, sometimes I need to talk to the native English speakers, like talk about whether the grammar is right or the structure of the essay is right ... the feedback I got from seminar leaders, ... like it's too short, you need to make it longer ... So I will ask my like classmates to read it and check it out like ... like one sentence by one sentence and give me like more detailed advice.
>
> (Student C, March 2012)

In the UK, students with language difficulties are often referred to language centres where they have to pay additional fees that many cannot afford. The same Chinese student remarked:

> Since in our department we have so many like international students who it's the first time we're using English ... I think that like for our department we should have like an English teacher, like sitting in the general office who we can like ask for help any time ... not like ask classmates instead.
>
> (Student C, March 2012)

Postgraduate students also turn to international peers for advice (McAlpine and Turner 2012), which may not be the best solution where language issues are concerned.

Varying Assessment Tasks

Glonacal universities can draw on global, national and local resources to create authentic assessment for learning environments. Students can work together on carefully designed projects that mirror real life tasks. These should ideally involve students in taking on different roles, communicating with others, locally, nationally and internationally, using blogs, chats, developing concepts based on mind maps, and searching for information rather than listening passively to lecturers. This type of learning and assessment is already taking place (see for example Kali et al. 2009). Provided students demonstrate that they have attained learning outcomes, why should they be constrained as to the tasks they choose to make their learning visible?

The reliability of assessment is considered to be problematic when students work in flexible ways, but a simple pass/fail would be sufficient for this type of assessment task. Potential employers in the competitive global job market would value graduates who had used their university knowledge in creative ways, working with peers from diverse cultural backgrounds.

Reflective Prognosis – Assessment in Glonacal Universities

The assessment experience of international students is as diverse as the universities and the students themselves. Their experience will be shaped by myriad influences. Their home culture, their personality and chosen subject area, their approach to their studies, and the ease with which they adapt to new study and assessment systems, all have an impact on their learning.

Knowledge is provisional. Continuing professional development to keep up with the accelerating pace of global change is essential for success. Assessment tasks must therefore be designed to equip students to evaluate their own learning needs and be sensitive to the requirements of others so they can work together across cultures.

A variety of approaches that have the potential to initiate a paradigm shift in assessment have been proposed in this chapter. Assessment systems can prepare students for challenging yet rewarding lives. At present, universities often subject students to assessment as passive victims in an unequal power structure where academic staff dictate the terms and conditions. It would be better if learners were active participants in assessment systems, taking more responsibility for their development and that of their peers. Students can be offered more choice as to how they evidence their attainment of university learning outcomes. Flexibility encourages creativity and innovation, which is much needed in our crisis-ridden world.

References

Arambewela, R. and Hall, J. (2009) An empirical model of international student satisfaction. *Asia Pacific Journal of Marketing and Logistics*, 21(4), 555–569.

Barrett, P. (2012) *Introducing the ISB International Student Barometer*. Available at: http://www.aascu.org/uploadedFiles/AASCU/Content/Root/ConferenceLeadershipDevelopment/2012_Presentations_and_Handouts/Barrett-Friday–3pm.pdf (accessed 16 April 2012).

Biggs, J. (2003) *Teaching for quality learning at university* (2nd edn). Buckingham: The Society for Research into Higher Education, & Maidenhead: Open University Press.

Black, P. and Wiliam, D. (1998) Assessment and classroom learning. *Assessment in Education*, 5(1), 7–74.

Black, P., Harrison, C., Lee, C., Marshal, B. and Wiliam, D. (2003) *Assessment for learning: Putting it into practice*. Maidenhead: Open University Press.

Bloxham, S., Boyd, P. and Orr, S. (2011) Mark my words: The role of assessment criteria in UK higher education grading practices. *Studies in Higher Education*, 36(6), 655–670.

Brattin, M. (2008) Grade non-disclosure. *Study abroad blog.* Available at: http://www.internationalstudent.com/study-abroad/blog/2008/01/grade-non-disclosure/ (accessed 22 April 2012).

British Council (2012) *Going Global 2012: Internationalising higher education.* Available at: http://ihe.britishcouncil.org/going-global/going-global-2012 (accessed 5 September 2012).

Brown, L. (2009) The transformative power of the international sojourn: An ethnographic study of the international student experience. *Annals of Tourism Research*, 36(3), 502–521.

Collom, C. (2011) Getting into the swing of things … *Study in the UK.* Available online at: http://uk.internationalstudent.com/blog/ (accessed 22 April 2012).

Colvin, J. W. and Ashman, M. (2010) Roles, risks, and benefits of peer mentoring relationships in higher education. *Mentoring & Tutoring: Partnership in Learning*, 18(2), 121–134.

Coughlan, S. (2008) Whistleblower warning on degrees. British Broadcasting Company (BBC). Available online at: http://news.bbc.co.uk/1/hi/health/7358528.stm (accessed 16 April 2012).

Duhs, R. (2010) 'Please, no exams!' Assessment strategies for international students. *Educational Developments*, 11(4), 3–6.

Dysthe, O., Engelsen, K. S. and Lima, I. (2007) Variations in portfolio assessment in higher education: Discussion of quality issues based on a Norwegian survey across institutions and disciplines. *Assessing Writing*, 12(2), 129–148.

The Economist (2012) Pretty polys: The new universities are 20 years old and still spry. 20 March 2012. Available at: http://www.economist.com/node/21549955 (accessed 9 November 2012).

European Union (2011) *Clearer property rights for Europe's 16 million international couples – frequently asked questions* Available at: http://europa.eu/rapid/pressReleasesAction.do?reference=MEMO/11/175&format=HTML&aged=0&language=EN&guiLanguage=en (accessed 17 April 2012).

Fetherston, B. and Kelly, R. (2007) Conflict resolution and transformative pedagogy. *Journal of Transformative Education*, 5(3), 262–285.

Hattie, J. A. (1987) Identifying the salient facets of a model of student learning: A synthesis of meta-analyses. *International Journal of Educational Research*, 11, 187–212.

Hill, G. W. and Zinsmeister, D. D. (2012) Becoming an ethical teacher, in: W. Buskist & V. A. Benassi (Eds) *Effective college and university teaching: Strategies and tactics for the new professoriate*, Thousand Oaks, CA: Sage Publications Inc., 125–133.

Hofstede, G. (2001) *Cultural consequences: Comparing values, behaviors, institutions and organizations across nations* (2nd edn). Thousand Oaks, CA: Sage.

Huang, J. (2007) Should Chinese students study abroad? Available at: http://www.jameshuang.co.uk/articles/chinese_students_abroad/ (accessed 9 November 2012).

Institute of International Education (2011) *Project atlas: Trends and global data 2011.* Available at: http://www.iie.org/en/Research-and-Publications/~/media/Files/Services/ProjectAtlas/Project-Atlas-Trends-and-Global-Data-2011.ashx (accessed 22 April 2012).

Johnson, D. W., Johnson, R. T. and Smith, K. (2007) The state of cooperative learning in postsecondary and professional settings. *Educational Psychology Review*, 19, 15–29.

Juwah, C., Lal, D. and Beloucif, A. (2006) *Overcoming the cultural issues associated with plagiarism for international students.* Available at: http://www.heacademy.ac.uk/assets/bmaf/documents/projects/TRDG_projects/trdg_0506/Juwah_trdg2006_finalreport_webversion.pdf (accessed 15 April 2012).

Kali, Y., Levin-Peled, R. and Dori, Y. J. (2009) The role of design-principles in designing courses that promote collaborative learning in higher-education. *Computers in Human Behavior,* 25(5), 1067–1078.

Kingston, E. and Forland, H. (2008) Bridging the gap in expectations between international students and academic staff. *Journal of Studies in International Education,* 12(2), 204–221.

Knight, P. T. (2002) Summative assessment in higher education: Practices in disarray. *Studies in Higher Education,* 27(3), 275–286.

Krause, S. D. (2007) How to collaborate and write with others. *The Process of Research Writing.* Available at: http://www.stevendkrause.com/tprw/ (accessed 9 November 2012).

Kuznetsov, A. and Kuznetsova, O. (2011) Looking for ways to increase student motivation: Internationalisation and value innovation. *Higher Education Quarterly,* 65(4), 353–367.

Laal, M. and Ghodsi, S. M. (2012) Benefits of collaborative learning. *Procedia – Social and Behavioral Sciences,* 31(0), 486–490.

Marginson, S. and Rhoades, G. (2002) Beyond national states, markets, and systems of higher education: A global agency heuristic. *Higher Education,* 43(3), 281–309.

Mauranen, A., Hynninen, N. and Ranta, E. (2010) English as an academic lingua franca: The ELFA Project. *English for Specific Purposes,* 29(3), 183–190.

McAlpine, L. and Turner, G. (2012) *International students.* Available at: http://www.learning.ox.ac.uk/supervision/dphil/international/ (accessed 22 April 2012).

McMahon, W. W. (2009) *Higher learning, greater good: The private and social benefits of higher education.* Baltimore, MD: Johns Hopkins University Press.

Mentowski, M. and Associates (2000) *Learning that lasts: Integrating learning development, and performance in college and beyond.* San Francisco, CA: Jossey-Bass.

Meyers, N. M. and Nulty, D. D. (2009) How to use (five) curriculum design principles to align authentic learning environments, assessment, students' approaches to thinking and learning outcomes. *Assessment & Evaluation in Higher Education,* 34(5), 565–577.

Mezirow, J. (1991) *Transformative dimensions of adult learning.* San Francisco, CA: Jossey-Bass.

Mori, S. (2000) Addressing the mental health concerns of international students. *Journal of Counseling and Development,* 78, 137–144.

Muttaqi (2010) *The pressures of studying a masters degree at a British university.* Available at: http://www.heacademy.ac.uk/resources/detail/internationalisation/case_story_supervision_staff_muttaqi_masters (accessed 16 April 2012).

Olds, K. (2011) *International student mobility highlights in the OECD's education at a glance 2011.* Available at: http://www.insidehighered.com/blogs/globalhighered/international_student_mobility_highlights_in_the_oecd_s_education_at_a_glance_2011 (accessed 19 April 2012).

Pecorari, D. (2003) Good and original: Plagiarism and patchwriting in academic second-language writing. *Journal of Second Language Writing,* 12(4), 317–345.

Pelletier, C. (2003) *The experiences of international students in UK higher education: A review of unpublished research.* Report for UK Council for International Student Affairs (London).

Peters, S. J. (2010) *Democracy and higher education: Traditions and stories of civic engagement*. East Lansing, MI: Michigan State University.

Pilcher, N., Smith, K. and Riley, J. (2009) *An 'unturned stone'? Exams and international students. Final report*. Report for Edinburgh Napier University, Glasgow Caledonian University (Edinburgh and Glasgow).

QAA (2011) *UK quality code for higher education: Chapter A6 assessment of intended learning outcomes* Available at: http://www.qaa.ac.uk/Publications/ InformationAndGuidance/Documents/Quality-Code-Chapter-A6.pdf (accessed 21 April 2012).

Richards, J. C. and Renandya, W. A. (2002) *Methodology in language teaching: An anthology of current practice*. Cambridge: Cambridge University Press.

Rojstaczer, S. and Healy, C. (2010) Grading in American colleges and universities. *Teachers College Record*, 4, 1–6.

Rust, C., Price, M. and O'Donovan, B. (2003) Improving students' learning by developing their understanding of assessment criteria and processes. *Assessment and Evaluation in Higher Education*, 28(2), 147–164.

Sadler, D. R. (2009) Indeterminacy in the use of preset criteria for assessment and grading. *Assessment & Evaluation in Higher Education*, 34(2), 159–179.

Shimazoe, J. and Aldrich, H. (2010) Group work can be gratifying: Understanding & overcoming resistance to cooperative learning. *College Teaching*, 58(2), 52–57.

Sweeney, A., Weaven, S. and Herington, C. (2008) Multicultural influences on group learning: A qualitative higher education study. *Assessment & Evaluation in Higher Education*, 33(2), 119–132.

Tom (2011) Response to 'Chinese students want American schools'. *Seeing Red in China blog*. Available at: http://seeingredinchina.com/2011/05/09/chinese-students-want-american-schools/ (accessed 9 November 2012).

US Department of State (2011) *Open doors 2011: International student enrollment increased by 5 percent in 2010/11*. Available at: http://www.iie.org/en/Who-We-Are/ News-and-Events/Press-Center/Press-Releases/2011/2011–11–14-Open-Doors-International-Students (accessed 16 April 2012).

Volet, S. E. and Ang, G. (2012) Culturally mixed groups on international campuses: An opportunity for inter-cultural learning. *Higher Education Research & Development*, 31(1), 21–37.

Yeh, C. J. and Inose, M. (2003) International students' reported English fluency, social support satisfaction, and social connectedness as predictors of acculturative stress. *Counselling Psychology Quarterly*, 16(1), 15–28.

8

Globalised Undergraduate Curriculum

CAMILLE B. KANDIKO

The curriculum is at the heart of learning and teaching in all institutions of higher education. The curriculum can be considered at several different levels, from the micro environment of the module through to programme, degree, and up to university, national and supra-national curricula. There are convergent and divergent influences on curricula. For example, national policies may tend to regulate and standardise the curriculum, whereas disciplinary and professional organisations may contradict national agendas. The introduction of a more globally oriented curriculum needs to account for national and international policies and trends, the local context and disciplinary differences. University-wide curriculum models often cede control of disciplinary content to the local level, but work across schools and faculties to enhance student learning experiences through broader and interdisciplinary content, more innovative pedagogies and integration with the co-curriculum.

Changes in the curriculum in major universities can be understood in relation to global shifts in society, politics, economics and education. In the competitive global knowledge economy, nations and institutions compete to attract the best and brightest staff and students. There is a worldwide trend toward mass enrolment in higher education, knowledge and skill specialisation, and credentialing. Employers expect, and often require, students to graduate with various skills, attributes and aspects of knowledge, many of which did not exist a generation ago. Many universities have restructured, reconceptualised or reviewed their curriculum to compete for high achieving students, recruit international students and provide all students a more globally oriented student experience. This chapter explores a series of broad curriculum models, or orientations, in the context of globalisation, and resulting issues of intellectual and practical coherence and curriculum structures.

The Curriculum

There are many broad influences that shape a curriculum, set its scope and provide a sense of coherence throughout the educational experience. How such factors play out varies across regions, countries and institutions, but regardless, the curriculum is always experienced by individual students and strongly influenced by the local context. The sources of information about the curriculum are varied, often restricted-access, in addition to being sensitive and often work in progress, as is particularly the case for university-based documents. This chapter draws on a project based on visits to a number of universities around the world that were engaging in international discussions and debates about large-scale curriculum change (King's Learning Institute [KLI] 2010; Blackmore and Kandiko 2012). Over 25 research universities were visited across five different countries. This allowed the heart of the curriculum – the intersection of its purposes, the forces affecting it, and the intended goals and the actual outcomes – to be surfaced and analysed. Drawing on the findings from the project, this chapter explores the process of developing a more globally oriented curriculum, in terms of structure, content and outcomes and the increase in international opportunities for students within and beyond the formal curriculum.

Here the term 'curriculum' is used to include all of the intended learning experiences, both within and beyond formal teaching. This also acknowledges the importance of the co-curriculum – that range of experiences that students may gain through participation in, for example, voluntary and service activities (Kandiko and Blackmore 2012). Many world-leading institutions have reviewed the ways in which the formal curriculum is structured, in terms of both content and processes. This has raised questions about coherence, particularly where a traditional emphasis on the learning of a discipline as the principal purpose of a higher education has been challenged. The process of change raised many tensions, including: challenges between breadth versus depth; structure versus choice; provision in the formal versus co-curriculum; disciplinary versus professional education; and theory versus practice. These issues are explored here in the context of the curriculum, and the students experiencing it, becoming more globally oriented.

The purpose grounding a curriculum varies across countries, institutional types and missions as well as within various colleges, schools and faculties. Some institutions have a narrow and focused aim for the curriculum, for example military service academies and institutes of technology, and others have a broad aim of knowledge creation and dissemination, such as with liberal arts institutions and often in the case with research-intensive universities that promote 'academic excellence' in the broadest sense of the term. The purpose of the curriculum can cohere around: the subject or discipline; graduate attributes; vocational proficiency; professional competence; personal development; and university mission and values. These are obviously overlapping categories and any curriculum would contain elements of many of these areas, but some institutions prioritise some to offer a 'distinctive' curriculum. Many institutions throughout the world are branding themselves as offering a particularly global and international experience, through the mix of the staff and student bodies, the curriculum content, co-curricular offerings, locations in major global cities and partnerships with universities around the world.

Throughout the cohering principles listed above is a fundamental debate about how much a curriculum focuses on content (what is designed and delivered) versus capacity (what students learn and how they are empowered). This becomes intertwined with arguments for curriculum structures and prescriptions on one hand and creating an environment for desired outcomes to occur on the other. Models that seek to balance these tensions are discussed further below. First, how the content of a curriculum can become more 'global' in universities, within and across disciplines, is explored.

Internationalising the Curriculum

The curriculum has become more global in three primary, yet divergent ways. The first is through disciplines entering the global marketplace – competing for funding, students and prestige. The second is through institutional structures and processes, such as offering enhanced content in traditional courses, often through use of international and comparative research, perspectives or internationally themed degrees in language-based or area and cultural studies' fields. The third is through an internationalisation of the student experience.

Disciplines in the Global Marketplace

Academic discipline has important effects during a student's university career; indeed, some assert that the academic field of study has a larger effect on student learning and outcomes than the type of institution attended (Ewell 1989; Davies and Hammack 2005). Faculty within a discipline often share levels of expectations for students; in fields of study where faculty expect students to study more, students actually do study more (National Survey of Student Engagement 2004). This highlights the importance of expectations and the context for how content is delivered. The perceived economic differential of disciplines is growing; already, varying levels of tuition are charged for graduate field of study in many countries, and similar trends are occurring at the undergraduate level in Canada and the US.

Certain disciplines, particularly business studies, are in high demand from international students, and may be offered with a target audience of high fee-paying students. Many disciplines that have favoured status in the marketplace may not provide undergraduates with the best education for the modern knowledge economy. Rhoades and Slaughter (2006) observed that colleges and universities have been disciplined by the logic of the private marketplace; policies advocated by governments and external groups often vary from what students want. Through the curriculum, and what is offered to students, such dimensions and purposes of higher education are structured into the student learning experience.

In a large scale comparative study of undergraduates in the US and Canada, students in the most popular fields of study (with the highest enrolments) in both countries had the lowest engagement across a number of educational benchmarks, including academic challenge, active and collaborative learning, and student–faculty interaction (Kandiko 2008). A worrying finding was that disciplines close to the market with rich research potential (particularly science, engineering and technology) are opposite from the fields of study that are attracting the most students (social sciences and humanities). This has the potential to polarise academic staff teaching and research, with the associated deterioration of the student–faculty relationship. Increasingly interdisciplinary curricular offerings have been seen as a way to bridge gaps across disciplines, with a global orientation a common linking theme. However, interdisciplinary efforts have also introduced their own associated challenges for curriculum design and teaching.

Institutionalising Internationalisation through Interdisciplinarity

Interdisciplinarity is often used as a vehicle for embedding international and global elements into the curriculum. Interdisciplinary work is constantly breaking down the boundaries of disciplines through borrowing tools and concepts, combining methodologies, and reconceptualising epistemologies. However, there need not be a strict dichotomy between disciplines and interdisciplinarity. Interdisciplinary work has developed to answer a wide variety of objectives: to address complex questions; to address broad issues; to explore disciplinary and professional relations; to solve problems that are beyond the scope of any one discipline; and to achieve unity of knowledge, whether on a limited or grand scale (Klein 1990: 11). Interdisciplinarity is the basis of many programmes with an international orientation, for example European studies and diaspora studies, as well as 'global issues' oriented programmes, such as poverty studies, climate change and sustainability. Such offerings draw on a number of disciplines to provide a range of perspectives on an issue. There are four primary contexts for globally oriented interdisciplinary work in higher education, although there are large variations across institutional settings.

- Content. The most basic form involves enhancing traditional disciplinary-based education with globally themed content, through international examples, comparative research and through assessments for a defined project, for example UN-style debates. This effort is usually locally based and led by individual academics or departments. Examples of modules include global health education, war and global conflict in the contemporary world, global child dental health, and social change in global cities. This can also include using international experiences of staff and students in the classroom. While good practice at the local level can have great benefits for the students involved, it can be challenging to scale up across different fields and schools.

- Programmes. The second common context is creating an interdisciplinary degree programme (either a unique formal course or an amalgamation of existing offerings). These can range from semi-formal options to large, advanced programmes with their own permanent staff and infrastructure. Traditional examples of this include language-based courses, such as French or Farsi, and discipline-based degrees in comparative literature or international business. As noted above, such programmes are often locally organised, and may place a heavy administrative burden on a few academics. They can also be challenging to scale up beyond a few high profile programmes run by committed individuals. They may also suffer from constant restructuring.

- Structures. The last two contexts of internationalising the curriculum involve more of the theoretical spirit of interdisciplinarity. The third context, reconceptualising and restructuring the undergraduate curriculum, often happens on a university-wide scale. Examples range from general education requirements or core courses with a strong international focus, to required second-language proficiency or the adoption of intercultural graduate attributes. This can also happen through study abroad requirements and jointly offered degrees through institutional partnerships. Curricular changes can present challenges of synthesis and depth (Klein, 1990); interdisciplinary courses based on global themes are sometimes charged with lacking the proper synthesis of ideas. Because of this, additional language training is increasingly offered in addition to another disciplinary focus, as seen in the curriculum changes at the University of Aberdeen and at University College London.

- Policies. The final context of internationalising interdisciplinarity in higher education goes a step further, pushing for a reorientation of university structures and policies. This often happens with new institutions, for example the new Yale-NUS College, a partnership between Yale University and National University of Singapore, or in developing international hubs, such as Education City in Qatar. These options combine approaches to higher education from different countries, often working in new ways across disciplines and recruiting diverse groups of students. Similar policies are adopted for international research institutes and centres. All of these interdisciplinary contexts present challenges for academic leaders and managers. The next section explores how curriculum structures and plans have changed to accommodate a globally oriented student experience.

Global Orientation of the Student Experience

Approaches to internationalisation often involve efforts to equip students with knowledge and skills to be global workers and global citizens, appreciative of the interconnectedness of the world and able to take a global perspective. Many of these skills are developed beyond the domain of the formal curriculum. Some have argued that exploring global dimensions within the curriculum and co-curriculum is 'one of the most powerful forces for change in contemporary education' (Taylor 2004). This can include training graduates for the global workforce in the modern knowledge economy as well as educating all students in the context of a globalised world. Knight (2004) defines internationalisation as, 'The process of integrating an international, intercultural or global dimension into the purpose, functions or delivery of post-secondary education" (11).

Drawing on the curriculum project mentioned above, internationalisation encompasses:

- the experience of students studying abroad (both home students going overseas and international students)
- students based in their own countries becoming familiar with and experiencing other cultures, languages and nationalities
- the international aspects of all curricula and co-curricular activities
- the learning of foreign languages
- awareness of one's culture and its relationships and interactions with other cultures.

Approaches to the process of internationalisation include increasing international mobility of students (incoming and outgoing), adopting international perspectives in the formal curriculum and through co-curricular activities, and developing intercultural sensitivity and competence of staff and students. Important notions include developing the global orientation of all students, and not isolating international students or limiting opportunities to students in internationally oriented degree programmes. Students are far more likely to adopt a positive outlook towards internationalisation and global connectedness if staff demonstrates such attitudes (Johnson 2009), which can be a useful starting point for change. Efforts also work to go beyond the employability benefits and to engage students to develop broader world views. There is a concern that curricular internationalisation efforts become a 'tick-box' exercise and students are not encouraged to engage in the way and at the level they desire. The next section provides an overview of embedding a global orientation into the curriculum and providing the environment for students to acquire the desired outcomes of it.

Curriculum Change

It can be argued that most students do not become disciplinary-based academics or do postgraduate research and so need a more general education that prepares them for a work environment in which they are likely to change jobs and careers. Thus they need a broad range of abilities and the capacity to think clearly. A common approach for this is through the specification of general education requirements, introduced in a way that allows an institution to retain traditional disciplinary degree structures whilst offering exposure to other ways of thinking. A broad intellectual base rather than a narrow disciplinary one is the foundation of general education requirements. Many universities that conducted a university-wide curriculum change spoke of wanting common learning experiences for all students, including features such as experiential learning, common core courses, interdisciplinary exposure, increased elective options and a more global orientation.

Coherence in the Curriculum

University-wide initiatives can lead to coherence being a major issue in curriculum design, referring to the way in which the component parts of the curriculum fit together into a cohesive whole. Most institutions ensure coherence within disciplines through sequencing of knowledge and skill development. The availability of less structured elective options raises questions not just about the relationship between electives and the primary field of study, but about degree programmes themselves. There is a tension between student choice on the one hand and intellectual coherence on the other.

In analysing global practices in curriculum development, how such curriculum designs were put into practice was looked at across institutions. Three main frameworks emerged for enhancing existing curricula with broader choice, structuring curriculum characteristics, and increasing cross- and interdisciplinary provision. First, features and characteristics could be infused in the existing curriculum or embedded in new modules (e.g. communication and intercultural skills). Second, these could be structured as required elements, again through existing courses or through new developments (e.g. foreign language requirements). Lastly, they could be structured throughout a degree programme, such as in core modules for all students or through distributed elective elements (e.g. 'Solving World Problems' courses). Institutions often placed the responsibility to meet such requirements on students, although some provided more support to embed these in the curriculum and assist students in meeting them.

The major challenge with offering provision beyond the discipline is the challenge of breadth versus depth in the curriculum. Many academics feel that undergraduate students do not have the disciplinary knowledge and understanding of subject methodology in one area to sufficiently engage with interdisciplinary learning or to be able to apply such knowledge to tackle global issues. However, most practical societal concerns and methodological approaches do not fit within disciplinary boxes, such as 'Global Sustainability' courses or foundational 'Cultures of the World' modules. Furthermore, globally themed courses, whether infused into traditional structures or added through core modules, are often seen as taking away from traditional disciplinary learning and rigour in the curriculum. This said, across the institutions that were studied, some were able to implement university-wide globally oriented, interdisciplinary-based modules, courses and programmes with great success, others had to scale back grand plans, and some initiatives never made it into the classroom.

Some features can be added to the formal curriculum (through the types of activities listed above) whilst others can be offered as optional elements or though the co-curriculum. Several institutions included work experience, internships, placements or community volunteering experience in the curriculum. To link with the academic curriculum, this has to be organised at the local (school, department or discipline) level, and therefore is very difficult to universalise across the university. Such activities are standard in some fields and disciplines, but do not align with other areas of study, further highlighting tensions listed above. In part this relates to the purpose of a degree. For example, some curricula include a significant level of vocational and professional training whilst others lend themselves more to a liberal arts 'learning how to learn and think' approach.

Coherence beyond the Curriculum

How the goal of embedding a global curriculum orientation was interpreted varied immensely across disciplinary, institutional and national settings, highlighting some of the key challenges of curriculum change initiatives. This brings to mind the normative cultural aspects of curriculum design, reform and processes of change. Although the curriculum can be researched and explored comparatively, historical contexts, current issues, local structures and political tensions always factor in curriculum change.

A further challenge for enhancing curriculum content is the increased diversity of students' prior learning experiences. With the massification of higher education (Trow 1974, 2006), and efforts towards access and widening participation, all institutions face incoming students with very different educational backgrounds. It can be daunting enough to get all students caught up to basic levels. As student bodies become more globally diverse, universities have to account for students whose secondary schooling content and structure may vary immensely from the home country. And in the case of several of the site visits, such as Hong Kong and South Africa, major changes to the primary and secondary schooling curriculum made universities unsure of the incoming knowledge base and skill level of home students as well.

Many institutions' curriculum change efforts were limited by graduation standards, particularly for professional and pre-professional-based education. This challenge is faced in fields such as medicine, law and engineering around the world. There can be less flexibility in what can be required in the formal curriculum. However, as seen during the site visits there were many examples of creative ways that universities engaged with professional and accrediting bodies to include curriculum features such as language provision and globally themed courses into existing structures. For this to happen, the case had to be made for the employability enhancement and increased skill attainment of the new content and provision. This put pressure on curriculum models to provide coherence within and beyond the institutional context and a clear set of developmental skills and graduate attributes.

Curriculum Models

Looking across hundreds of different curriculum plans, a number of different models were identified. However, each model has myriad different curricular processes, content, pedagogies and outcomes. Rather than analysing particular structures, these models focus on the broad ethos of the curriculum, and how that is enacted in practice. Three models are briefly discussed below, followed by a final model that takes a more integrated approach.

Subject-centred

A subject-centred approach is often viewed as a rigorous and traditional curriculum model. The focus is on depth within a particular discipline. The curriculum is often highly structured, with content set by disciplinary experts. Academically, there is interest in the formal curriculum only, with any extracurricular activities separate from the academic sphere. Assessments are often based on analysing major themes within the discipline, working towards developing expertise and creating new knowledge within the discipline. Occasionally these have interdisciplinary foundations, but they tend to be tightly bound programmes. Globally themed content is included at the individual module level, done at whim of individual academics. Students may take a global orientation within their own work, but there may be little tutorial support.

Market-orientated

A market-oriented model is usually externally driven. It is often promoted by governments, higher education agencies and speaks to 'stakeholders' generally. There is a focus on application, both within content and assessments.

Flexibility is a key component, in terms of courses, how credit can be granted and with external partnerships such as placements and internships. The structure is largely outcomes-based, with a focus on the skills and attributes that graduates attain. This is often positioned in contrast to a subject-centred model, which is criticised for catering to academics' interests rather than needs of employers and businesses. Global attributes, both academically oriented and personal skills, are increasingly seen as necessary for graduates to succeed in the connected world of today. Such efforts can be resisted by academics, particularly when curriculum changes are seen to be managerial and not linked in with academic content. If global attributes are left to the domain of co-curricular activities, students can struggle to relate them to their formal course of study.

Student-centred

A student-centred model can be seen as situated between a subject-centred and a market-oriented model. There is a mix of depth and breadth in the curriculum. There is 'structured choice' with students choosing from combinations of disciplinary areas of study, complemented with general education requirements. These are often theme-based, such as: selections based on particular cultures in world; modules exploring major world questions and global problems; distribution models, with students required to take one or more courses exploring global issues; interdisciplinary modules; modules that focus on a particular location, such as urban environments; connecting liberal studies with life beyond university; and placing disciplines in a wider global context (KLI 2010). This model often integrates the co-curriculum, through credit for additional activities and courses that incorporate study abroad, service-learning and community work. Although the focus is on the student and student choice, this is often tightly bound within institutional structures, with courses developed by academics with little student input. A student-centred model can be created through 'carving out' space in a subject-centred model and opening that up for globally themed general education requirements. However, as discussed above, this can lead to a lack of coherence in the curriculum.

Network-integrated Model

In 1990, Powell advanced the idea of network forms of organisation, which are typified by reciprocal patterns of communication and exchange. This notion was applied to a variety of industries and has since been widely adopted as a useful organisational structure. Network forms of organisation bridge theoretical and practical gaps between structure-dominated views of organisation with a broader context by viewing exchange as embedded in a social-structural context (Powell, 1990). Network theory draws in many of the features of higher education, such as status hierarchies and reputational concerns, non-easily measured exchange (such as staff and student flows across departments), long-term relations (necessary for developing interdisciplinary programmes and research), and interdependent relationships (Podolny and Page, 1998). Networks highlight the relationships between different units, shared benefits and burdens, and flexible notions of reciprocity. Powell (1990) highlights four aspects of network forms of organisation, all of which have implications in higher education settings:

1 cooperation can be sustained over the long run as an effective arrangement
2 networks create incentives for learning and the dissemination of information, thus allowing ideas to be translated into action quickly
3 the open-ended quality of networks is most useful when resources are variable and the environment uncertain and
4 networks offer a highly feasible means of utilising and enhancing such intangible assets as tacit knowledge and technological innovation (322).

A network-integrated curriculum model focuses on how to keep the benefits of disciplines but also enhance student learning and the student experience (Blackmore and Kandiko 2012). Rather than a linear view of the curriculum, there is a focus on reflection and integrating what is learnt inside and outside the classroom. This adopts a view that what is 'educative about the curriculum is the area of overlap, that is to say simultaneous engagement and interaction, between the domains of knowledge, activity and self' (Parker 2003: 542).

A network-integrated model merges the foundation of the subject-based curriculum with the student-focused breadth component and integrates them in the context of the external environment. This links notions of breadth and depth through curriculum structures and activities such as study abroad, applied global projects, interdisciplinary options and undergraduate international research projects. Tensions between structure and choice can be mediated through options including first-year seminars, internships and placements, and final year projects. Furthermore, integration within and beyond the curriculum can be supported through service learning projects and courses, community engagement activities, study abroad and enhanced transcripts. Such activities need to be complemented by advising and mentoring systems to support a learning environment that promotes repeated cycles of engagement and critical reflection throughout a student's course. The network-integrated model works to draw in students' past experience, which can promote diversity from within the curriculum.

A Globally Oriented Engagement-based Curriculum

All the curriculum models above set out to engage students through different foci and structures. Each has advantages and disadvantages, particularly for different types of students. However, variations in prestige and status markers can lead to some models being valued more than others. Within the context of globalisation, although some institutions are positioning themselves by offering a particular curriculum, or promoting distinctive traditions, there is a strong convergence on curricular processes that engage students in their learning. These include:

- Active learning – application-based assignments.
- Collaborative learning – getting students working together.
- Cooperative education – group-based projects with particular attention to interpersonal skills.
- First-year seminars – shared learning experiences, often developing a variety of academic capabilities, including academic and digital literacies, and used to explore topics from an interdisciplinary perspective.
- Final-year seminars and capstone courses – provide coherence to increasingly broad undergraduate degrees. Allows students to design and create projects that can extend the boundaries of the university, for example writing up a business plan for a local charity or designing a smart phone application.
- Intercultural education – diversity embraced throughout the curriculum, through content, process and outcomes.
- Learning communities – can be residential-based but can also be done in virtual or blended formats. Allow students from a variety of settings to work together and share experiences.
- Writing across the curriculum – promotes intensive writing across all fields of study.

Such engagement-based curriculum practices can be used as a vehicle for promoting global and international education, enhancing the experience of both home and international students, and to support diverse students within and beyond the formal curriculum. This includes paying attention to the experience of students studying abroad, both home students going abroad and international students, and students based in their own countries becoming familiar with and experiencing other cultures, languages and nationalities. There are international aspects to many curricula and extra-curricular activities that can be enhanced, through the global-themed practices listed above and through promoting activities such as the learning of foreign languages. There can also be holistic attention to student development including the awareness of one's own culture and its relationships and interactions with other cultures.

Processes of internationalisation include increasing the number of international students, adopting international perspectives in the curriculum and in co-curricular activities and developing the intercultural competence of students and staff. Curricular initiatives can include international research collaboration and exchange and travel programmes. A considerable potential resource at most institutions is the international staff and students, and in many cases a diverse local community as well. For a truly global experience, it is important to pay attention to staff and home students, not only international students.

Conclusion

In curriculum planning, there is a constant tension between separation, through modularisation and education credits schemes, and cohesion, through group seminars, capstone courses and integrative projects. Although the activities listed above have sound pedagogical foundations, they are often shelved in favour of cost-saving large lectures accompanied by occasional seminars, and seen in the development of massive online open courses (MOOCs). Adopting such practices as listed above is expensive and time-consuming; higher education becomes more staff-intensive, through administration to set up and coordinate programmes and the advising and tutorial support necessary. Furthermore, such activities may not receive student support, especially when they are seen as carrying a higher workload with more challenging assessments. If not adequately supported and integrated into institutional practices, such activities can lead to a lack coherence in the curriculum and inhibit student success and timely completion. Developing such activities may lead to extended degree lengths. This can be 'in practice', such as in the US, where a majority of four-year degrees take at least five years to complete, and 'in policy', seen in the move to four-year Bachelor degrees in Hong Kong and current initiatives underway to extend some Indian degrees to four years.

Following on from discussions about divergence in response to global forces, there are several policies and initiatives that have unintended consequences. In regards to the drive for students to become more mobile and to study abroad, very low proportions of students in some countries take up such opportunities: in Europe, less than one per cent of students are in a study abroad programme compared to home students enrolled, less than one per cent engage with European Community Action Scheme for the Mobility of University Students' (ERASMUS) schemes, and most students that study in Europe are clustered in three countries: the UK, France and Germany (ACA Report 2011).

External stakeholders often want graduates with proscribed skills and attributes, such as 'critical thinking skills' and the 'ability to think outside the box'. However, academics argue that it is through in depth disciplinary study that such outcomes are obtained. The network-integrated model goes some way to addressing this, but nevertheless the tension remains and there is often much debate in curriculum change discussions. A challenge remains for globally oriented courses and world questions' modules to be designed and developed to have rigorous learning outcomes and coherence with degree programmes.

Additionally, external demands and desires often lack student and institutional support or interest. This was discussed earlier in relation to science, technology, engineering and mathematics (STEM) fields, where there is often high external demand for more students in these subjects but often low student interest. This leads to a tension between student choice versus national and economic need. This is also the case with many of the global curricular elements. Although foreign language study is widely seen as beneficial, few students opt for it even when it is available. Similar issues arise with study abroad programmes.

As with many other trends, a paradox of globalisation remains that as higher education becomes more integrated locally, it also becomes harder to expand globally. As it becomes more global in its orientation, it is in danger of becoming locally irrelevant. For myriad reasons discussed throughout this book, many students see their best option for higher education outside their home country – for all or part of their study. Countries and institutions react by changing to attract local and international students. One can only hope that in the fury of competition the curriculum can be the driver of effective educational practice and education, retaining its distinctive position as the academic link between students and teachers, discipline and outcomes, and engagement and learning.

References

ACA Report (2011). Mapping mobility in European higher education, in U. Teichler, I. Ferencz and B. Wächter (eds.). A study produced for the Directorate General for Education and Culture (DG EAC), of the European Commission. Brussels: European Commission

Blackmore, P. and Kandiko, C. B. (2012). *Strategic curriculum change in universities: Global trends.* London: SRHE/Routledge.

Davies, S. and Hammack, F. (2005). The channeling of student competition in higher education: Comparing Canada and the U.S. *Journal of Higher Education,* 76(1), 89–106.

Ewell, P. T. (1989). Institutional characteristics and faculty/administrator perceptions of outcomes: An exploratory analysis. *Research in Higher Education,* 30(2), 113–136.

Johnson, M. (2009). *Student success in community colleges: The effect of intercultural leadership and relationships.* Ed.D. Dissertation, Azusa Pacific University.

Kandiko, C. B. (2008). Student engagement in two countries: A comparative study using National Survey of Student Engagement (NSSE) data. *Journal of Institutional Research,* 14(1), 71–86.

Kandiko, C. B. and Blackmore, P. (2012). Strategic curriculum change. In J. Groccia. M. Alsudairy and W. Buskist (eds.), *Handbook of college and university teaching: Global perspectives* (pp. 293–311). Thousand Oaks, CA: Sage Publications.

King's Learning Institute (KLI) (2010) Creating a 21st century curriculum: The King's-Warwick project. London: King's Learning Institute.

Klein, J. T. (1990). *Interdisciplinarity: History, theory, and practice*. Detroit, MI: Wayne State University Press.

Knight, J. (2004). Internationalization remodeled: Definition, approaches, and rationales. *Journal of Studies in International Education*, 8(1), 5–31.

National Survey of Student Engagement (NSSE) (2004). *Student engagement: Pathways to collegiate success*. Bloomington, IN: Indiana University Center for Postsecondary Research.

Parker, J. (2003). Reconceptualising the curriculum: From commodification to transformation. *Teaching in Higher Education*, 8(4), 529–543.

Podolny, J. M. and Page, K. L. (1998). Network forms of organization. *Annual Review of Sociology*, 24, 57–76.

Powell, W. W. (1990). Neither market for hierarchy: Network forms of organization. *Research in Organizational Behavior*, 12, 295–336.

Rhoades, G. and Slaughter, S. (2006). Academic capitalism and the new economy: Privatization as shifting the target of public subsidy in higher education. In R. A. Rhoades and C. A. Torres (eds.), *The university, state, and market: The political economy of globalization in the Americas* (pp. 103–140). Stanford, CA: Stanford University Press.

Slaughter, S. and Leslie, L. L. (1997). *Academic capitalism: Politics, policies, and the entrepreneurial university*. Baltimore, MD: The Johns Hopkins University Press.

Taylor, J. (2004). Toward a strategy for internationalisation: Lessons and practice from four universities. *Journal of Studies in International Education*, 8(2), 149–171.

Trow, M. (1974). Problems in the transition from elite to mass higher education. In OECD (ed.), *Policies for Higher Education* (pp. 51–101). Paris: OECD.

Trow, M. (2006). Reflections on the transition from elite to mass to universal access: Forms and phases of higher education in modern societies since WWII. In J. J. F. Forest and P. G. Altbach (eds.), *International handbook of higher education* (pp. 243–280), Dordrecht, The Netherlands: Springer.

Part 2
Exploring the Student Experience
International Perspectives

9

EU and Bologna
A New Educational Agenda for the Knowledge Society and its Global Students

LENA ADAMSON AND ANDERS FLODSTRÖM

Historically, the most important asset to a society at that time has often been used to identify the age, the epoch or the era. The ages of bronze and iron, the revolutions of industry and science, the digital and knowledge societies are all such examples. Today we consider knowledge and the ability to use knowledge to be the most important assets to mankind, only challenged by the access to food, energy and raw materials.

Knowledge is in one fundamental aspect different to any other asset though. It cannot be used up and its sustainability depends on being used, actually the opposite to other assets, for our vital resources. Competent users of knowledge will attract new users resulting in a benign spiral. Knowledge users start new ventures and create new infrastructures and companies by inventing, using and understanding the social and societal context of new technology. This is the knowledge society: a society which is dependent on its citizens and their willingness to develop and use their competencies both for individual and collective purposes, and thus also dependent on its own ability to create educational systems and contexts that let every individual fully develop their potential. But what knowledge and what educational systems does a knowledge society need?

The view of knowledge and education has changed considerably over time. Knowledge was for a long time defined as the codified factual content in books disseminated by reading and memorising, or by students listening to more knowledgeable people lecturing and, again, memorising. From a student perspective, before Gutenberg and the invention of the printing press, the codified knowledge and the non-codified knowledge and skills (such as learning the skills to become a sailor, a carpenter or a blacksmith) in a sense were taught in similar ways. The master taught in a person-to-person way, with one or a few students or apprentices.

Knowledge codification was essentially manual and cumbersome work by a single person, which limited the possibility of teaching many students at one time. Gutenberg radically changed this situation, resulting in the increase and spread of universities around Europe, and the numbers of students increased dramatically. The consequences for teaching and learning methods and the student experience were equally dramatic in the sense that the individual person-to-person learning situation now was replaced by learning in groups. The positive development with provision of learning materials and the possibility of self-study alongside meetings with teachers did unfortunately also lead to an almost singular focus on content knowledge, resulting in a passivation of students. The marriage between codified knowledge and skills into competencies did not occur until the beginning of the 20th century when the scientific revolution created the academic professions we still have, such as medical doctors, engineers, psychologists, academically educated teachers, etc. The passive learning approach in higher education has prevailed though, specifically in the 'traditional academic' contexts. However, the development of the knowledge society and the need to combine new knowledge with new competencies highlights the importance of integrating skills training into the educational programmes for these professions.

The Bologna Process and the creation of the European Higher Education Area (EHEA) can be considered the European response to this development. It was initiated in 1998 by the ministers of education from France, Germany, the United Kingdom and Italy and through signing the Sorbonne Declaration. It was further formalised a year later, in 1999, via the Bologna Declaration. Here 30 countries expressed their wish to participate in a voluntary harmonisation process of the European higher education system, which at the time was segmented and thus seen, by many, as both outdated and harmful. The process has since been driven via minister conferences every second year (at the moment comprising 47 countries), each conference resulting in a communiqué. The work in between these meetings has been driven by the Bologna Follow Up Group (BFUG) and many others, where reports are written and provided as decision material for the coming conference and communiqué. Although there has been criticism at times and in places, the Bologna Process has been a remarkably effective process in driving the development of European higher education systems. This is most probably explained by the process being initiated and largely owned by the higher education sector itself and also engaged with students from the very beginning.

Bologna is probably best known for its objective to structure higher education along three cycles (bachelor's, master's, PhD), in order to ensure more comparable, compatible and coherent higher education systems. The target has been to create a EHEA, which was considered accomplished in March 2011 at the ministry conference in Budapest-Vienna where it was officially launched.

However, in addition to structural changes, Bologna also includes a radical shift in higher education where the learning outcomes paradigm, with active learning and a student-centred approach, was put on the agenda almost right from the start. The intentions were, and are, to move higher education from being knowledge-based to instead being competence-based. These policies are now shaping a higher education system that serves the needs of a modern knowledge society and at the same time promotes the integration of all member states. It also represents a shift to education starting from student and societal *needs*, rather than from knowledge to be imposed. These changes have been much promoted within the context of quality assurance via the European Association for Quality Assurance in Higher Education (ENQA), European Quality Assurance Register (EQAR), European Student Union (ESU), European University Association (EUA), Council of Europe (CoE) and others. However, true links in *the actual practice* between the move from teacher-driven to student-centred teaching and learning on the one side, and quality assurance systems on the other are not yet truly developed. This we come back to further below.

To conclude this section, the knowledge society is truly global. Wherever people live, a knowledge society can be created and can be made to grow, eradicate poverty and increase the quality of life of people. Globalisation with its expansion and intensification of social relations and consciousness across world-time and world-space is the vehicle for this. Silicon Valley and Route 124 are often talked about as hotspots for creativity, innovation and entrepreneurship, where stakeholders such as universities with their academics and students meet venture capitalists with 'intelligent' money and where the culture, lifestyle and society is open and multicultural and designed for social interaction. But examples of the knowledge society are not always or only found among the very best; it can also be found where the needs are the greatest like Monkey Hill in the slum of Rio de Janeiro. Today the knowledge society can be found everywhere – where there are people, possibilities to communicate, questions to be answered and needs to be satisfied.

Bologna and Mobility

Looking back at the Bologna Process (probably the biggest reform process that has ever 'hit' European higher education), the overarching goals of higher education were originally formulated in four points. Higher education should serve as preparation for the labour market and for life as active citizens in a democratic society, it should promote students' personal development and the development and maintenance of a broad, advanced knowledge base for Europe (Danish Ministry of Science Technology and Innovation 2005). Although the Sorbonne Declaration (1998) expresses mobility both for students and staff as one key component in higher education studies[1], and one of the original eight Bologna action lines refers to mobility, we observe that the internationalisation aspects are not visible in the Bologna overarching goals. In addition, mobility in the Sorbonne Declaration refers to European mobility, that is, deliberately or not, an intra-European perspective on internationalisation. The tool for this has primarily been exchange schemes often supported by the European Community Action Scheme for the Mobility of

University Students (Erasmus) initiative with students doing part of their study programme at another European university. According to Wächter (2008) the Erasmus statistics do not give us any evidence that this intra-European non-degree mobility has increased in any dramatic way during the Bologna period. Further, it is impossible to speak of a European picture. Different countries have very different mobility profiles. This applies also to the other student group, the 'free movers', which are mainly non-European students coming to Europe for a full education programme and a degree, most often a master's level degree or a PhD. Also here the country profiles differ a lot, where UK, France and Germany account for the majority of incoming degree mobility compared to the other member states.

Nations with keen and motivated students with good primary and secondary schooling, but with less developed higher education systems, quality- or quantity-wise, of course try to utilise more developed higher education systems to educate students and hope that other mechanisms bring them back home. The students themselves and their parents may see this as an opportunity to climb a social ladder at home or elsewhere. Europe had for a long time a much more altruistic view of this compared with the US. Exchange programmes for aid and cultural reasons and filling empty places within science and engineering have been considered to be enough. In a Europe with almost 100 per cent state-financed universities, England being the exception, the mental distance to viewing higher education as a service market is rather long. However, the 'free movers' and their parents do look upon higher education as a market and are, as in any market, sensitive to brand, quality and price. The market has been created by a lack of student places in the economically fast growing countries such as the BRIC (Brazil, India, Russia and China) countries, but also many other countries in the Middle East and Africa. Europe's main competitive advantages here can probably be attributed more to low tuition fees, good university quality and democratic societies with inclusive social systems, rather than to Bologna reforms. That 'money talks' here becomes evident when you look at the consequences of introducing tuition fees for non-European students in Sweden in 2011. The number of students that applied to international master's study programmes (taught in English) decreased from 92,000 to 25,000 (a drop of 73 per cent), and the number of admitted students dropped from 16,600 to 1,200. Similar patterns were observed for Switzerland, Denmark and The Netherlands when tuition fees were introduced.

Thus, and to conclude, our opinion is that the Bologna Process does not (at least yet) succeed in its internationalisation and/or mobility activities. In fact the internationalisation agenda can even be somewhat questioned since, for a long time, it primarily concerned intra-European mobility, and it could also be labelled a tool for increasing European cohesion and the European identity. It will not significantly increase the global collaboration and competition needed to drive European higher education quality. Instead, we now want to highlight Bologna's impact on curriculum development and quality assurance policies. This is where students, whether national or international, can be said to have made the greatest wins and still have the largest gains to come.

Bologna and Curriculum Reform: From Knowledge Possession to Knowledge Performances and Competences

The Bologna Process started out as a structural reform, working towards European degrees becoming similar in terms of length and credits in order to obtain greater compatibility and comparability between the systems. The two cycle model (bachelor's and master's) was adopted in the Bologna Declaration, 1999, and the need for including a third cycle (doctoral) studies was first mentioned in the Berlin communiqué 2003, and later adopted in Bergen 2005.

These structural issues, length of time for degrees (especially master's degrees) and the European Credit Transfer System (ECTS), for a long time took most of academia's attention – this *was* for many the Bologna Process. However important these issues were and are, both for transparency and mobility reasons, they did for some time shadow the real radical change that was underway: the move into new ways of looking at knowledge and equally new ways of planning and performing teaching and learning. The terms *learning outcomes* (statements of what a learner is expected to know, understand and/or be able to do at the end of a learning period) and *competences* were first mentioned in the Berlin communiqué (2003) where it was said that:

> Ministers encourage the member States to elaborate a framework of comparable and compatible qualifications for their higher education systems, which should seek to describe qualifications in terms of workload, level, learning outcomes, competences and profile. They also undertake to elaborate an overarching framework of qualifications for the European Higher Education Area.
>
> (Berlin communiqué 2003: 4)

Two years later, in Bergen, the so called Dublin Descriptors, originally created by the Joint Quality Initiative (2004), was presented and adopted as the basis of this framework, the Qualification Framework of the European Higher Education Area (QF-EHEA, not to be confused with a later framework initiated by the European commission, the European Qualification Framework [EQF] 2005). Ministers here said:

> We adopt the overarching framework for qualifications in the EHEA, comprising three cycles (including, within national contexts, the possibility of intermediate qualifications), generic descriptors for each cycle based

on learning outcomes and competences, and credit ranges in the first and second cycles.

(European Qualification Framework 2005: 2)

Looking back, this was probably one of the most important steps on the road 'towards student-centred higher education and away from teacher-driven provision' as it was later formulated in the London Communiqué (2007: 2).

Two things were new with this framework. First, the level descriptors of all three cycles were formulated as overarching learning outcomes, clearly positioning the student as focus for educational activities. Instead of focusing on what the course or module should give, and what teachers should do – mirroring the aforementioned view of knowledge as the codified content in books disseminated by teachers lecturing and student memorising – they instead focused on what the students should be able to do after completion of a study period.

Learning outcomes and student-centred learning leads to a number of important changes. To start with, for students it (can) create a more understandable learning chain, tying the teaching–learning–assessment relationships clearly together, instead of the course or the module just being a sequence of lectures sometimes rather unattached (at least to the student) to both course literature and outlines (see Figure 9.1). To teachers it highlights the fundamental links between the design, delivery, assessment and measurement of learning, and when presented is often seen as a very helpful tool for both planning and performing teaching.

When aligning teaching in this way it also leads to a number of important shifts of perspectives; from the teacher's activities to those of the student,

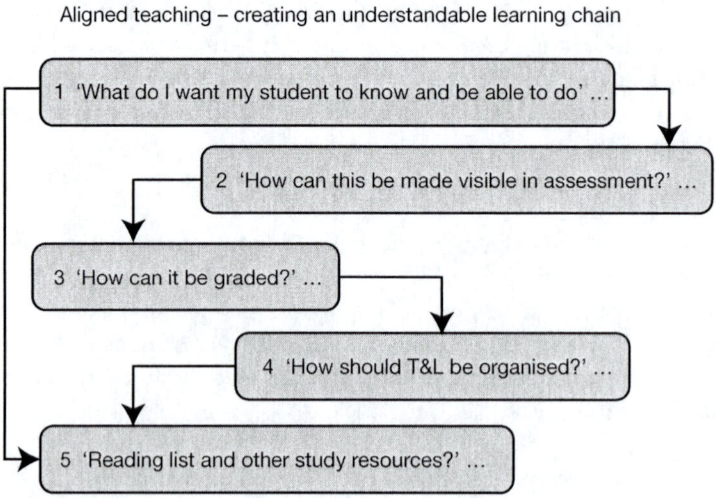

Aligned teaching – creating an understandable learning chain

Figure 9.1 Aligned teaching: a student-centred approach to programme planning

from planning the module, course or programme 'from beginning to end', to a reversal of the process (in the US and other parts of the world this is most often called Outcome Based Learning [OBL]), but maybe most important and connected to the second goal of higher education mentioned earlier: fostering students to become active citizens in a democratic society. This represents a change of relationship, from teachers talking *to* students to teachers talking and interacting *with* students. The last shift leads to empowering students, transforming them from passive respondents into active subjects, with both rights and responsibilities in their own learning processes.

The second new aspect of the QF-EHEA has been less discussed: the way the level descriptors were structured and presented. The Dublin Descriptors were built on the following five forms of knowledge: knowledge and understanding; applying knowledge and understanding; making judgements; communications skills; and finally, learning skills (Joint Quality Initiative 2004), for the first time formally articulating the need for also focusing on more than just factual content knowledge, that is, generic and transferable (transversal) skills, previously at best embedded or implicit in the assessment values and practices, but just as often fully ignored. Although the learning outcomes clearly moves students' learning from knowledge possession to knowledge performances, they do not, in fact, by themselves guarantee that these knowledge performances cover much else than the application of knowledge and understanding, that is, the use of pure factual content knowledge. The explicit use of different types of knowledge forms brings these issues up to a meta-level, and here we have the true key of moving from content-based to competence-based education. It is surprising that this point has not received more attention. In fact, when the learning outcomes of the Dublin Descriptors were adopted into the formal QF-EHEA these knowledge forms were removed (although kept but often in altered forms in national qualification frameworks [NQF], e.g. in Norway and Sweden). In addition to securing that higher education includes aspects such as making value judgements, communication and learning skills, knowledge forms can also be used as profilers of specific degrees, and this we address later, but before that we address the issue of quality assurance.

Bologna and Quality Assurance

Quality assurance was mentioned in the Bologna Declaration but was expressed primarily as the need for European cooperation in developing comparable criteria and methodologies. The subject was revisited in Prague, in 2001, where in addition to cooperation between the countries, the relationship between recognition and quality assurance was also emphasised. The big leap came at the ministerial meeting in Bergen, in 2005, where, as already mentioned, the QF-EHEA was adopted together with the so-called European Standards and Guidelines (ESG) proposed by the ENQA. The ESG has since become a very important document addressing both higher education institutions and the quality assurance agencies. A further step was taken in London where the EQAR was endorsed and later founded by the E4 group (ENQA, ESU, EUA and the European Association of Institutions in Higher Education [EURASHE]) in 2008. This register now includes 28 European quality assurance agencies. Since 2006 the E4 group has also jointly organised the European Quality Assurance Forum (EQAF), which is where the European developments in quality assurance are discussed on different themes on a regular basis.

Two of the main issues that have been discussed during these years have concerned the relationship between the higher education institutions and the quality assurance bodies, and the balance, especially in national systems, between accountability and promoting quality. A general consensus between most parties exists in that higher education institutions are the ones that carry the main responsibility for quality assurance and that the ultimate goal of all quality assurance, internal or external, is to enhance quality and the quality culture.

With such a strong focus on learning outcomes and the shift towards student-centred teaching and learning in both the ministers' communiqués and in a number of other Bologna documents and conferences, a logical assumption would be that these concepts would be especially prominent features in the quality assurance contexts. This is not so. The ESG, although having a clear student focus and stating as the first of three purposes in the document that it is 'to improve the education available to students in higher education institutions' (ENQA 2009), only mentions the term intended learning outcomes once, and then only in relation to institutions' internal quality assurance systems, not in relation to the responsibilities of external quality assurance bodies. This lack of linkage between the learning outcome paradigm, the need for student-centred teaching and learning and the (minister-) agreed requirements for students to receive a degree expressed as learning outcomes, is also mirrored for instance in the themes of the EQAF where very little attention has been given to this subject over the years. The reasons for this we can only speculate, but a reasonable guess is that work and development of quality assurance systems, and work, research and development of teaching and learning methods, has for a long time been done in separate contexts by people with separate professional backgrounds. The former has been done mainly by staff at quality assurance agencies and the latter by academic staff at universities.

The first initiative on a Bologna-wide level that we are aware of – to discuss how to join quality assurance mechanisms to actually drive development towards a more student-centred approach – was a conference in 2010 arranged by ESU together with Teachers' International. Here two of the conference speakers came to very different conclusions on the conference question 'QA and Student Centred Learning – Is QA a tool that can bring about more incentives in shifting the paradigm?' The first, answered *no* just as clearly as the second speaker answered *yes*. The difference in approach between the speakers was whether the starting point was quality assurance via institutional audits (no) or programme evaluations (yes). The conclusion is that difficulties in making assumptions about educational quality from a learning outcome perspective will increase, the further away from the teaching and learning situation the evaluation is carried out. Between the choices of audits versus evaluations of study programmes and subjects, there is a need to choose the latter in order to tackle the issue at its source: the teacher–student situations where both intended and achieved learning outcomes are applied in actual practice (Adamson, 2011).

On a national level, few external quality assurance agencies have focused on learning outcomes, whether intended (written statements in educational documents) or achieved (student products) when creating their systems. Haakstad (2011) found three examples, The Netherlands, Denmark and Sweden, where the Swedish example at that time was constituted only of a proposal from the Swedish National Agency of Higher Education to the Swedish Government (Högskoleverket [Swedish National Agency of Higher Education] 2009). This proposal (which was developed together with the Association of Swedish Higher Education and the National Student Union) was, however, rejected, this after a prolonged conflict between the Ministry of Education on the one side and the Agency, the higher education sector and the students on the other hand (Myklebust 2010). It was replaced by a model produced at the ministry bringing the so called 'result dimension', one could say, to its extreme: only achieved learning outcomes (here student final theses/projects) were to be (re-) evaluated and seen as the indicator of programme or subject quality, methods-wise a highly questionable assumption and heavily critisised by ENQA. The model should, according the government bill, 'Focus on Knowledge – quality in higher education', explicitly not take into account the planning and/or performing of teaching since this 'would endanger institutional autonomy' (Utbildningsdepartementet [Swedish Ministry of Education and Culture] 2011). Consequently it would not be able to give any information to institutions on where to make corrections and adjustments in order to promote student learning, thus leaving the student completely out of sight. The Danish and Dutch-Flemish systems have not adopted this type of approach.

In sum, the Bologna Process, in particular members of the E4 group but also many others, have truly put quality assurance issues on the agenda as one of the key drivers for educational quality. However, there is still some way to go when it comes to linking quality assurance models to students' achievements of intended learning outcomes and driving the development towards more research-informed teaching and learning methods, putting the student in the centre.

Bologna and the Knowledge Triangle. Higher Education for the Future: Creativity, Innovation and Entrepreneurship as the New Knowledge Forms – the European Institute of Technology and Innovation

The knowledge society is characterised by a paradox: at the same time as a rapid increase of international cooperation and collaboration takes place – academic institutions and their researchers, their teachers and students are more agile and mobile than ever, creating new networks and mixing personal and professional relationships in totally new ways – the race where regions and nations compete about how to generate the best academic education, research and innovation activities to gain a global competitive advantage is stronger than ever. The four goals for higher education according to Bologna can be said to illustrate this paradox, simultaneously expressing the need for a democratic society with European cohesion and harmony, and at the same time the need for developing itself in the arena of global competition.

Another paradox we need to take into account is what sometimes is called the European paradox: Europe is good at generating scientific results but not as good at transforming these into innovations and new business. Why? The mindset of Europeans and European students, compared to many other regions of the world, is a lot less entrepreneurial in its character. In other parts of the world, one meets students with a sense of urgency to finish their education in order to make a difference in their societies and to create value for themselves and for others. In Europe, this spirit is less often met and the educational programmes at European universities seldom help students to gain that spirit. European universities are focused on research as their main task, and higher education is viewed mostly as an individual project. There is obviously a lack in the European educational systems of promoting the development of an entrepreneurial mindset in its pupils and students. High quality teaching for competencies rather than the mere acquisition of knowledge is now developing via the Bologna Process, but teaching from which students also develop their competencies in creativity and innovation is scarcer. Education that starts from challenges, questions, problems and projects, not from knowledge and curriculum, is strongly promoted by using the learning outcomes paradigm. Maybe the next step on this road is the transformation of learning outcomes to 'learning enquires' or 'learning problems', stimulating students' curiosity and their abilities to think beyond boundaries and systematically explore and generate new ideas.

In March 2008, the European Parliament and the Council of the European Union launched the European Institute of Innovation and Technology (EIT), a new initiative at the EU-level intended to complement existing EU and national policies in increasing European innovation and business. EIT can be said to be a 'new animal' in the European educational landscape, it is an independent community body based on *the knowledge triangle*, which means to foster the integration between research, higher education and innovation/business (see Figure 9.2). The mission of EIT concerns both creating new innovations and businesses, but, equally importantly, also fostering and developing students through master and doctoral programmes focused on creativity, innovation and entrepreneurship (Adamson and Flodström 2011). EIT is a distributed organisation with currently three so-called Knowledge and Innovation Communities (KICs), a new type of legal entity with common governance where businesses, industry, universities and research institutes collaborate within a common legal framework.

EIT is a new innovation infrastructure where higher education plays an important role. It is not a new infrastructure for higher education. All the three current KICs involve top European universities, and their faculties execute the EIT-labelled educational programmes. In addition to the learning outcomes expressed in the QF-EHEA, the EIT label imposes additional overarching learning outcomes. These overarching learning outcomes were developed by the EIT Educational Working Group. As a foundational issue and starting point, knowledge forms were discussed. What types of knowledge forms were needed to distinctly profile these educational programmes in line with the knowledge triangle, earlier mostly presented as a theoretical concept? Three questions were formulated in order to transform theory into action: first, what are the best ways of linking research to education; second, what are the best ways of teaching creativity, innovation and entrepreneurship; and lastly, how can optimal conditions be created for returning students', entrepreneurs' and innovators' experiences from business and the 'real world' back into research? (Flodström et al. 2011).

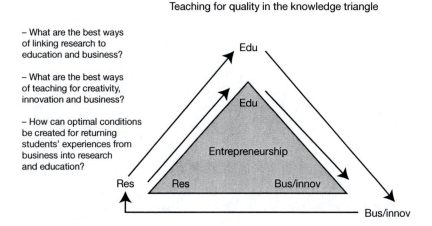

Figure 9.2 The knowledge triangle

These questions, in turn, generated the first five EIT and knowledge triangle knowledge forms: *creativity skills and competencies, innovation skills and competencies, entrepreneurship skills and competencies, intellectual transforming skills and competencies and research skills and competencies*, all connected to the three sides of the triangle. Finally, *leadership* and *making value judgements* were added since the EIT degrees also are geared towards educating a new brand of leaders. After this framework was created the formulation of the EIT overarching learning outcomes commenced (overarching to fit and guide all KIC programmes, regardless of theme). It is this framework, these knowledge forms, that in fact profile the EIT master and doctoral degrees most clearly and bring these programmes one step further into the future, reflecting new societal needs, fostering a new generation of students. The goal is to develop students with an integrated view of research, education, innovation and business, combined with the spirit to transform ideas into business and to make a societal difference.

Quality Assurance for Learning – The EIT Quality Assurance and Learning Enhancement Model

Background and Basic Principles

EIT's mission, in addition to creating new innovations and businesses and developing students' skills and competences in creativity, innovation and entrepreneurship, is also to elaborate on the models that enable this impact to materialise – to work towards becoming a role model for integrating all parts and all actors of the knowledge triangle. This also applies to the development of an internal quality assurance model for its educational activities.

The natural starting point for a quality assurance system based on learning outcomes is a qualification framework combined with a definition of high educational quality as simply the goal that as many students as possible achieve (at least) the intended learning outcomes of the educational program they take part in. A 'high quality' quality assurance system for the future also needs to be evidenced-based in the sense that it should rest on knowledge and research concerning *both* evaluation and teaching and learning. Optimally the system should also be constructed in such a generic way so that with simple adjustments it can be contextualised and applied to all types of programmes regardless of content and/or level; the same principles but different applications in different settings. It should also include the professionals that are involved in order to create a trust base and motivation to use the system and, as for any modern quality system, have a clear stakeholder perspective. In addition it should be designed to support faculty in their daily work when teaching and planning teaching, avoiding becoming just an administrative burden arriving at regular intervals. The ESG explicitly express the need for external quality assurance to be fit for its purpose and to place only an appropriate and necessary burden on institutions for the achievement of its objectives. Reichert and Tauch (2005) showed in a survey of 29 European higher education institutions that, in many of them, external quality assurance tended to be seen as a bureaucratic burden of only limited use for development. This must be considered a failure of these systems.

Finally, the system should be transparent, easy to work with and easy to understand, thus it needs to be based on a clear logic giving evidence to its purpose, and have a clear structure. The results of an evaluation should never come as a surprise for the teachers involved. If students benefit from teaching and learning characterised by aligned teaching and fit for purpose assessment methods, including transparent grading systems and assessment criteria, we believe higher education institutions and their teachers will benefit from quality assurance procedures characterised in the same way.

The Model

The EIT Quality Assurance and Learning Enhancement Model (EIT-QALE; Adamson 2012) has a strong focus on the promoting and enhancing aspects of a quality assurance model in addition to that of accountability. It builds on the same basic principles as the previously mentioned proposed Swedish model, which combined the evaluation of intended learning outcomes (then based on the Swedish National Qualification Framework) and fit for purpose assessment, achieved learning outcomes and stakeholder opinions.

The question the model is to answer, the logic of the model, is 'do programmes ensure that students attain the EIT learning outcomes?' That is, that the programmes provide students with opportunities to develop a true entrepreneurial mindset combined with the knowledge triangle skills and competencies. The structure consists of a total set of five quality indicators each comprised of a number of assessment fields, where the first indicator consists of obligators that must be fulfilled (see Figure 9.3).

The first three indicators are used in the labelling process (cf. accreditation of a new programme) and the two remaining more result-oriented indicators are added when ongoing programmes are reviewed. For transparency, predictability and also for workload reasons each indicator is evaluated by the reviewer with the aid of a checklist focused on each assessment field. Each indicator (except the one for obligators) is graded on a four-point scale, which will be added up for each indicator. In addition to text reports on quality, this indicator structure creates the possibility of presenting the results in quality profiles (see Figure 9.4). These reports and profiles provide students and stakeholders with clear and easy to comprehend quality information, a previously very neglected area in the quality assurance context. The quality of higher education institutions is currently mainly judged by and presented in

The 1 + 4 quality indicators of the EIT quality assurance and learning enhancement model

Q indicators: Assessment areas:	Q indicator 0 compulsory requirements	Q indicator 1 aligned teaching and content coverage	Q Indicator 2 Learning environment and facilities	Q Indicator 3 Results	Q Indicator 4 Stakeholder experiences
Ass area 1	0.1 Mobility	1.1 EIT overarching learning outcomes coverage	2.1 Robus entrepreneurship education	3.1 Student creativity	3.1 Students
Ass area 2	0.2 Business partner curriculum collaboration	1.2 General quality of learning outcomes	2.2 Highly integrated innovative "learning-by-doing curricula	3.2 Achieved learning outcomes	3.2 Alumni
Ass area 3	0.3 ECTS, DS and recognition	1.3 Fit for purpose assessment	2.3 Mobility, European dimension and openness to the world	3.3 R&D projects on KIC educational activities	4.3 Other stakeholders
Ass area 4	0.4 Application, selection and admission	1.4 Grading criteria		3.4 Retention rates	
Ass area 5	0.5 English denomination, EIT logo	1.5 Active and appropriate teaching methods			

Figure 9.3 EIT-QALE review model

the shape of international rankings of individual universities. These rankings promote research and the recognition associated with research. Educational quality is often said to be too difficult to include. As a consequence the contribution to the knowledge society made by higher education, its academic teachers and students is ignored. Also the stakeholders that utilise the new knowledge gained by research for innovation and creation of new products and businesses, and who employ the new skilled students, are ignored. Still, the branding of knowledge from these rankings is as strong as the branding of national soccer teams by the World Cup. EIT highlights the importance of information to students and stakeholders about educational quality with these quality profiles. They can also be aggregated on, for instance, KIC level, giving a 'bigger picture' of all its programmes. Rankings are here to stay and have come to symbolise the global competition that is a part of the global knowledge society. Applied in other contexts (departmental, university or even national levels) these types of profiles could become the basis for making more meaningful comparisons of educational quality.

To Conclude: Bologna, Europe and the World

In moving ideas, people and goods, national, cultural and geographical borders have always been hindrances. The history of internationalisation

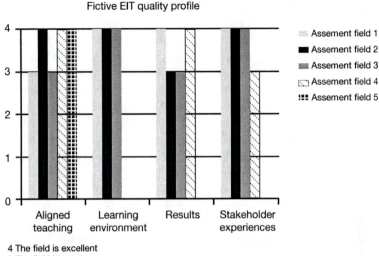

Fictive EIT quality profile

Assement field 1
Assement field 2
Assement field 3
Assement field 4
Assement field 5

4 The field is excellent
3 The field is good
2 The field meets the minimum criteria but still needs improvement
1 The field does not meet the minimum criteria

Figure 9.4 Draft example of a detailed quality profile on a four-point scale

includes the discovery of America (1492) by Christopher Columbus and the seaway to India (1498) by Vasco da Gama. Actually, Columbus looked for a seaway to India and believed he found it. The reason for these discoveries was simply to find a simpler, faster and safer way to trade with India and China. The Age of Discovery is seen as a bridge between the Middle Ages and the Modern Era along with its contemporary renaissance movement. Accounts from distant lands and maps spread with the help of the new printing press and fed the rise of humanism and curiosity about the world, ushering in a new age of scientific and intellectual enquiry. European overseas expansion led to the rise of colonial empires. The contacts between the Old and New Worlds produced an exchange of a wide range of plants, animals, foods, human populations (including slaves) and diseases, between the Eastern and Western hemispheres, in one of the most significant global events concerning ecology, agriculture and culture in history. European exploration continued until the global mapping of the world was accomplished, resulting in a new world view and distant civilisations acknowledging each other, and later reaching even the most remote boundaries. The growth of the global knowledge society holds a promise to be as exploratory as the era of geographical exploration. The vehicles for the exploration now are not sailing ships but surfing the Internet and the opportunities for people to travel and communicate in ways unseen before.

The global dissemination of new ideas and mobility of skilled people are necessary for global knowledge society advancement. Hindrances created by national or any other border will hamper progress. The international dimension of Bologna was already noted in the Bologna Declaration in that the need for increasing the international competitiveness of the European system of higher education was pointed out as an important objective to pursue. At the Bergen meeting work with a strategy for what was then called Bologna's external dimension was initiated and this was later adopted in London as 'The European Higher Education Area in a Global setting'. Five policy areas were proposed: improving information on the EHEA; promoting European higher education to enhance its worldwide attractiveness and competitiveness; intensifying policy dialogue; strengthening cooperation based on partnership; and furthering the recognition of qualifications. The document also includes an action plan for each of these areas, specifically pointing out mobility programmes between EHEA and non-EHEA countries, foreign language learning and a number of issues to do with further recognition of qualifications, all important enablers for students to move freely across borders.

In all, the Bologna Process has been a great step forward towards creating a curriculum and educational systems that are congruent with the needs for the knowledge society; one where national boarders are losing their importance and distance is measured in time and access to communication tools rather than kilometres or miles. In spite of hindrances still existing, not geographical today but instead political, social, ethnic and cultural, Bologna has created the possibility for many students to move freely between European universities, either through joint programmes set up by the different universities or by adding a European dimension and experience to their own local/national programme. The natural way to move from joint programmes and joint degrees is now to also aim towards a European degree. This would increase both the competition and the collaboration among European universities and hence increase both quality and diversity. A European degree, preferably combined with a European loan scheme, would also truly establish the EHEA, creating a higher education area both for European and non-European students: the global students. Students who by the end of their studies can go out in life and society not only knowing things, but also knowing what to do and how to solve real life problems.

Note

1   '... At both undergraduate and graduate level, students would be encouraged to spend at least one semester in universities outside their own country. At the same time, more teaching and research staff should be working in European countries other than their own. The fast growing support of the European Union, for the mobility of students and teachers should be employed to the full' (Sorbonne Declaration, 1998: 2).

References

Adamson, L. (2011). On Quality Assurance and Learning Outcomes: Evaluating students' work or institutional work with students? In *Quality Assurance and Learning Outcomes*, European Network for Quality Assurance, ENQA, publications. Available from http://www.enqa.eu/pubs_workshop.lasso (accessed 24 January 2012).

Adamson, L. (2012). Quality for Learning – EIT Quality Assurance and Learning Enhancement Model. Handbook for planning and monitoring EIT educational programmes. European Institute of Innovation and Technology, http://eit.europa. eu/education/eit-labelled-programmes/

Adamson, L. and Flodström, A. (2011). Teaching for Quality in the Knowledge Triangle – European Institute of Innovation and Technology's (EIT) coming Quality Assurance and Learning Enhancement Model. Conference proceedings *The Future of Education*, Florence, Italy, 16–17 June, 2011. Available from http://www.pixel-online.net/edu_future/common/download/Paper_pdf/ITL50-Adamson.pdf (accessed 24 January 2012).

Bergen Communiqué (2005) *Bologna Official Website 2010 and onwards.* Available from http://www.ehea.info/article-details.aspx?ArticleId=43 (accessed 4 April 2012).

Berlin Communiqué (2003) *Bologna Official Website 2010 and onwards.* Available from http://www.ehea.info/article-details.aspx?ArticleId=43 (accessed 4 April 2012).

Danish Ministry of Science Technology and Innovation (2005). A Framework for Qualifications of the Higher Education Area, 18 February. Available from http:// www.bologna-bergen2005.no/ (accessed 4 April 2012).

European Association for Quality Assurance in Higher Education (ENQA) (2009). *Standards and Guidelines for Quality Assurance in the European Higher Education Area* (Helsinki, 3rd edition). Available from http://www.enqa.eu/files/ ESG_3edition%20%282%29.pdf (accessed 24 January 2012).

European Qualification Framework (2005). *Bologna Official Website 2007 – 2010.* Available from http://www.ond.vlaanderen.be/hogeronderwijs/bologna/qf/over-arching.asp (accessed 4 April 2012).

Flodström, A., Colombo, G., Adamson, L. and Fammels, M. (2011). *EIT's Strategic Innovation Agenda (SIA) Investing in Innovation Beyond 2014.* Available from http://eit.europa.eu/fileadmin/Content/Downloads/SIA/EIT_Strategic_Innovation_ Agenda_Final.pdf (accessed 24 January 2012).

Haakstad, J. (2011). New Paradigm for Quality Assurance. In *Building Bridges: Making sense of quality assurance in European, national and institutional contexts.* European University Association, the 5th Quality assurance Forum 18–20 November, 2010. Available from http://www.eua.be/Libraries/Publications_homepage_list/EUA_Building_Bridges_ web.sflb.ashx (accessed 24 January 2012).

Högskoleverket (Swedish National Agency for Higher Education) (2009). *Quality Evaluations in Learning*, Report 2009, 25 R. Available from http://www.hsv.se/aboutus/publications/reports/reports/2009/qualityevaluationsinle arning.5.747d95e41276be05d697ffe244.html (accessed 24 January 2012) and http:// www.hsv.se/download/18.d09bd2412506e25d637ffe2385/QA_new_system_hsv_ eng.pdf (accessed 24 January 2012).

Joint Quality Initiative (2004). The Dublin Descriptors. Available from www.joint-quality.org (accessed 24 January 2012).

London Communiqué (2007) *Bologna Official Website 2010 and onwards.* Available from http://www.ehea.info/article-details.aspx?ArticleId=43 (accessed 4 April 2012).

Myklebust, J. P. (2010). Sweden: Protests against Government Reward System. University World News. Available from http://www.universityworldnews.com/article.php?story=20100429204512982) (accessed 4 April 2012).

Reichert, S. and Tauch, C. (2005). Trends IV: European universities implementing Bologna. *Brussels, European University Association.* Available from http://www.eua.be/eua/jsp/en/upload/TrendsIV_final.1114509452430.pdf (accessed 24 January 2012)

Sorbonne Declaration (1998). Joint Declaration on Harmonisation of the Architecture of the European Higher Education System. Available from http://www.bologna-bergen2005.no/Docs/00-Main_doc/980525SORBONNE_DECLARATION.PDF (accessed 24 January 2012).

Utbildningsdepartementet (Swedish Ministry of Education and Culture) (2011). Government Bill 2009/10:139. *Focus on Knowledge – Quality in Higher Education.* Fact sheet in English. Available from http://www.sweden.gov.se/content/1/c6/14/30/86/358bd536.pdf (accessed 24 January 2012).

Wächter, B. (2008). Internationalisation and the European Higher Education Area. *Academic Cooperation Association (ACA).* Available from http://www.aca-secretariat.be/?id=4 (accessed 24 January 2012).

10

The Student Experience in the UK

MARK WEYERS

This chapter reports on a pilot study done in 2006 (Ainley and Weyers 2008; Weyers 2007) that collected quantitative data from a sample of 1000 students to investigate the home student experience in the United Kingdom (UK). Initial differences in students' socio-economic backgrounds, perceptions and experience (especially motivations, approaches to study and conceptions of learning) were investigated. The sample was divided into four subgroups (Russell Group, non-Russell Group institutions, high and low socio-economic status [SES]). Forty students (10 from each sub-sample group) were interviewed by telephone. The second part of the chapter uses secondary sources to draw some comparisons to the experiences of international students studying in the UK and the experience of UK students who have chosen to study abroad.

Universities in the UK over the past decade have been investing heavily in the implementation of 'internationalisation' strategies. To date, the globalisation of higher education in the UK has predominantly involved the marketing of UK education to overseas consumers while attracting thousands of international students. The government's policy on internationalising higher education was launched through the Prime Minister's Initiative on International Education (PMI) (1999–2004) and PMI2 (2006–2011). PMI2 was a five-year strategy that built on PMI1 with the aim of ensuring the UK becomes a leader in international education by attracting an additional 70,000 international students to the UK and significantly growing the number of partnerships between the UK and other countries (British Council 2012). However, currently, no UK policy exists that takes a position on the desirability of UK students studying abroad.

The Bologna Process has also impacted higher education in the UK. While the basic framework outlines three cycles of higher education qualification (bachelor, master and doctorate) it has also created a shift in higher education through the implementation of the learning outcomes paradigm, which has put a focus on student-centred active learning. This moves the focus of university education from being knowledge and subject content-based to including a competence-based framework. However, the didactic teaching and passive learning approach in higher education has prevailed, specifically in the traditional academic disciplines. The development of a knowledge society and the need to combine new knowledge with specific graduate attributes highlights the need to integrate key skills training into the academic programmes.

The large numbers of prestigious highly ranked research-intensive institutions in the UK are in a unique position to make their teaching equivalent to their world-class research profile. The key to achieving this goal is to enhance and strengthen the link between research and teaching. Ramsden (2001) asserts that if universities want to encourage a genuine student-centred undergraduate education, then they must 're-engineer' the teaching–research nexus. Scott (2002) argues that in modern universities teaching and research are becoming intimately related and that in the knowledge economies of the future all students need to be researchers and engage in the production and dissemination of knowledge.

The UK Higher Education Context

Universities in the UK have generally been instituted by an Act of Parliament under the Education Reform Act 1988. The government coordinating body for universities is Universities UK (UUK). Most universities in the UK share an undergraduate admission system that is operated by the Universities and Colleges Admissions Service (UCAS). In 2011–2012, undergraduate fees were set at a maximum of £3,375 per year and were repayable following graduation. Undergraduates admitted in 2012–2013 pay fees set at a maximum of up to £9,000, with many institutions in the UK charging the maximum. Students from Scotland attending Scottish universities do not pay fees and fees for students from Northern Ireland are also capped at £3,465. An independent commission on fees found that the fees increase in England has led to 15,000 fewer applications to university from UK students (Vasagar 2012). However, it is not clear whether this is a temporary drop or if the fee increase will have long-term consequences for university applications.

Most universities in the UK can be categorised into the one of the following membership groups:

1   Russell Group – an association of 24 British public research universities.
2   1994 Group – a coalition of 15 of the top smaller research-intensive universities in the UK, founded in 1994.
3   Post-1992 universities – new universities formed from polytechnics or colleges of higher education, established through the Further and Higher Education Act of 1992.

There are also two other categories of membership that have some overlap with the previous categories:

4   University Alliance – formed in 2007 it is a group of 23 major, business-engaged universities committed to delivering world-class research and a quality student experience (Universities Alliance 2012).
5   Million+ – was formed in 1997 as the Coalition of Modern Universities, but in November 2007 was rebranded with the name Million+. It seeks to solve complex problems in the higher education sector. It currently is composed of 22 post-1992 institutions (Million+ 2012).

Russell Group Versus 1994 Group Universities

The Russell Group has 24 member institutions and was established in 1994 to represent its members' interests to the UK government. As of 2008, while it only represents 15 per cent of the higher education sector by student population, Russell Group universities accounted for 67 per cent (£2.7 billion) of UK universities' research grant and contract income and 68 per cent (over £1.0 billion) of the total income from the government-funded UK Research Councils (Russell Group 2012). They drew in 62 per cent (over £1.1 billion) of the total quality-related research funding (QR) that was allocated by the Funding Councils. They also won 75 per cent (over £0.6 billion) of the funding from UK charities for their research. They account for 57 per cent (10,105) of all doctorates awarded in the UK and have over 30 per cent of all students studying in the UK from outside the EU (Russell Group 2012).

Two thirds of the UK's very best research takes place in the Russell Group's 24 universities. They also have a highly successful track record of entrepreneurialism and in 2008 maintained 64 per cent of the total UK higher education sector income from intellectual property, with 58 per cent of the spin-out companies coming from Russell Group institutions. These spin-outs also had a total estimated annual turnover of £724 million, which represented 70 per cent of the total turnover for the entire UK higher education sector (Russell Group 2012).

In 1994, in response to the formation of the Russell Group, the 1994 Group was formed by a coalition of 15 of the top 'smaller' research-intensive universities, many of which are represented in the top 20 universities in UK league tables. The group was formed to represent the interests of Britain's smaller institutions who share the same aims, values and standards. The 1994 Group aims to increase their global visibility and attract the highest calibre of staff and students. By working together they can share best practice, respond efficiently to key government policy and be more adaptable in a rapidly changing global higher education landscape while also maximising research income (1994 Group 2012).

The 1994 Group achieved excellent results in the 2008 Research Assessment Exercise (RAE), demonstrated by the fact that 57 per cent of the Group's research is rated 4* (world-leading) or 3* (internationally excellent).

Research-led teaching is central to their mission and a large proportion of the top research active staff in these institutions teaches. Further, the student experience is a key part of the group's mission, and many of their institutions often rated in the top 10 in the UK National Student Survey (NSS). However, institutions in both groups share more commonalities than differences. For the most part, the key difference tends to be that Russell Group institutions have medical schools and a strong emphasis on science and technology (1994 Group 2012).

The UK Home Student Experience

Research on the learning environment in higher education has stemmed strongly from Scandinavian, British and Australian research (Nield 2007). Biggs's (1978) seminal work of study processes incorporates presage factors and product factors. Presage factors include the learning environment and individual characteristics of a student that exist prior to the learning event. The product factors are the learning outputs (e.g. grades, satisfaction). Thus, research on student learning at university has explored the relationship between the teaching–learning environment (teaching methods, resources, etc.) and student learning outcomes.

The key concepts emerging from this large body of research are the categories of deep and surface approaches to studying (Marton and Säljö 1976, 1997). Deep, surface and strategic approaches to learning and studying have been identified in a number of studies (Biggs 1989a; Entwistle and Ramsden 1983; Entwistle et al. 2002). Following them, deep approaches to studying are student-centred and emphasise understanding while, conversely, surface learning uses reproductive strategies (e.g. rote memorisation) to absorb information with limited attention paid to the integration of newly acquired knowledge (Marton and Säljö 1976, 1997; Thomas and Bain 1984). Although students may be classified as deep or surface learners these classifications are not fixed attributes and a student may use both approaches at different times depending on the context (although they may also have a predisposition for a particular approach).

Biggs identified prior motivations (intrinsic and extrinsic) to be a strong indicator of which approach to learning a student takes. Simply passing an examination or test motivated students to take a surface approach, as it can be achieved with minimal effort through rote learning. Studying for the intrinsic enjoyment of engaging with information and knowledge in one's course typically encourages students to take a deep approach, while extrinsic motivations such as 'getting into a good course' and then 'making a lot of money' once one graduates is strategic and students can employ a combination of methods (deep or surface) depending on the situation.

Instruments

Data collection involved the use of a questionnaire and a semi-structured inter-view schedule (Ainley and Weyers 2008). The questionnaire was composed of subscales taken from the Approaches and Study Skills Inventory (ASSIST), the Learning and Studying Questionnaire (LSQ) and the Experience of Teaching and Learning Questionnaire (ETLQ), which were initially developed to indi-cate students' overall approaches to studying and their perceptions of and attitudes towards the teaching–learning environment in higher education (Entwistle et al. 2002). A correlational analysis investigated the relationship between the various questionnaire factors for the four subgroups.

Students responded to each questionnaire item on a 1–5 scale (1 = strongly disagree, 2 = disagree, 3 = unsure, 4 = agree, 5 = strongly agree). Each subscale score was formed by adding together the responses of the items that form that subscale. Table 10.1 outlines the conceptual underpinnings of the factors investigated in the questionnaire.

Participants

One thousand students, divided into four sub-sample comparison groups (Russell and non-Russell higher education institutes and high and low SES), took part in the questionnaire with approximately 250 students from each of the four subgroups (see Figure 10.1). Qualitative data was collected from a sample of 40 students (10 from each group) who were interviewed by tele-phone. The gender composition of the study participants was 454 males (45 per cent) and 556 females (55 per cent) for a total of 1000 students. The sample population represented the full range of academic subjects and disciplines across the higher education sector in England. The purposive sample was obtained through the independent market research company, Opinionpanel Research, drawing upon their 40,000-strong representative online panel of UK higher education students derived from UCAS sources. SES was assessed from the participants' parental occupations following the standard UK Office of Population and Census Statistics' measures of occupational status divided in two (Ainley and Weyers 2008).

Views on UK Home Students' Approaches to Studying and their Conceptions of Learning

Many home students come from a UK further education system that is strongly built on formal standardised testing through General Certificate of Secondary Education (GCSE) and Advanced Level General Certificate of Education (A levels). Students that are applying to university generally take three A levels. Each one consists of three separate modules that are assessed predominantly by a three-hour unseen written examination. Those that have

Table 10.1 Questionnaire factors and their conceptual basis

Subscales	Definition
Conceptions of learning	*Characterised by students who see learning as:*
Reproducing	Building up knowledge by acquiring facts and information so that they can remember and use the information.
Understanding/ Conceptual change	Understanding new material for yourself so that you can develop as a person and see the world in a different way.
Approaches to learning and studying	*These approaches are characteristic of students who:*
Deep	Attempt to understand the material for themselves by relating new information to practical or real-life contexts or to other topics within the course while looking for evidence to reach their own conclusions
Surface	Often have trouble in making sense of the things they have to remember because they concentrate on memorising a good deal of what they have to learn *(Unrelated memorising)*. Much of what they learn seems no more than lots of unrelated bits and pieces *(Fragmented knowledge)* and they tend to read very little beyond what is actually required to pass *(Syllabus-boundedness)*.
Strategic	Are quite systematic and organised in their studying, prepare for class and prioritise time, they work steadily during the course and they look carefully at tutors' comments on course work to see how to get higher marks next time.
Reasons for studying course	*Characteristic of students who:*
Intrinsic	Find the subject interesting and want to learn things to develop as a person and which might allow them to help people and/or make a difference in the world.
Extrinsic	Feel they need to prove themselves to other people. They feel studying the course will look good on their CV, which will enable them to get a good job when they finish.
Preferences for teaching method	*Characteristic of students who prefer:*
Supporting understanding	Lecturers who encourage them to think for themselves by modelling thinking in the discipline. They prefer courses where they are encouraged to read around the subjects that challenge them and provide explanations that go beyond the lectures.
Information transmission	Lecturers who tell them exactly what to put down in their notes. They prefer exams that need only the material provided in the lectures, and books that give definite facts and information that can easily learnt.

Subscales	Definition
Demands made by course	*Students were asked to rate:*
Acquiring knowledge and skills	The amount of work they were expected to complete; the amount of information they were expected to know to begin with; the rate at which new material was introduced and the ideas/problems or technical skills they needed to acquire while studying their subject.
Ratings of learning achieved	*Students were asked to rate:*
Acquiring knowledge and skills	The level of knowledge/understanding/skills or technical procedures they feel they achieved and their ability to think about ideas or to solve problems in their discipline.

Source: Weyers 2007.

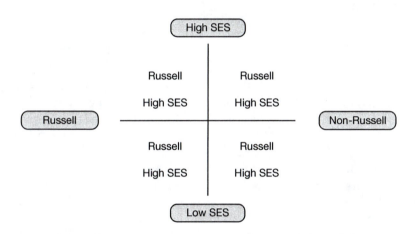

Figure 10.1 Sample breakdown of study participants into Russell and non-Russell and low and high socio-economic status subgroups

Source: Ainley and Weyers 2008.

achieved high grades tend to go to Russell Group institutions while those that have not achieved high grades tend to go to lower ranked institutions. Russell Group students therefore tend to be the students that have done well when writing these examinations, which indicates that they have certain academic attributes such as: good organisational skills, motivation to succeed and the capacity to retain large amounts of information.

However, the results of this study suggest that regardless of which type of institution or socio-economic background the students originate from, those students that see learning as an act of reproduction tend to take a strategic approach, while those that see learning as a process to understand the material tend to take a deep approach when they study their subjects. Interestingly, non-Russell students from low socio-economic backgrounds that view learning as a process to understand also tended to be more strategic in their approach to studying. During the interviews, when students were asked to choose whether they preferred structure and direction from their lecturers (related to a strategic approach) or whether they preferred lecturers who encourage them to seek out information for themselves (related to a deep approach) two students commented (cited in Ainley and Weyers 2008):

> It depends what subject it is … Some of the really hard subjects 'Yes'. Sometimes you can go away and write your own notes. Some of the easier subjects you can go away and do it for yourself; however, hard subjects in which you are really struggling you need more guidance. I don't want to be told everything all the time because that is not what you go to university for. At university it is time to think for yourself and if you want your degree you are going to have to work for it.
>
> Student 32 (NR-L-SES)

> I prefer the free thinking methods when it's not as important and crucial for examinations. I like both structures. But when it is more important [it will be examined] I like structure and guidelines.
>
> Student 31 (NR-L-SES)

These students demonstrate both a preference to achieve and a preference to engage with their course at a deeper level when the opportunity permits them. This also seems to suggest that a student's discipline or subject area has a fundamental impact on the approach they take to their studying and their views on the purpose of learning in higher education. Many disciplines have teaching approaches that are common across the subject area, they have been shown to be effective in the past and they now permeate the way courses are structured and taught in that discipline. For example, in hard science subjects like chemistry, it is common to have a practical laboratory class where students are given the opportunity to work hands-on with the kinds of chemicals that they are learning about in their lectures. In many social science subjects large group lectures are followed up with smaller tutorial sessions in the same week that complement the lectures. These approaches are not just structural, because physicists teach physics students the way that they have been taught and engineers teach engineering students the way they were taught when they were students. We teach the way that we have been taught. Similarly, Bekhradnia et al. (2006) found that the variation in workloads between subjects was large while the differences between old and new universities in each subject were relatively small. In light of this, it would seem that the type of institution may have a much smaller impact on the student experience than the subject area.

UK Home Students' Preferences for Teaching Method

The results indicated that students that prefer a transmission model of teaching (a didactic lecture style) tend to adopt surface learning strategies (e.g. rote memorisation) and those students that prefer teaching methods that focus on understanding (e.g. student-centred learning approaches) tend to employ learning strategies that are student centred. Generally, there were no significant differences between the groups on their preferences for either method of teaching (i.e. teaching for understanding versus a transmission model of teaching). However, Russell Group students from lower socio-economic backgrounds seemed to prefer more didactic methods (i.e. information transmission) of teaching. However, the results also indicated that Russell Group students from low socio-economic backgrounds who preferred information transmission teaching were not deterred from taking a deep approach when studying. This, again, is counter-intuitive as you would think that students that prefer their teachers to lecture and transmit information would prefer to focus on memory strategies for learning the subject content. However, this anomaly may be explained by the following student who comments:

> I like a mixture to be honest. I like when they give you a certain amount of information in the lecture that will be on the exam and then they leave it to you to back it up. When they give you a bit more than the outline, you know the general information, then you use books to go over it after the lecture ... I think that is the best way to learn.
>
> Student 15 (R-L-SES)

This comment suggests that while lectures cover the content of the course and tend to focus on what students are be examined on, some students prefer to be able to seek out information to expand on their own understanding. Russell Group students tend to have well developed organisational and study skills and are accustomed to independent study outside class time. Thus, while information transmission teaching tends to be associated with students engaging in surface learning, this relationship does not exist for Russell low SES students. They appear to be more strategic in their approaches and while they at times prefer information transmissions teaching they also engage in student-centred approaches to learning when the opportunity permits. It is probable that this is related to their motivations for attending university. While they want to know what is in the exam and how they can achieve the best results, they are also intrinsically interested and motivated in the subject they are studying. Coming from a low socio-economic background and having the opportunity to attend a prestigious university likely has both strong intrinsic and extrinsic drivers.

Comparing UK Home Students' Intrinsic and Extrinsic Motivations to Study

Looking at the differences across the four groups there appears to be a significant difference on why students are going to university. Non-Russell Group students ranked their extrinsic reasons and intrinsic reasons for taking their course of study higher than Russell Group students. Non-Russell high SES students rank their extrinsic reasons for studying higher than Russell high SES students. Non-Russell low SES students rank their intrinsic reasons for studying their course higher than Russell high SES students. This suggests non-Russell students, especially from lower socio-economic areas, may have a stronger motivation to study at university. This finding may be explained by the non-Russell Group student who stated:

> We probably have just as good a time, but I think because we're not one of the elite universities we have more people that come here and work harder for it. Some of my friends that go to the elite universities have an attitude that daddy's paying for it and I'm here to have a good time and the school-work comes second. There are a lot of people at this university that are paying their own way who work harder when they are here because they have come here to get a good education.
>
> Student 27 (NR-H-SES)

Non-Russell low SES students rank their extrinsic reasons for studying higher than Russell Group students. Thus, it may be that low SES students, especially non-Russell, see education as a stronger determining factor for achieving their life goals.

The Experience of International Students Studying in the UK

The globalisation of higher education in the UK has focused strongly on the recruitment of international students. Higher Education Statistical Agency (2011) statistics indicate that international student numbers increased by six per cent between the academic years of 2009–2010 and 2010–2011. PMI2, a five-year strategy, aims to attract an additional 70,000 international students to the UK. The export earnings in the UK from international students are expected to grow to £17 billion by 2025 (*The Economist* 2012). However, with this comes a multitude of difficulties for institutions when trying to ensure a positive student experience for the thousands of international students that UK higher education attracts to study in UK universities. The top 10 countries sending the highest number of students to the UK are listed in Table 10.2.

China and India top the list of international student coming to the UK for higher education. Many British universities have experienced a significant increase in the number of Chinese students studying in their universities. Therefore, while the number of students coming from China has dropped since 2005 (Tysome 2005, 2006), there is still a significant number of international students that come to the UK to study.

The learning approach of Chinese students studying in the UK has been widely researched (Biggs 1996; Branine 2005; Nield 2007; Watkins and Biggs 1996). A great deal of the research takes a deficit model and looks at the perceived difficulties of students' adjustment to higher education in the UK and suggests various ways that the learning environment can be adapted to support international learners (Leonard et al. 2004). Au and Entwistle (1999) noted that at an early age Chinese children are taught to memorise and copy Chinese characters, while Biggs (1996) has suggested that in universities Chinese students are prone to rote memorisation (often associated with a surface approach to learning). Liu (2006) has argued that rote learning is a distinct characteristic of the Chinese education system and when they come to the UK they bring these approaches to studying with them. The Chinese student's preference for an information transmission model of teaching would encourage a tendency to focus on concrete answers to specific questions in an environment where collaborative work is not considered important and critical and creative thought is discouraged. This is supported by Branine (2005) who found that limited resources, strong views on traditional approaches to learning and student–teacher power relations were all obstacles to the facilitation of interactive teaching environments in China.

Table 10.2 Higher Education Statistical Agency (2011) figures on the top 10 countries sending students to university in the UK

Country	Number of students	EU or Non-EU
China (PRC)	67,325	Non-EU
India	39,090	Non-EU
Nigeria	17,585	Non-EU
Republic of Ireland	16,855	EU
Germany	16,265	EU
United States	15,555	Non-EU
Malaysia	13,900	Non-EU
France	13,325	EU
Greece	11,630	EU
Cyprus	11,320	EU

Thus, such findings have led to the idea in the wider pedagogical literature that Chinese students are generally passive learners, engage less in
classroom activities and tend to have an over-reliance on rote memorisation (Biggs 1996; Kember and Gow 1991; Samuelowicz 1987). However, their
level of achievement is high (Garden 1987; Stigler and Perry 1990) and they
have also been shown to have higher deep and strategic inventory scores
in comparison to Western students (Biggs 1989b, 1990, 1991; Kember and
Gow 1990, 1991) despite their perceived reliance on rote memorisation strategies. Watkins and Biggs (1996, 2001) have coined this phenomenon the
'paradox of the Chinese learner'. This is supported by Lee (1996) when investigating preferences for deep and surface approaches to learning who found
a consistent preference for understanding over surface learning. However,
this finding is not surprising given that surface learning is 'unreflective'
rote memorisation. Therefore, it is not memorisation that is the problem
in learning because a learner must remember the facts, information and
knowledge to be able to work with it at a higher level (e.g. problem solving
and critical thinking).

Further research indicates that Chinese students combine memorisation
with understanding, which contradicts earlier research on student learning
among Western students (Kember 1996). For Chinese students understanding
is synonymous with remembering (Marton et al. 1997: 32) and being able
to remember course content that assists them in understanding it as well
(Marton et al. 1996). Tang (1991) labels the combination of remembering and
understanding 'deep memorising'.

Confusion arises when there is an implied link between approaches to
studying and culture. A 'deep' approach seems to be associated with Western
culture while 'surface' approaches (i.e. rote memorisation strategies) seem to
be associated with Asian cultures. This often happens in the literature when a
further link is made between culture and nationality. Confucian philosophy
is often attributed with infusing rote learning into the Chinese education
system. However, there are many other influences on Chinese philosophical
thought from Taoism to Buddhism that have influenced Chinese culture
and society. To argue that the Chinese education system and its students are
largely governed by Confucian ideologies is synonymous with suggesting
British education is governed solely by 'empiricism' as outlined by John Locke
and David Hume.

As noted in the previous section, the most fundamental impact on the
student learning experience is not the type of institution attended, but the
discipline and subject area within which teaching takes place. While the
data suggests that there is some variation in disciplinary teaching environments, it is important to note that it is not just the learning environments that
are found to be socially constructed within a discipline, it is the assessment
regime as well. Pilcher et al. (2009) point out that traditional timed, written

examinations are still the most predominant approach to assessment in the UK and account for a large majority of students' overall grade. It is also widely regarded by international students as the most stressful form of assessment that they face (Kingston and Forland 2008: 215) and, as Biggs and Tang (2007) point out, assessment has one of the most dramatic impacts on the student learning experience.

Therefore, as Roberts (2006) suggests there is still an 'ideal student experience' shared by students, both home and international, in the UK. Often in the classroom, poor quality teaching impacts international students much more dramatically. Home students have the advantage of understanding the regulations and local system while also speaking the local language. Many academics would argue that to ensure both home and international students gain a valuable learning experience, you do not have to 'adapt' your teaching and assessment for international students you simply have to create pedagogically sound learning environments for all your students.

The Experience of UK Students Internationally

To date, research on international students has generally focused on flows from non-Western countries to English-speaking countries such as the United States (US), the UK and Australia (Waters and Brooks 2010). There is little research on the experience of UK students studying abroad. According to the OECD the number of UK students studying abroad rose from 16,866 in 1975 to 22,405 in 2005 (Findlay et al. 2010). UK students often take a 'gap year' in between further and higher education (i.e. between A levels and university study). This is a term used to describe taking time out from curricular activities to travel and see the world. Many gap year students work and travel during the 12 months between finishing their A level education and applying to university. This may include volunteer activities and working abroad. This may partly explain why UK students tend to study abroad less.

Waters and Brooks (2010) point out that to middle-class decision making around university and employment is strategic (for example, Bourdieu 1984; Brown et al. 2003). International student migration and the accumulation of capital (Balaz and Williams 2004; Findlay et al. 2006; Waters 2006, 2008) are intertwined as an international degree is highly valued in the labour market (Bourdieu 1986).

This strategy is played out by parents paying for their child's private education or families moving house to be within a specific school catchment area. Within higher education, choosing an institution for a graduate degree is a way of distinguishing oneself above one's peers with an equivalent undergraduate degree (Brown and Hesketh 2004).

However, Waters and Brooks (2010) argue that in the case of UK students, seeking cultural capital BY gaining an international degree is not strategic, rather it is accidental. UK students tend to seek adventure from overseas study and often use it to prolong a carefree student lifestyle. UK students that move internationally to study tend to be high achieving school leavers and often come from independent schools and high income (professional and managerial) families (Findlay et al. 2010).

Findlay et al. (2010) found there is some degree of selective differentiation by destination. Some students were seeking an international career following graduation. UK students studying in Australia were often interested in a permanent move while those studying in Ireland were more likely to choose to return to the UK following graduation. Students from families with parents who themselves have gained an undergraduate or postgraduate degree were more likely to go abroad looking for a world-class university education. Further, UK students studying in the US often came from privileged backgrounds and their move in search of an elite university, for some, is due to their failure to gain a place at their preferred UK university.

These sentiments are supported by comments from students in the Ainley and Weyers (2008) study that show the mindset of UK students in relation to the differences between Russell Group and non-Russell institutions. Differences were noted by students in the value of their degrees depending on from which institution the degree was granted. For example one student commented (cited in Ainley and Weyers 2008):

> If I had gone to a more prestigious university, I would know I could walk into a career, show someone my CV and they would be immediately impressed by the university that I attended. They wouldn't be so concerned with me as a person. I feel I will be prejudiced against.
>
> Student 26 NR H-SES

While another student from a non-Russell institution commented that, 'The graduates at this university get into non graduate-based jobs' (Student 11 NR L-SES).

The idea of human capital is supported by some interviewees who regarded the payment of fees as an investment in their own human capital – 'like an investment for the company's future' (Student 8 R H-SES). For some paying fees was natural: 'I went to private school anyway so as long as the service we are getting is good, there is no harm in paying for it' (Student 15 R L-SES) (cited in Ainley and Weyers 2008).

Conclusion

While the research suggests that approaches to studying and perceptions of teaching are two of the most direct influences on the quality of student learning at university (Prosser and Trigwell 1999), it is clear that these influences cannot account for the large variation in the student experience and the effects on student learning outcomes. Importantly, regardless of which type of institution they attend, the socio-economic background or their cultural background they originate from, a large part of the student experiences of teaching and learning remain somewhat similar. What is fundamental is the context, both the discipline and subject area, in which the students are learning.

The increasing competition between universities not only within the UK but globally is leading to what Leys (2001) calls 'market-managed consolidation' in which departments within 'weaker' institutions either merge or close. However, Jary argues that despite all of the dramatic changes that have occurred in the UK over the past decade, 'the fundamental unity of the UK higher education system remains intact' (2006: 96). Ringmar (2006) argues that what makes the student experience at an institution unique is its student body. Ainley supports this position and also suggests that 'staff and students collude in consolidating institutional identities which are socially distinctive' (1994: 120). Russell Group institutions attract a certain demographic of student while former polytechnics attract another. Russell Group institutions tend to be highly focused on the sciences while former polytechnics often market courses that are vocationally based. This also explains how qualifications are ranked subsequently by employers (Brown and Hesketh 2004).

The impact of international students on UK higher education is strong, particularly in relation to assessment. The challenges for international students are complex but the experience can also be extremely valuable. Coping with cultural differences increases the confidence in students. Students who choose to study internationally select their destination of choice based on perceptions of teaching quality, then for the reputation of the institution. Therefore, while research-intensive institutions may have some initial advantage over former polytechnics that are teaching focused, the importance of the student experience and a high quality learning environment is increasingly important to students that are paying increasingly higher fees. However, UK institutions must be careful in their competition for fee-paying overseas students that they continue to provide a high quality academic infrastructure and the kind of support that assists international students to settle into the UK academic culture.

References

1994 group. (2012). Available at: http://www.1994group.ac.uk/ (accessed 3 October 2012).

Ainley, P. (1994) *Degrees of Difference: Higher Education in the 1990s*, London: Lawrence and Wishart.

Ainley, P. and Weyers, M. (2008) The variety of student experience: Investigating the complex dynamics of undergraduate learning in 'The Times Top 30' and other universities in England. In Canaan, J. and Shumar, W. (Eds) *Subject To Change, Structure and Agency of Students and Faculty in the Neo-Liberal University* (pp.131–152), London: Routledge.

Au, C. and Entwistle, N. (1999) Memorisation with understanding in approaches to studying: A cultural variant or response to assessment demands? European Association for Research on Learning and Instruction Conference, Gothenburg, August 1999.

Balaz, V. and Williams, A. (2004). 'Been there, done that': International student migration and human capital transfers from the UK to Slovakia, *Population, Space and Place*, 10, 217–237.

Bekhradnia, B., Whitnall, C. and Sastry, T. (2006) *The Academic Experience of Students in English Universities*, Oxford: Higher Education Policy Institute.

Biggs, J. B. (1978) Individual and group differences in study processes, *British Journal of Educational Psychology*, 48, 266–279.

Biggs, J. B. (1989a) Approaches to the enhancement of tertiary teaching, *Higher Education Research and Development*, 8, 7–25.

Biggs, J. B. (1989b) Approaches to learning in two cultures. In Bickley, V. (Ed.) *Language Teaching and Styles Within and Across Cultures* (pp. 421–436), Hong Kong: Institute of Language in Education.

Biggs, J. B. (1990). Effects of language medium of instruction on approaches to learning, *Educational Research Journal*, 5, 18–28.

Biggs, J. B. (1991). Approaches to learning in secondary and tertiary students in Hong Kong: Some comparative studies, *Educational Research Journal*, 6, 27–39.

Biggs, J. B. (1996) Western misperceptions of the Confucian-heritage learning culture. In Watkins, D.A. and Biggs, J. B. (Eds.) *The Chinese Learner: Cultural, Contextual and Psychological Influences* (pp. 45–68), Hong Kong: CERC; and Melbourne: ACER.

Biggs, J. B. and Tang, C. (2007) *Teaching for Quality Learning*. Maidenhead, UK: SRHE Open University Press.

Bourdieu, P. (1984). *Distinction: A Social Critique of the Judgement of Taste*. Cambridge, MA: Harvard University Press.

Bourdieu, P. (1986) The forms of capital. In Richardson, J. G. (Ed.) *Handbook of Theory and Research for the Sociology of Education* (pp. 241–258), New York: Greenwood Press.

Branine, M. (2005) Cross-cultural training of managers: An evaluation of a management development programme for Chinese managers, *Journal of Management Development*, 24, 459–472.

British Council (2012). PM2. Available at: http://www.britishcouncil.org/eumd-pmi2-about.htm (accessed 10 September 2012).

Brown, P. and Hesketh, A. (2004) *The Mismanagement of Talent: Employability and Jobs in the Knowledge Economy*, Oxford: Oxford University Press.

Brown, P., Hesketh, A. and Williams, S. (2003) Employability in a knowledge-driven economy, *Journal of Education and Work*, 16, 107–126.

The Economist (2012) Pretty polys: The new universities are 20 years old and still spry. Available at: http://www.economist.com/node/21549955 (accessed 10 September 2012).

Entwistle, N., McCune, V. and Hounsell, J. (2002) *Approaches to Studying and Perceptions of University Teaching-Learning Environments: Concepts, Measures and Preliminary Findings*. Occasional Report 1. University of Edinburgh: Teaching and Learning Research Program.

Entwistle, N. J. and Ramsden, P. (1983) *Understanding Student Learning*, London: Croom Helm.

Findlay, A., King, R., Stam, A. and Ruiz-Gelices, E. (2006) Ever reluctant Europeans: The changing geographies of UK students studying and working abroad, *European Urban and Regional Studies*, 13, 291–318.

Findlay, A., King, R., Geddes, A., Smith, F., Stam, A., Dunne, M., Skeldon, R. and Ahrens, J. (2010) *Motivations and Experiences of UK Students Studying Abroad*, BIS Research Paper No.8. Dundee: University of Dundee.

Garden, R. A. (1987). The second IEA mathematics study, *Comparative Education Review*, 31, 47–68.

Higher Education Statistics Agency. (2011) International students in UK higher education: Key statistics. Available online: www.ukcisa.org.uk/about/statistics_he.php (accessed 30August 2012).

Jary, D. (2006) Contribution to Universities of East London and Staffordshire dilemmas of the new governance, 10th International Research Conference, 1 September, Conference Proceedings.

Kember, D. (1996) The intention to both memorise and understand: Another approach to learning, *Higher Education*, 31, 341–354.

Kember, D. and Gow, L. (1990) Cultural specificity of approaches to study, *British Journal of Educational Psychology*, 60, 356–363.

Kember, D. and Gow, L. (1991) A challenge to the anecdotal stereotype of the Asian student, *Studies in Higher Education*, 16, 117–128.

Kingston, E. and Forland, H. (2008) Bridging the gap in expectations between international students and academic staff, *Journal of Studies in International Education*, 12(2), 204–221.

Lee, W. O. (1996) The cultural context of Chinese learners: Conceptions of learning in the Confucian tradition. In Watkins, D.A. and Biggs, J. B. (Eds.) *The Chinese Learner: Cultural, Contextual and Psychological Influence*, Hong Kong: CERC; and Melbourne: ACER.

Leonard, D., Pelletier, C. and Morley, L. (2004) *The Experiences of International Students in UK Higher Education: A Review of Unpublished Material*. London: UKCOSA.

Leys, C. (2001) *Market-Driven Politics: Neoliberal Democracy and the Public Interest*, London: Verso.

Liu, S. (2006) Developing China's future managers: Learning from the West, *Education and Training*, 43(1), 6–14.

Million+. (2012). Available at: http://www.millionplus.ac.uk/ (accessed 3 October 2012).

Marton, F. and Säljö, R. (1976) Symposium: Learning processes and strategies. On qualitative differences in learning. II: Outcome as a function of the learner's conception of the task, *British Journal of Educational Psychology*, 46, 115–127.

Marton, F. and Säljö, R. (1997) Approaches to learning. In Marton, F., Hounsell, D. J. and Entwistle, N. J. (Eds.) *The Experience of Learning* (2nd ed.) (pp. 39–58). Edinburgh: Scottish Academic Press.

Marton, F., Dall'Alba, G. and Tse, L. K. (1996) Memorizing and understanding: The keys to the paradox? In Watkins, D. A. and Biggs, J. B. (Eds.) *The Chinese Learner: Cultural, Psychological and Contextual Influences* (pp. 69–83). Hong Kong: Comparative Education Research Centre and The Australian Council for Educational Research.

Marton, F., Watkins, D. and Tang, C. (1997). Discontinuities and continuities in the experience of learning: An interview study of high-school students in Hong Kong, *Learning and Instruction*, 7, 21–48.

Nield, K. (2007). Understanding the Chinese learner: A case study exploration of the notion of the Hong Kong Chinese learner as a rote or strategic learner, *Education*, 6(1), 39–48.

Pilcher, N., Smith, K. and Riley, J. (2009) *An 'Unturned Stone'? Exams and International Students. Final Report.* Report for Edinburgh Napier University, Glasgow Caledonian University (Edinburgh and Glasgow).

Prosser, M. and Trigwell, K. (1999) *Understanding Learning and Teaching. The Experience of Higher Education.* Buckingham: SRHE and Open University Press.

Ramsden, P. (2001) Strategic management of teaching and learning. In Rust, C. (Ed.) *Improving Student Learning Strategically* (pp.1–10), Oxford: Oxford Centre for Staff and Learning Development, Oxford Brookes University.

Ringmar, E. (2006) Slip of the tongue betrays true quality of elite, *The Times Higher*, 18 August.

Roberts, K. (2006) Sociology and the present day student experience in the UK. Paper presented to the Researching Students Study Group at the British Sociological Association 2006 Conference.

Russell Group. (2012). Available at: http://www.russellgroup.ac.uk/ (accessed 2 October 2012).

Samuelowicz, K. (1987) Learning problems of overseas students: Two sides of a story, *Higher Education Research and Development*, 6, 121–132.

Scott, P. (2002) A lot to learn: We are all researchers now, *Education Guardian*, 8 January. Available at: education.guardian.co.uk/egweekly/ story/0,,628918,00.html (accessed 12 November 2012).

Stigler, J. W. and Perry, M. (1990) Mathematics learning in Japanese, Chinese, and American classrooms. In Stigler, J. M., Shweder, R. A. and Herdt, G. (Eds.) *Cultural Psychology: Essays on Comparative Human Development* (pp. 328–353), Cambridge: Cambridge University Press.

Tang, K. C. C. (1991) Effects of different assessment methods on tertiary students' approaches to studying. Unpublished PhD thesis, University of Hong Kong.

Thomas, P. R. and Bain, J. D. (1984) Contextual dependence of learning approaches: The effects of assessments, *Human Learning*, 3, 227–240.

Tysome, T. (2005) UK's Chinese bubble bursts. *Times Higher Education Supplement*, 21 October.

Tysome, T. (2006). Foreign students put off by cost of living in the UK. *Times Higher Education Supplement*, 2 November.

University Alliance. (2012). Available at: http://www.unialliance.ac.uk/about/ (accessed 3 October 2012).

Vasagar, J. (2012) Tuition fees increase led to 15,000 fewer applicants, *The Guardian*, 9 August.

Waters, J. and Brooks, R. (2010) Accidental achievers? International higher education, class reproduction and privilege in the experiences of UK students overseas, *British Journal of Sociology of Education*, 31(2), 217–228.

Waters, J. L. (2006). Geographies of cultural capital: Education, international migration and family strategies between Hong Kong and Canada, *Transactions of the Institute of British Geographers*, 31, 179–192.

Waters, J. L. (2008). *Education, Migration and Cultural Capital in the Chinese Diaspora: Transnational Students Between Hong Kong and Canada*, New York: Cambria Press.

Watkins, D. A. and Biggs, J. B. (Eds.) (1996) *The Chinese Learner: Cultural, Contextual and Psychological Influences*. Hong Kong: CERC; and Melbourne: ACER.

Watkins, D. A. and Biggs, J. B. (2001) The paradox of the Chinese learner and beyond. In Watkins, D. A. and Biggs, J. B. (Eds.) *Teaching the Chinese Learner: Psychological and Pedagogical Perspectives* (pp. 3–26), Hong Kong: CERC; and Melbourne: ACER.

Weyers, M. (2007) An analysis of the undergraduate student experience in London universities. Paper presented at the Society for Research into Higher Education Annual Conference.

11

The Student Experience in India

PRITI CHOPRA, SAVITA DATTA AND VEENA MISHRA

Understanding the student experience of global education and internationalisation in twenty-first century Indian higher education is marked by three significant issues for ongoing critical conversation: the development of good quality inclusive processes contributing to the successful progression and employability of heterogeneous students in a rapidly transforming economy; the implementation of reform agendas striving to enhance the purpose, functions and delivery of higher education provision; and the changing requirements for institutions, academics, learners and administrators under conditions of globalisation. As a part of its reforms in higher education the Indian government sanctioned the establishment of a US$5 billion National Knowledge Network (NKN) in March 2010 (India Edunews 2010). The vision of NKN is to provide a network through which Indian institutions of higher learning and research would be able to engage in knowledge sharing and collaborative research (Ministry of Communications and Information Technology 2012). Approximately 1,500 institutions form a part of the initial target for the NKN reach (National Knowledge Network Programme and Implementation Unit 2012). The main subjects currently prioritised for implementation and delivery through NKN are in the areas of: health, education, computing, agriculture and e-governance.

NKN enables the use of specialised online applications for sharing and developing effectively functioning and accessible computing facilities, e-libraries, virtual classrooms and very large databases (Lin and Yen 2011). Since early 2012, more than 681 institutions of higher learning and advanced research have been connected to the network and fifty-two virtual classrooms have been established (National Knowledge Network Programme and Implementation Unit 2012). Applications such as nationwide virtual classrooms aspire to address the issue of shortage in teaching faculty and ensure the delivery of quality education across the country (Indian Institute of Public Administration 2010). NKN also aims to assist the growth of quality institutions with necessary research facilities and contribute to building a resource bank of highly trained professionals (*Business Standard* 2011a).

In addition, international partnerships have become increasingly important for promoting global education through curriculum, pedagogy, research and institution, programme, staff and student mobility (Brennan, King and Lebeau 2004). In India, the Foreign Educational Institutions Bill 2010 (Regulation of Entry and Operations, Maintenance of Quality and Prevention of Commercialization) may facilitate the development of international partnerships and collaborations in order to support the alignment of the Indian higher education sector with global standards (*The Economic Times* 2010). According to the Ministry of Human Resource Development (MHRD), the Foreign Educational Institutions Bill 2010 has encouraged global higher education institutions, including Massachusetts Institute of Technology, Yale University, Virginia Tech, Columbia University, University of Southern California and University of Alabama, to deliver their higher education provision through India (Pathak 2011). Over fifty overseas universities have expressed an interest in setting up campuses in India. These overseas education providers may also contribute to increasing the gross enrolment ratio in the country (*Business Standard* 2011b).

In the next section an overview of the Indian higher education system takes account of some of these outlined issues in more detail. Following this, the experience of Indian students, within examples of current national higher education provision, are considered. Correspondingly, the experience of international students, within the same Indian higher education context, is then discussed. Finally, the experience of Indian students as international students in different countries is described. This chapter ends with a conclusion that provides a reflective analytical account of emerging factors for further consideration and research.

An Overview of Indian Higher Education

The Indian higher education system is one of the largest in the world with around forty central universities, 234 state universities and 128 'deemed' universities (Indian universities are established by an Act of Parliament or State Legislature; however, the Indian government can, through an executive order, grant the status of 'deemed-to-be-universities' to higher education institutions through the recommendation of the University Grants Commission [UGC]) (UGC 2011a: 3). In total, there are over 20,000 higher education institutions, inclusive of a combination of universities (awarding their own degrees) and colleges (awarding their degrees through an affiliated university), with just over twelve million students and 505,000 lecturers (Thorat 2008). Conversely, according to the UGC (2005), with an estimated gross enrolment ratio of 11 per cent of students between 18 and 23 years of age, India is relatively small in terms of percentage of student enrolment (Agarwal 2009: 36). The wide ranging diversity and complexity of Indian higher education, across different linguistic and geographical regions, faces the challenge of strategically embracing growth, improving quality and raising standards of academic provision in the current competitive international context of globalised higher education. In 2007 Prime Minister Manmohan Singh during his speech at the 150th Anniversary Function of University of Mumbai stated,

> Our university system is, in many parts, in a state of disrepair ... In almost half the districts in the country, higher education enrolments are abysmally low, almost two-third of our universities and 90 per cent of our colleges are rated as below average on quality parameters ...
>
> (Mattoo 2009: 1).

Agarwal (2009: 29) describes these challenges as the consequence of 'chaotic and unplanned expansion'. He succinctly explains that:

> In an effort to meet rising aspirations and to make higher education socially inclusive, there has been a sudden and dramatic increase in [the] number of institutions without a proportionate increase in material and intellectual resources ... Several problems that the system faces include: inadequate infrastructure and facilities, large vacancies in faculty positions and poor faculty, outmoded teaching methods, declining research standards, unmotivated students, overcrowded classrooms and widespread geographic, income, gender and ethnic imbalances. But, this is not unique to India. Most systems of higher education in the world have expanded fast over the past few decades and are in quasi-crisis and need reform.

In order to gain an insight into the context of the Indian higher education system it is important to consider topical issues related to: structure; social exclusion; employability; and changes in the regulatory system and quality management.

Structure

Ancient Indian universities can be traced back to forest *ashrams* (the Hindu tradition of adult learning) and *Takshashilas* (Buddhist institutions for higher education aiming at spiritual and philosophical development) established during the fifth century (Scharfe 2002; Narlikar 2003). Nalanda in Bihar, India, flourished as a university during the fifth to twelfth centuries and is historically recognised as one of the first residential international universities in the world (Nalanda Digital Library 2012).

In 1857, during colonial rule, a British model of higher education was imitated when establishing universities in Kolkata, Mumbai and Chennai.

The mission of the colonial higher education system, for these three universities, was to provide predominantly high caste Indian men, from affluent socio-economic backgrounds, with undergraduate level British education in English. The aim was to develop cost-effective employable Indians for serving the British administration in India (Viswanathan 1990).

The time period, from post-Indian independence in 1947 till the 1980s, remained significantly influenced by the colonial legacy of higher education and witnessed a gradual increase in a small number of high quality institutions such as the development of five Indian Institutes of Technology (IITs) and two Indian Institutes of Management (IIMs). Several private institutions, financially supported by government grants, also came into existence (Lahiri 2004). As Agarwal states; 'By 1980, there were 132 universities and 4,738 colleges in the country, enrolling around 5 per cent of the eligible age group in higher education. Almost one-third of all colleges were private aided colleges' (2009: 21). Therefore, the persistence of challenges regarding the relationship between processes for expansion and processes for quality management, as well as the enhancement of student enrolment numbers, can be traced back to a history of over fifty-five years of higher education following Indian independence.

The post-1980s phase of Indian higher education has been impacted by a rapidly growing public demand for access to good quality higher education that would contribute to enhanced employability in industry and business (Tilak 2004, 2005). This has led to an increased diversification and augmentation in the number and types of higher education providers. According to Agarwal (2009: 21):

> Private institutions proliferated, distance education programmes gained wider acceptance, public universities and colleges started self-financing programmes, and foreign institutions started offering programmes either by themselves or in partnership with Indian institutions … As a result the entire higher education landscape got transformed over the past 25 years.

For example, well-known to the global higher education community, there are now sixteen IITs established to provide high quality education for Indian scientists and engineers. IITs have a common admission process for undergraduate admissions titled the 'Indian Institute of Technology Joint Entrance Examination (IIT-JEE)', which, in 2011, had a very low acceptance rate, only 9,618 out of 485,000 applications were accepted (Indian Institute of Technology Delhi 2011). Furthermore, there are sixty-six distance education institutions governed by the Distance Education Council functioning in about sixty universities and twelve Open Universities (Indira Gandhi National Open University 2011). As such, the School of Open Learning at the University of Delhi enrols around 100,000 students every year (University of Delhi 2011). Moreover, Indira Gandhi National Open University (New Delhi), one of the largest universities in the world, offers 338 programmes of study through more than 3,500 courses to approximately three million students (Indira Gandhi National Open University 2011).

Similar to the academic structure of European higher education institutions, under the Bologna Process, Indian academic qualifications require three academic years for the completion of an undergraduate degree, two academic years for a master's degree and a further three academic years for the completion of a PhD degree. Recent developments for introducing integrated, flexible and modular programmes are initiatives, embracing the requirements for open and flexible provision, to facilitate opportunities for student choice and mobility. However, the implications and impact of these initiatives still require deeper analysis and further research (Chakrabarti, Bartning and Sengupta 2010). In addition to structure, it is also essential to examine issues related to social exclusion and how this may have an impact on the gross enrolment ratio in Indian higher education.

Social Exclusion

India has a diverse culture comprised of different religions and castes. Indian society is stratified in terms of socio-economic background, caste, religion, urban–rural divide and gender. There are significant disparities across and within diverse socio-economic, caste and religious groups. The enrolment rate is considerably less than the national average for women, people with special educational needs and disability, marginalised caste and socio-economic groups, religious minorities (such as Muslims) and those who live in rural areas (Thorat and Kumar 2008). Several government policies and programmes have been implemented to address these inequalities. The Persons with Disabilities Act 1995 ensures that people with special educational needs and disabilities have the right to access education at all levels. In the higher education sector, the UGC has been supporting universities and colleges in the country to develop inclusivity and equality within higher education provision. The UGC introduced the scheme of Teachers Preparation in Special Education (TEPSE) and Higher Education for Persons with Special Needs (HEPSN) during the Ninth Five-Year Plan, which has been extended to the Eleventh Five-Year Plan (UGC 2011a).

Furthermore, through positive discrimination, the Indian government aims to facilitate equality in access to higher education for under-represented groups of people that are categorised by the Indian Constitution as Scheduled Castes and Scheduled Tribes. An Act of Parliament in 2007 reserved an additional positive discrimination quota of 27 per cent for higher education institutions to enrol students belonging to Scheduled Castes and Scheduled Tribes. This reservation is in addition to an existing reservation quota of 22.5 per cent for the enrolment of marginalised caste and tribe groups, in all educational institutions, making the existing requirement for positive discrimination reservations 49.5 per cent. This has contributed to a net increase in enrolment by approximately 54 per cent in 2010; the Eleventh Five-Year Plan aspires to provide enough resources to support a further increase in the national enrolment rate to 15 per cent by 2012 (UGC 2011a), from 10 per cent in 2010.

Gender disparities in higher education enrolment have been evident throughout history and across all religions, mainstream and minority groups (Umashankar and Dutta 2007). In order to achieve and promote education for women, the UGC has introduced scholarship schemes for prospective female candidates with an aim to take responsibility for the direct cost of their education at all levels (UGC 2011a). Historically, the development of university practices, such as the establishment of a Non-Collegiate Women's Education Board (NCWEB) in 1946, were a step towards making higher education accessible to more women. Post-1947, Indian higher education displayed a gradual increase in the enrolment of women (Sachdeva 1999; UGC 2010). However, the real growth in the enrolment of women has been significantly substantial over the past decade following the Tenth and Eleventh Five-Year Plans (UGC 2010, 2011a). In 2009–2010, women constituted 41.6 per cent of total student enrolment in some areas (UGC 2011a).

Faculty ratios of men and women, in a number of disciplines, have also become more balanced over the years (UGC 2011a). At the Indian Institute of Technology in Delhi, during the academic year 2010 to 2011, the enrolment of women in undergraduate courses increased by 3 per cent and a marginal increase was visible in postgraduate courses (*Hindustan Times Reporter* 2011; Indian Institute of Technology Delhi 2011). Nevertheless, the national gross enrolment ratio for women is currently 9.11 per cent, which is comparatively lower than the gross enrolment ratio of 12.42 for men (UGC 2011b). The national gross enrolment ratio for women belonging to marginalised caste groups and religious minority groups (especially Muslims) remains, disturbingly, lower (UGC, 2011b).

Current higher education expansion in provision, policy and programme initiatives to facilitate equality in provision, as mass education in India, demonstrates progress and achievements. Yet, there are still essential issues that remain to be addressed. These issues shift the focus beyond equality in access to equity in provision, achievement and progression. There is substantial lack of equity in all aspects of higher education provision; challenges encountered in the progress and achievement for marginalised groups of people; and difficulties experienced in the substantial improvement of the gross enrolment ratio (reaching the currently excluded 7.5 million potential students for higher education), which remain just some areas of immediate concern (Agarwal 2009). Equally, though the government intends to increase the gross enrolment ratio by 15 per cent in 2012, there are still concerns regarding the employability of higher education students (ibid.).

Employability

Despite having a population of over one billion people there is a shortage of highly competent professionals for the emerging industry sectors in India (*Financial Express* 2011). The education system needs to be transformed to encourage vocational skills development through higher education providers (UGC 2003). According to the Confederation of Indian Industry (CII), only 25 per cent of technical graduates and 15 per cent of other graduates can be readily employed in the jobs that recent economic developments have generated in retail, banking, telecommunications, health care and the information technology sectors (Planning Commission Report of the Task Force on Employment Opportunities 2001).

During 2008, the Ministry of Labour and Employment allocated the responsibility to CII to become the national assessing body for the development of modular employability skills in all higher education and vocational courses. The CII National Education Committee identified the need to build soft skills, as demanded by the impact of global developments, in order to construct bridges where gaps exist between industry, education and skill providers. These soft skills have been categorised as: communication skills, teamwork, problem solving, and applied research skills. All these skills are not, presently, adequately developed at university level and an emphasis has been placed on curriculum reform in order to embed this within programme provision (CII 2012). In addition, the National Policy on Skill Development, approved by the Cabinet in 2009, aims at empowering all individuals through improved skills, knowledge and internationally recognised qualifications in order to enable approximately 500 million people to access enhanced employment opportunities by 2022 (National Policy on Skill Development 2009).

Changes in the Regulatory System and Quality Management

There are mainly three dominant agencies in India, under the Ministry of Education, which regulate higher education: the UGC, the All India Council for Technical Education (AICTE) and the Distance Education Council (DEC). Since 1956, the UGC, along with fourteen statutory central professional councils, has tightly managed the entire higher education system. The UGC is responsible for overseeing the curricula, degrees, fees, faculty qualifications and the approval for new universities. Developed in 1987, AICTE has managed the bureaucratic administration and implementation of virtually all aspects of technical education. AICTE facilitates the standardisation of courses, curricula, teaching and learning provision, faculty roles, staff qualifications and formal summative assessment criteria in all vocational subject areas. The National Board of Accreditation (NBA), legitimised in 1994, is also entrusted with the task of quality assessment in the technical education sector (Prakash

2005; Kaul 2006). The DEC, under Section 25 of the Indira Gandhi National Open University Act 1985, established through the Ministry of Human Resource Development, has a prominent role in the promotion, coordination and establishment of standards for open universities and distance education provision in the country.

Since 1956, the Medical Council of India (MCI) has controlled all aspects of medical education. The Council of Architecture, established in 1972; Ministry of Urban Development; Indian Nursing Council (1947); Ministry of Health; Rehabilitation Council of India (1992); Ministry of Social Justice; National Council For Teacher Education (1993); Indian Council for Agricultural Research; and the Ministry of Agriculture are a few other influential administrative bodies that impact on the governance and management of Indian higher education (Prakash 2005). Historically, the role of the state in the regulation of higher education worked effectively when the state was the primary funding source for higher education. In today's context, with growth and the contemporary influence of variety in higher education providers, the role of the state in regulating Indian higher education has come under persistent scrutiny (Agarwal 2009). According to Agarwal, the:

> UGC Act may be replaced by a more comprehensive and umbrella Higher Education Act to provide [an] overall unambiguous framework for development, regulation and financing of higher education in the country. Unnecessary regulations need to be terminated. There is a need to relook at the entire recognition and approval system so that baseline standards are met.
>
> (2009: 356)

Similarly, in terms of quality management, the emphasis on processes for stakeholders to ensure accountability in exchange for financial investment and autonomy, in an academic milieu where students require high-standard internationally valued qualifications, has been an ongoing challenge and an area of development since 1998 (*The Times of India* 2007). Increasing and sustaining good quality academic faculty and integrating technology-enhanced learning effectively in higher education also face constraints that need to be consistently recognised and addressed in order to improve quality and standards of education (Stella 2001; Hattangdi and Ghosh 2008). Two new bills brought forward by the Indian Ministry of Human Resource Development titled the National Accreditation Regulatory Authority for Higher Educational Institutions Bill and the Universities of Innovation Bill are currently under consideration in the Government of India Cabinet. According to Dhawan (2012: 7),

> Presently, accreditation is voluntary as a result of which less than one-fifth of the colleges and less than one-third of all universities have obtained

accreditation. Mandatory accreditation will enable the higher education system in the country to become part of the global quality assurance system.

The National Accreditation Regulatory Authority for Higher Educational Institutions Bill aims to establish a statutory authority that that will ensure quality management in the assessment and accreditation of all higher educa-tion institutions (apart from agricultural institutes) and the Universities of Innovation Bill will enable universities to gain greater academic freedom if they demonstrate required standards in infrastructure, academic provision and faculty (Dhawan 2012).

In the next section, the impact of technology supported learning on the quality of learning and assessment is described further through an example of the experience of students in Indian higher education.

The Experience of Indian Students in Indian Higher Education

The experience of Indian students within the national higher education context is significantly shaped by the opportunities for minority and marginalised groups to have equitable access to academic success and the enhancement of quality education provision through technology-enhanced learning. This section draws upon two case studies developed under the UK-India Education and Research Initiative (UKIERI) to describe the experiences of students in different higher education institutions in the abovementioned areas.

Case Study 1

As a part of a UKIERI three-year project (2007–2010) on 'Widening Participation: Diversity, Isolation or Integration in Higher Education' conducted, in collaboration, by the University of Hertsfordshire (UK), University of Bradford (UK), the Tata Institute of Social Sciences (India), and Guru Nanak College of Education and Research (India), this case study exam-ines the influences of socio-cultural factors such as caste, language, religion and gender on group interaction in the classroom (Thornton and Wankhede 2012). The study is based on research data collected in four higher education institutions in Mumbai, India: the Tata Institute of Social Sciences (25 post-graduate students); University of Mumbai (25 postgraduate students); Guru Nanak College of Arts, Science and Commerce (49 undergraduate students); and Guru Nanak College of Education (100 undergraduate students) (Iyer 2012). Data analysis of student groupings revealed that:

- Mutual pairs and groups were predominantly formed between higher caste groups and between religious groups where the student numbers of particular religious groups were high.

- Inter-religious mutual pairs and groups were formed where there was religious diversity in the class.
- Caste category was a common factor in the formation of groups.
- Common linguistic background was a factor determining the formation of mutual pairs and groups.
- Heterogeneous gender pairing was not a prevalent aspect of classroom interaction. (Iyer 2012: 52)

The case study concluded that caste categorisation and English language proficiency contributed to the level of bonding students experienced in the classroom context. Students who completed their schooling in a vernacular language and faced challenges in communicating in English, and students who belonged to the Indian government categorisation of Scheduled Castes (historically marginalised and disadvantaged groups of people also known as Dalit) frequently experienced isolation. The research study signals value in the need for strategic interventions to facilitate purposive bonding and to confront such sociocultural barriers to integration and cohesion in higher education (Iyer 2012: 53).

Case Study 2

During 2007 a curriculum development project based on blended learning was introduced in the University of Delhi in collaboration with The Open University, UK, under the UKIERI. Following the completion of this project a survey to determine the impact of blended learning was implemented with 140 undergraduate attending students and 200 undergraduate distance learning students. Seventy per cent of the participants were female and 30 per cent of the participants were male. The students came from different socio-economic backgrounds, religions and caste groups.

The survey revealed that course choices were made on a personal basis and 45 per cent of students stated that they chose the course for good career prospects. Fifty per cent of the students were interested in jobs after completion of the course whereas 45 per cent of the students wanted to pursue higher studies. The survey also established that the students favoured blended learning as, they believed, it contributed to developing a better understanding of their learning material. Sixty-three per cent indicated that they felt they had an enhanced learning experience through blended learning with the use of multimedia. Statistical evidence collated over a period of three years also indicated that there has been a substantial impact on the achievement of students in the written component of their first year practical exams for the BSc Physics (Hons) programme. Every year approximately 90 per cent of enrolled students complete these essential summative assessments. The integration of information and communications technology has helped to facilitate an improvement in these results, which is illustrated in Table 11.1.

Table 11.1 Improvement in the scores of BSc Physics (Hons) first-year students (in the written component of practical exams)

% Average aggre physics, chemistry, maths finalschool exam results at the BSc Physics (Hons) degree at University of Delhi	*Cohort*	*Scoring less than 40%*	*Scoring above 50%*	*Scoring above 70%*	*Scoring above 90%*	*Scoring 100%*
78	2006–07	26	25	20	0	0
74	2007–08	18	36	36	0	0
70	2008–09	0	38	45	8	4

The Experience of International Students in Indian Higher Education

India has the third largest English speaking population in the world (Bateman 2008) and offers quality education at a lower cost compared to other countries (Education Consultants India Limited Report 2011). International students from over 145 countries are enrolled in different Indian universities (SRM University 2011; University of Delhi 2012). International students studying in India mainly belong to the following categories: students supported through government scholarships provided by their country or through the Indian Council for Cultural Relations (ICCR) and self-funding students. A few students may be funded by their employers for upgrading their qualifications. Every year ICCR sponsors 2,325 international students from more than eighty different countries by providing scholarships under twenty-one different schemes (Indian Council for Cultural Relations 2010a).

Indian educational institutions such as the Indian Institute of Technology, Indian Institute of Science, Indian Institute of Management, National Institute of Technology, Birla Institute of Technology and All India Institute of Medical Sciences are renowned for a provision of high level quality education (Educations.com 2011). For example, India's IIT graduates are amongst the most successful engineering, software and entrepreneurial professionals in the world and IIT graduates are highly sought after by Western companies (Lahiri 2004). Some Indian universities also offer unique courses that are based on traditional Indian knowledge systems, such as Ayurveda, Sanskrit, Yoga and Hindi. These courses are also popular with many international students (Educations.com 2011). A majority of international students enrol on undergraduate programmes and approximately one fourth of the international student population enrol on postgraduate programmes (Agarwal 2007: 87). In terms of a gender profile, in excess of 70 per cent of international students are male (ibid.).

In recent years, there have been over 13,627 international students enrolled in Indian universities (Dongaonkar and Rai Negi 2009). According to Agarwal (2009: 12), 'More than 90 percent of the international students were from ... Asia ... and Africa ... Only 8 percent of students were from Europe, Australia and the Americas ... The majority of international students ... come from Nepal.' The latest study on the profile of international students in India confirms that Indira Gandhi National Open University (IGNOU) enrols the highest number of international students through its distance education provision (Vishnoi 2009).

In terms of pastoral care, international students are received on arrival after obtaining information through the Indian Mission in their country. Several camps are organised by ICCR to introduce international students to Indian historical and cultural places of interest. ICCR also provides temporary accommodation on their arrival in India. Most of the institutions in India provide accommodation facilities for all students. International students have some reserved places in university hostels and there are a few student hostels that are exclusively for international students. If students find it difficult to secure accommodation in a university hostel they are supported through additional advice and assistance. Regarding affordability, accommodation in Indian universities is less expensive compared to other countries (Educations.com 2011). ICCR also offers financial assistance to low income self-financing students in cases of emergency (Indian Council for Cultural Relations, 2010b).

For admissions, international students require a valid passport and student visa to study in India. A few universities require a health certificate (Jawaharlal Nehru University 2012) or medical insurance in advance; others require students to provide them with this documentation at the time of admission. International students are expected to abide by the same set of rules and code of conduct applied to Indian students (Vidyapeetham 2012). Students coming from non-English speaking countries can be expected to provide English proficiency scores such as International English Language Testing System (IELTS) or Test of English as a Foreign Language (TOEFL), but this is not an essential requirement in all universities. In general, Graduate Record Examinations (GRE)/TOEFL/IELTS or other such tests are not a compulsory prerequisite for studying in India (Education Consultants India Limited Report 2011). Presently, increasing initiatives are being undertaken by universities to provide enrolled non-English speaking international students with additional short-term English Language courses.

During September 2011 the results of an online questionnaire with forty-two international student respondents studying at the University of Delhi confirmed that most of the students chose the university because they believed they would gain access to a good quality education at a relatively low cost. The profile of the respondents corresponds with the generic profile of international students in India (see Agarwal 2007), as 85 per cent of the respondents were undergraduate students and 76 per cent were between 18 and 25 years of age. Nearly 90 per cent of the respondents were male and over 70 per cent of the respondents were of Asian origin. Over 50 per cent of the respondents confirmed that extra-curricular activities presented an enriching platform to engage with various cultural practices and to interact with students from India and other countries. A respondent from Nepal found it easy to interact socially with fellow students through cultural activities, as he commented: 'Very helpful and understanding student body. Thumbs up.' However, regarding interaction with faculty, he stated that: 'Friendliness of the teachers would be appreciated. The more peer like the relation between teachers and students, the more harmonious would be the academic atmosphere.'

In contrast, a respondent from Afghanistan commented that he was not comfortable with group interaction in his college. He said: 'The College I'm studying in, almost all students are Indian and they have good interaction with each other, but I'm a foreigner and not familiar with their manners, I feel a little bit alone.'

Several respondents, especially those from Vietnam and Korea, chose to study Buddhist Studies at the University of Delhi (see Figure 11.1). A majority of respondents chose to study at University of Delhi due to a combination of factors such as affordability, quality of education and to gain the experience of studying in a different cultural environment (see Figure 11.2).

The Experience of Indian Students as International Students

The experience of Indian students as international students can be summarised with regards to three areas: destinations for study abroad; the quality of experience; and the role of international degrees within and beyond the country.

Destinations

According to the UNESCO Institute for Statistics (2011), during 2009 there were 195,107 Indian students studying overseas. The most popular destinations for their overseas higher education are: the United States, the United Kingdom, Australia, New Zealand, Canada and Ireland. Though the most frequented destinations are primarily English speaking countries, Indian students are also pursuing studies in non-English speaking countries that are offering academic programmes in English such as: Sweden, Norway, Denmark, Germany, France and Holland (ibid.). According to Agarwal students are also attracted to: 'Top hotel management schools in Switzerland; medical institutes in China, Russia, Eastern Europe and the Commonwealth of Independent States … Indians now find universities in Singapore and Malaysia equally good, less expensive and closer [to] home' (2009: 13–14).

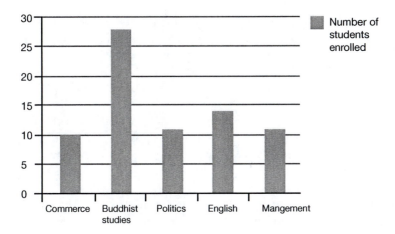

Figure 11.1 Number of international students enrolled in postgraduate programmes, 2011– 2012 (University of Delhi)

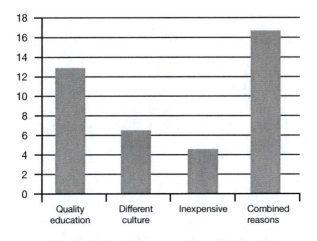

Figure 11.2 Reason for choosing to study in India (University of Delhi)

The Quality of Experience

Access to a good quality globalised higher education experience, in an academic institution that has an internationally recognised reputation for world-class high standards and well resourced provision, has been a persistent attraction and motivation for Indian students to study in other countries. Sejal Shah Gulati, president of Time Analytics Services and alumni from Princeton University and Harvard University, described her experience as the following:

Speaking for myself, I can say that Princeton gave me a true liberal arts education. It taught me how to think, the art of writing, speaking, analysis and to be solution oriented. You study with very bright people. The peer group is incredibly smart and accomplished.

(*The Times of India* 2011: 1).

Indian students who gain admission to universities ranked at the top of global league tables predominantly belong to affluent backgrounds. A *Times of India* interview with a recruitment representative in Princeton University illustrated this, as he stated:

Applicants to Princeton mainly consist of students from solidly middle class families of bureaucrats and college professors. Throw in generous aid to the mix and 2011 saw a 23 per cent jump in the number of Indian students applying to Princeton for undergrad studies making it the largest application pool that we have ever seen from India.

(*The Times of India* 2011: 1).

Nonetheless, there are also several domains of discomfort encountered by Indian students undertaking study abroad. Many of the difficulties they experience are associated with: the high cost of fees and living expenses; stringent and complicated immigration rules impacting on access to student visas; insufficient enhanced employment opportunities following graduation; inadequate level of inclusivity and intercultural engagement in curriculum and academic provision; and intense isolation (see Andrade and Evans 2009; Montgomery 2010; Gunjan 2011).

The Role of International Degrees Within and Beyond the Country

According to De Wit (2007) the global mobility of students can be attributed to four key areas of motivation: strengthening mutual understanding (a socio-cultural and political factor); increasing revenue (an economic factor); creating opportunities for skill migration (an economic factor); and capacity building (educational factor). Indian students may choose to study abroad in order to enhance their employability in a competitive global environment. Anuja Master Bose, a former alumni from Harvard Business School, explains that:

One of the USPs [unique selling points] of the Ivy League system, the reason people are willing to mortgage their farmhouse to get in, is the 'network.' … It's the network that really counts. They are all old schools. The alumni are well placed … The HBS network gave me access to leaders in the social enterprise sector. I got my first job because the Fishers (founders of the Gap clothing stores) contacted my professor who reached out to me.

(The Times of India 2011)

Students could also be pushed to invest their resources in an overseas degree if access to admission in high quality Indian institutions, such as IIT, is over-subscribed (Cheney, Ruzzi and Muralidharan 2006). Moreover, students may be motivated by the belief that an overseas qualification has a prestige factor attached to it and would be regarded positively by employers within India (Gunjan 2011). As Agarwal (2009: 14) indicates, 'Large outward mobility from India is often seen as loss of revenue or brain drain.' Even so Freeman argues that:

> India can compete with the U.S. in high tech by having many … specialists although those workers are a small proportion of their work forces. This threatens to undo the 'North-South' pattern of trade in which advanced countries dominate high tech …
>
> (2005: 123)

Conclusion

Indian higher education is vast, diverse and complex. India has some world class institutions of higher learning in science and technology. Institutes such as IITs claim to produce graduates who have internationally leading calibre and are highly successful within a competitive global knowledge economy. On the other hand, with a small gross enrolment ratio and numerous challenges faced in reaching all eligible students, India still has a long way to go in developing an inclusive, good quality and equitable higher education provision suitable for the globalisation contexts of the twenty-first century. Chakrabarti, Bartning and Sengupta point out 'that the implementation of robust student support and quality-assessment methodologies in Indian universities is essential if India is to become an attractor as well as a source for international student and faculty circulation' (2010:183).

India's higher education system also depends on executive and senior management and leadership capacity development to help shape its future (there is now a recognition and emphasis on leadership capacity building in the national Twelfth Five-Year Plan 2012–2017) (UGC, 2011b). Furthermore, in the sudden transition from academic roles, located in specific disciplines, to higher education leadership and management positions managers often feel that their lack of training and adequate knowledge impacts on their potential to contribute to the growth of the faculty or institution that they are leading. There are a range of higher education administration and management areas that require more meticulous and vigorous consideration for capacity improvement such as: supporting strategic decisions for enhancing the quality of teaching and learning and student experience; developing effective mechanisms for maintaining high standards of quality assurance in national and borderless higher education programmes; and strengthening the implementation of high standards of professionalism and equal opportunity, in accordance with Indian government policies.

Integral to achieving this is the development and support for nationwide higher education administration, leadership and management capacity building for: strategic awareness to plan for change, improvement and growth; developing attitudes and approaches that facilitate sustainable change and growth; and strengthening aptitude to engage in critical analysis for implementing and monitoring change and sustainable growth. In terms of the student experience in the Indian higher education context, expanding applied, multi-sited, mixed-method, multidisciplinary and interdisciplinary research studies, conducted collaboratively by higher education practitioners, could inform and enhance the development and quality of teaching and learning provision. Strategically resourced national and regional opportunities for applied research may also offer further reflective and analytical insights into the disaggregated social equity profile of access, retention and progression across and within different disciplines. This may reveal much more enriched perspectives on students' engagement with teaching and learning practices (including technology enhanced learning), curriculum and assessment in order to strengthen and advance inclusivity and the quality of student experience within diverse Indian higher education institutions.

References

Agarwal, P. (2007) India in the Context of International Student Circulation, in De Wit, H. (Ed.), *The Dynamics of International Student Circulation in a Global context.* pp. 83–112. Rotterdam and Taipei: Sense Publishers.

Agarwal, P. (2009) *Indian Higher Education: Envisioning the Future.* New Delhi: Sage Publications.

Andrade, M. S. and Evans, N. W. (2009) *International Students. Strengthening a Critical Resource.* Lanham, MD: Rowman & Littlefield Education.

Bateman, M. (2008) *India or Philippines: Which Country is Asia's Largest English-speaking Nation?* Available at: www.groundreport.com/Arts (accessed 23/10/ 2011).

Brennan, J., King, R. and Lebeau, Y. (2004) *The Role of Universities in the Transformation of Societies.* Available at: www.open.ac.uk/cheri/documents/transf-final-report.pdf (accessed 23/10/ 2011).

Business Standard (2011a) *Pitroda for Early Passage Higher Education Bills.* Available at: www.business-standard.com/india/news/pitroda-for-early-passagehigher-education-bills/455302/ (accessed 23/10/2011).

Business Standard (2011b) *Foreign Universities in India.* Available at: www.icbse.com/ universities/foreign/ (accessed 23/10/2011).

Chakrabarti, R., Bartning, A. Sengupta, S. (2010) Developing Globally Compatible Institutional Infrastructures for Indian Higher Education. *Journal of Studies in International Education* 14(2), 183–199

Cheney, G., Ruzzi, B. and Muralidharan, K. (2006) *A Profile of the Indian Education System.* Washington: National Centre on Education and the Economy.

Confederation of Indian Industry (CII) (2012) Available at: www.cii.in (accessed 15/01/ 2012).

De Wit, H. (Ed) (2007) *The Dynamics of International Student Circulation in a Global context.* Rotterdam and Taipei: Sense Publishers.

Dhawan, H. (2012) Cabinet May Consider Accreditation Bill Today. *The Times of India Education* 10 May, New Delhi.

Dongaonkar, D. and Rai Negi, U. (2009) *International Students in Indian Universities.* Delhi: Association of Indian Universities.

Education Consultants India Limited Report (2011) Available at: http://edcilindia.in (accessed 15/01/2012).

Educations.com (2011) *Study in India.* Available at: www.educations.com/Study_in_India__d2067.html (accessed 15/01/2012).

Financial Express (2011) The Education System in India needs to be Transformed. 8 August, New Delhi.

Freeman, R. (2005) 'Does Globalization of the Scientific/Engineering Workforce Threaten U.S. Economic Leadership? *NBER Working Papers* 11457. Cambridge, MA: National Bureau of Economic Research, Inc.

Gunjan, S. (2011) Should I go or should I stay?: The making of a 'good' or 'bad' international student migrant. *Compare: A Journal of Comparative and International Education* 41(6), 850–853.

Hattangdi, A. and Ghosh, A. (2008) *Enhancing the Quality and Accessibility of Higher Education Through the Use of Information and Communication Technology.* Available at: http://www.iitk.ac.in/infocell/announce/convention/papers/Strategy%20Learning-01-Ashish%20Hattangdi,%20%20Atanu%20Ghosh.pdf (accessed 15/01/2012).

Hindustan Times Reporter (2011). At IIT-Delhi, More Girls than Boys in Engineering. 14 August, New Delhi.

India Edunews (2010) *Cabinet Approves Setting up of a National Knowledge Network.* Available at: www.indiaedunews.net/Today/Cabinet_approves_setting_up_of_a_'National_Knowledge_Network'_10332/ (accessed 15/01/ 2012).

Indian Council for Cultural Relations (2010a) *Scholarship Schemes.* Available at: www.iccrindia.net/scholarshipschemes.html (accessed 15/01/2012).

Indian Council for Cultural Relations (2010b) *Welfare of International Students.* Available at: www.iccrindia.net/studentwelfare.html (accessed 15/01/ 2012).

Indian Institute of Public Administration (2010) *IIPA News: 20/02/2010.* Available at: www.iipa.ernet.in/upload/IIPA-News%20Feb–2010-.pdf (accessed 15/01/ 2012).

Indian Institute of Technology Delhi (2011) Available from: www.iitd.ac.in/;IIT-JEE2011 (accessed 21/11/2011).

Indira Gandhi National Open University (2011) Available from: www.ignou.ac.in (accessed 14/01/2012).

Iyer, P. (2012) A Study of Students' Interaction in Higher Education in the Socio-cultural Context, in Thornton, M. and Wankhede, G. (Eds), *Widening Participation and Social Cohesion amongst Diverse, Disadvantaged and Minority Groups in Higher Education.* pp 47–53. Mumbai: TISS.

Jawaharlal Nehru University (2012) *International Students Association.* Available at: www.jnu.ac.in/main.asp?sendval=ISA (accessed 15/01/2012).

Kaul, S. (2006) *Higher Education in India: Seizing the Opportunity.* Available at: www. icrier.org/pdf/wp_179.pdf (accessed 21/09/2011).

Lahiri, K. (2004) *Higher Education Framework in India: From Preindependence to Post Independence.* Social Science Research Network (SSRN). Available at: http://ssrn. com/abstract=871024 or http://dx.doi.org/10.2139/ssrn.871024 (accessed 21/09/ 2011).

Lin, S. and Yen, E. (Eds.) (2011) *Data Driven e-Science: Use Cases and Successful Applications of Distributed Computing Infrastructure.* New York: Springer-Verlag Inc.

Mattoo, A. (2009) Greater Priorities – The Time Has Come for India to Transform Higher Education. *The Telegraph*, 18 June, Calcutta.

Ministry of Communications and Information Technology, Government of India. (2012) Available at: www.mit.gov.in/content/national-knowledge-network (accessed 15/01/ 2012).

Montgomery, C. (2010) *Understanding the International Student Experience.* New York: Palgrave/Macmillan.

Nalanda Digital Library (2012) Available at: Nalanda.nitc.ac.in (accessed 14/01/2012).

Narlikar, J. (2003) *The Scientific Edge: The Indian Scientist from Vedic to Modern Times.* New Delhi: Penguin Books.

National Knowledge Network Programme and Implementation Unit (2012) Available at: www.nkn.in (accessed 15/01/ 2012).

National Policy on Skill Development (2009) Available at: www.psscive.nic.in/pdf/ National%20Skill%20 Development%20Policy.pdf (accessed 14/01/2012).

Pathak, K. (2011). *Centre to Address Foreign University Bill Corpus Hurdle.* Available: www.business-standard.com/india/news/centre-to-address-foreign-university-bill-corpus-hurdle/445483/ (accessed 28/11/ 2011).

Planning Commission Report of the Task Force on Employment Opportunities (2001) Available at: http://planningcommission.nic.in/aboutus/taskforce/tf_skilldev.pdf (accessed 15/01/2012).

Prakash, V. (2005) *Internationalization of Higher Education: The Indian Context.* Paris: International Institute for Education Planning, UNESCO

Sachdeva, S. (1999) *Education Scenario and Needs in India – Planning Commission.* Available at: planningcommission.nic.in/reports/sereport/ser/vision2025/ edu2025.pdf (accessed 14/01/ 2012).

Scharfe, H. (2002) *Education in Ancient India.* Koln: Brill.

SRM University (2011) Available at: www.srmuniv.ac.in/admission.php?page=twining/ twining_overview (accessed 11/11/2011).

Stella, A. (2001) *Quality Assurance in Indian Higher Education: Issues of Impact and Future Perspectives.* New Delhi: Allied Publishers.

The Economic Times (2010) *Experts Speak on Foreign Educational Institution Bill.* 16 March, New Delhi.

The Times of India (2007) *Tax Students Taking up Foreign Jobs: House Panel.* 20 August, New Delhi.

The Times of India (2011) *In a League of its Own.* 28 May, New Delhi.

Thorat, S. (2008) Emerging Issues in Higher Education – Approach and Strategy in 11th Plan, in *Higher Education in India – Issues Related to Expansion, Inclusiveness, Quality and Finance.* New Delhi: University Grants Commission.

Thorat, S. and Kumar, N. (Eds.) (2008) *In Search of Inclusive Policy: Addressing Graded Inequality*, Jaipur: Rawat Publishers.

Thornton, M. and Wankhede, G. (Eds.) (2012) *Widening Participation and Social Cohesion amongst Diverse, Disadvantaged and Minority Groups in Higher Education*. Mumbai: TISS.

Tilak, J. (2004) Absence of Policy and Perspective in Higher Education, *Economic and Political Weekly* 39(21), 2159–2164.

Tilak, J. (2005) Higher Education in Trishanku. *Economic and Political Weekly* 40(37), 4029–4037.

Umashankar, V. and Dutta, K. (2007) Balanced Scorecards in Managing Higher Education Institutions: An Indian Perspective, *International Journal of Educational Management* 21(1), 54–67.

UNESCO Institute for Statistics (2011) Available at: www.uis.unesco.org/Education/Pages/ged–2011.aspx (accessed 21/11/ 2011).

University Grants Commission (UGC) (2003) *Higher Education in India*. Available at: www.ugc.ac.in/pub/heindia.pdf. (accessed 3/10/ 2011).

University Grants Commission (UGC) (2005) *Annual Report 2004/2005*. New Delhi: UGC.

University Grants Commission (UGC) (2010) *Annual Report*. New Delhi: UGC.

University Grants Commission (UGC) (2011a) *Annual Report*. New Delhi: UGC.

University Grants Commission (UGC) (2011b) *Inclusive and Qualitative Expansion of Higher Education 12th Five-Year Plan, 2012–2017*. New Delhi: UGC.

University of Delhi (2011) Available at: www.du.ac.in/;SOL.du.ac.in/about us.aspx (accessed 21/11/ 2011).

University of Delhi (2012) *Information Bulletin Foreign Students*. Available at: http://du.ac.in/fileadmin/DU/students/Pdf/du/inform_bulletin_foreign.pdf   (accessed 14/03/ 2012).

Vidyapeetham, A. V. (2012) *International Admissions*. Available at: www.amrita.edu/admissions/international-admissions.php (accessed 15/01/2012).

Vishnoi, A. (2009) *IGNOU Draws Most Foreign Students to India: Study*. 20 March. Available at: www.indianexpress.com/news/ignou-draws-most-foreign-students-to-india/436741/ (accessed 15/01/2012).

Viswanathan, G. (1990) *Masks of Conquest: Literary Study and British Rule in India*. London: Faber and Faber.

12

The Student Experience in China

SHUIYUN LIU

Chinese higher education has gradually changed its elitist nature since its birth a century ago and embarked on the internationally recognised path of massification of higher education as a result of the dramatic expansion of enrolment since the end of the 1990s. Currently, China has the largest higher education system in the world. In 2009, there were 2305 accredited universities and colleges with a total student enrolment of 21.4 million (Ministry of Education [MOE] 2009). Among these 2305 institutions, there are 1090 universities providing four-year undergraduate programmes with bachelor's degrees (*benke*), and the other 1215 colleges providing two- or three- year professional programmes (*zhuanke*) leading to diplomas. Most of these universities and colleges are public (1649), while only 656 of them are private. The Chinese central and local governments play the key role in directing the development of public higher education, and the autonomy enjoyed by these universities and colleges is relatively low. Students must pass the national higher education entrance examination (*gaokao*) before they are able to be enrolled into these universities and colleges, both public and private.

Like higher education institutions in other countries, Chinese universities and colleges have made great efforts to integrate themselves into the trend of internationalisation of higher education, especially since China joined the World Trade Organization (WTO) in 2001. Many strategies have been used to enhance international communication and cooperation, such as sending Chinese students and scholars to study and research abroad, recruiting foreign students to study in Chinese universities, inviting foreign researchers to work in Chinese universities, encouraging Chinese students studying abroad to return to China, holding international conferences and forums, and establishing cooperative programmes with foreign higher education providers. In 2009, there were about 229,300 students and scholars studying abroad. Among them, about 12,000 were state-funded, about 7200 were employer-funded, and the remaining students were self-funded (MOE 2011a). In the same year, a total of 108, 300 students and scholars returned from studying overseas (MOE 2011a).

Moreover, in order to promote Chinese language and culture, Chinese government started to establish Confucius Institutes across the world. Chinese universities also began to recruit foreign students. By the end of 2009, 282 Confucius Institutes and 272 Confucius Classrooms had been established in 88 countries and regions, and they were teaching roughly 260,000 students in 2009 (Hanban 2009). In the same year, more than 238,000 foreign students from 190 countries were recruited to 610 Chinese universities, colleges and research institutes (MOE 2011b). Among them, about 18,000 students benefited from the Chinese Government Scholarship, which covers tuition fees and/or living costs of students (MOE 2011b). Accompanying the development of international education, the recognition of international diplomas has also been initiated in China since the end of the 1980s. By the end of 2009, China had signed the agreement for the mutual recognition of academic diplomas and qualifications with 35 countries (China Academic Degrees and Graduation Education Information 2011). Furthermore, international influence can also be observed inside Chinese universities. For example, Chinese universities and colleges have enhanced foreign language training and established bilingual curricula. They have also tried to adjust the teaching and learning strategies to conform to traditions in Western education.

Many researchers have discussed the influence of internationalisation on Chinese higher education, while students' experience in this process has not been discussed adequately. This chapter explores the experience of Chinese students studying abroad, foreign students in China, and the Chinese students in domestic campuses, respectively, in the context of internationalisation. The previous studies on the experience of these three groups of students are reviewed (i.e. Holmes 2004; Chen 2007; Campbell and Li 2008; Xie and Liu 2010; Ding 2010), as the main evidence source of this chapter. Through examining their learning experience, especially the challenges they are facing in terms of language and pedagogy, the impact of internationalisation on students is explored in-depth. The similarities and differences among the experience of these three groups are also analysed.

The Experience of Chinese Students Internationally

China is the largest source country of overseas students in the world. As mentioned above, there were about 229,000 students and scholars studying abroad in 2009. English-speaking countries are the main destinations of Chinese students studying abroad. The top ten destinations of Chinese overseas students are, in order, the US, Australia, the UK, South Korea, Japan, Canada, Singapore, New Zealand, France and Russia (MOE 2011a).

Studying in a different country can be an exciting and challenging experience for international students, who often face many adjustment problems (Ward and Kennedy 1993; Campbell and Li 2008). The literature in the area of international students' adaptation has generally distinguished between psychological, soci-ocultural and academic adjustment (Zhou and Todman 2009). Studies found that international students' adjustment course was related to the cultural differ-ence between their own countries and the host countries (the greater cultural difference, the more difficult for students to adapt), the study environments (such as the supporting facilities for international students in the host universi-ties), and the characteristics of students per se (their motivation and abilities of adaptation). This paper focuses on the academic challenge for Chinese students studying abroad and their adjustment. Students in English-speaking countries (including the UK, Australia, New Zealand, the US, Canada, etc.) are used as an example. The difficulties that Chinese students in these countries are facing might be individual and context-dependent. Notwithstanding, this paper tries to show the widely acknowledged difficulties for Chinese students studying in English-speaking countries. Literature in this area shows that the academic shock for Chinese students primarily results from the difficulties in using the English language and the differences in the approaches to teaching and learning, such as independent learning, class participation of students, critical thinking and group work (Gu and Schweisfurth 2006).

Language Difficulties

Language difficulties are often cited in the literature as one of the biggest barriers for Chinese students' integration into Western education (Li et al. 2002; Salter-Dvorak 2004; Hills and Thom 2005). The language barriers prevent international students from effectively communicating with lecturers and other students, listening to lectures, following instructions, under-standing assessment criteria and procedures, taking notes, reading textbooks, completing assignments, and doing exams and tests (Andrade 2006; Campbell and Li 2008; Tian and Lowe 2009). The difficulties involve various dimensions of using language, including listening, speaking, reading and writing.

Listening and Speaking

Studies found that Chinese students had inadequate listening comprehension for extended lectures (Holmes 2004). Chinese students' listening and under-standing skills did not equip them for extended native-speaker delivery in lecture contexts (Du-Babcock 2002). Professors' accents and idiomatic styles posed further problems (Holmes 2004). They became particularly confused when teachers departed from notes projected overhead and began to enrich lectures by using humour and examples (Holmes 2004; Tian and Lowe 2009). At the same time, studies show that Chinese students' oral communication skills in English were also not adequate (Andrade 2006). They lacked confi-dence in their English speaking abilities and feared making mistakes (Senyshyn et al. 2000), and thus they were reluctant to ask lecturers for clarification or elaboration in class and to communicate with other students. The language difficulties inhibited their class participation (Tompson and Tompson 1996; Robertson et al. 2000).

Reading and Writing

The reading skills of Chinese students are also perceived to be inadequate to meet the requirements of the Western learning environment. Holmes (2004) found that Chinese students were surprised when they first arrived at the number of reading assignments given in Western universities. Limited by their English skills, they had to read more slowly than their native speaking classmates and read texts multiple times. This was time-consuming, and required a high level of abstraction that Chinese students were unfamiliar with (Holmes 2004). Moreover, Chinese students tended to regard writing assignments, essays and reports as the top academic difficulty (Campbell and Li 2008). Besides the inadequate language proficiency, the conventions of academic writing in Western countries were the greatest barrier for Chinese students (Holmes 2004; Campbell and Li 2008). They had no prior knowledge of Western academic conventions, such as writing literature reviews, critical reviews and essays, field research reports, research proposals, case study analysis, and making references (Andrade 2006), since these are not the regular academic tasks in Chinese universities.

Facing the language skills-related difficulties, students have made efforts to improve their English. Chinese students have often thought 'it would be easy to learn English in English-speaking countries', but after their arrival they have realised that this perception was far from correct (Zhang and Brunton 2007). Notwithstanding, their English is believed to have improved to various extents since they arrived in Western countries (Campbell and Li 2008). Studies found that for students who stayed longer in the English-speaking world, the language barrier for them tended to be less (Cheng and Erben 2011). On the other hand, Chinese students have also developed some strategies to cope with the language barriers (Holmes 2004). For example, many students tend to depend on same-culture classmates, pre-read, highlight and mark textbooks rather than taking notes, prioritise what to read, manage time more effectively and read only the abstract and conclusion or only the introduction and summaries in a book instead of every chapter (Holmes 2004). These strategies are believed to be helpful for them to bypass the language barrier and gain academic success.

Teaching and Learning

Pedagogy is context-dependent and value-laden (Ellsworth 1997). It is shaped by the specific cultural values and ideology suited to the society where it originates

(Barrow 1990; Campbell and Li 2008). Several researchers have noted differences in the learning styles between China and Western countries (Hammond and Gao 2002; Greenholz 2003; Holmes 2004). Western education is generally described as Socratic, where knowledge is generated or co-constructed through a process of questioning and evaluation of beliefs; problem solving and critical thinking skills are considered important (Greenholz 2003). Hammond and Gao (2002) described this as a dialogic learning model. The power distance between teachers and students is relatively low. Students are expected to be independent learners, to think critically, to challenge their teachers, and to be active participants in the class (Hofstede 1980). The learning process tends to be 'holistic, interactive, cooperative and diversified, emphasising critical thinking, real time evaluation, hands-on experience and overall education quality' (Hammond and Gao 2002: 228). Relatively speaking, the Confucian tradition regards knowledge as being passively absorbed by students in a more dialectic model. Chinese learners have been brought up to respect knowledge and wisdom (Chan 1999). The power distance between teachers and students is very high. Teachers direct the learning process and demand a high level of respect, and students are expected to be passive in class, only speaking by invitation (Hofstede 1980). The learning process tends to be 'fragmented, linear, competition-oriented, and authority-centered' (Hammond and Gao 2002: 228–229). Thus, with such big differences between the Western and Chinese teaching approaches, Chinese students arriving in Western classrooms are likely to experience learning and communication dislocation and they have to make every effort to adapt to the Western academic discourse (Holmes 2004; Kingston and Forland 2008). The adaptation mainly involves developing independent learning, class participation, critical thinking, and group discussion and group work.

Independent Learning

Chinese students have been used to being directed and pushed by teachers. As reported in a recent study, after they came into the new learning environment, the lecturers adopted some teaching methods to facilitate their independent learning skills, which were incompatible with their expectations; in this situation, they admitted that they felt disheartened (Campbell and Li 2008). However, after some time, when they realised that independent learning is important, they endeavoured to adapt to the new situation. Studies found that a profound change in Chinese students is the greatly increased independent learning skills (Campbell and Li 2008). This change was also noticed by the lecturers in Western universities. For example, British lecturers in the UK study have noticed that their Chinese students have started to take the initiative in doing research from the second semester (Gu and Schweisfurth 2006).

Class Participation

Chinese students were familiar with a one-way, directive communication style between teacher and students. They were often surprised by the dialogic nature of classroom communication in Western universities (Holmes 2004). Studies found that most Chinese students like the flat rather than hierarchical teacher–student relationships and felt satisfied with the patterns of teacher–student classroom interactions (Campbell and Li 2008). However, eliciting Chinese students' responses to these interactive activities seemed to be very difficult. Many students reported that they did not know how to involve themselves in the class learning activities. They were reluctant to ask questions during a lecture (Kingston and Forland 2008), and they felt uncomfortable when they were given opportunities to participate in classroom activities (Campbell and Li 2008).

Studies found that professors and students often had different views in terms of this adjustment challenge. International students attributed their lack of participation to language weaknesses and sensitivity to their ability (Robertson et al. 2000). Professors, conversely, perceived this lack of involvement to be cultural rather than linguistic (Tompson and Tompson 1996; Andrade 2006). Chinese students were not used to expressing their opinions in public, especially challenging their teachers, which is regarded as being disrespectful in Chinese culture (Chan 1999). On the whole, students enjoyed the interactive teaching approaches in Western universities, but they were reluctant to participate and contribute (Huang 2005; Campbell and Li 2008). When it comes to the effectiveness of the student-centred teaching approaches, studies found that not many Chinese students thought the student-driven teaching method was a more effective way for them to learn than the traditional teacher-centred methods. 'Uncertainty about the accuracy of the acquired knowledge' was most frequently mentioned by the respondents in Huang's (2005) research. This can be regarded as another reason why the Chinese students were not active in class participation. Chinese students tend to be more pragmatic in evaluating ideas than their Western counterparts (Huang 2008).

Critical Thinking

The technique of critical analysis, requiring the writer to discuss the strengths and weaknesses of an argument, was a great mystery to Chinese students especially when they first arrived in Western countries. Studies in this field show that Chinese students did not really understand the term and, instead, confused it with criticism or an attack on a person for the ideas they hold (Holmes 2004). Criticism of another person results in loss of face, which is an unacceptable communication practice in China (Gao and Ting-Toomey 1998). Chinese students have to reconstruct and renegotiate their primary learning and communication styles to accommodate the new way of thinking. Most students felt that they were learning to question knowledge and society (Holmes 2004). The process of reconstruction and renegotiation was best encapsulated by a Chinese student in Holmes's study:

> The education system here is different and I think opened my mind ... I find I'm now more critical in thinking ... If I read something I can have some very different thinking, and I think it's some valuable thinking.
>
> (2004, 303)

Group Discussion and Group Work

The teaching approaches of group discussion and teamwork are also not common in the Chinese education system. Research in this area shows that most Chinese students highly valued group discussions where they could interact with students from other cultures and backgrounds (Campbell and Li 2008; Kingston and Forland 2008). They saw them as opportunities to improve their English language skills, enhance their cultural understanding through such intercultural encounters, broaden the understanding of the course or assessment-related issues, and develop their negotiating, teamwork and inter-personal communication skills, and possibly make friends (Campbell and Li 2008; Kingston and Forland 2008). Staff also commented that though there was an initial dislike for group discussions, international students were highly adaptive and grew to enjoy them, as highlighted by Hills and Thom (2005).

However, some other studies also reported that rather than promoting intercultural exchange and understanding, intercultural group-based learning activities could easily become a source of discomfort and anger for some students (Tian and Lowe 2009). Sources of discomfort included a sense of lacking appropriate background knowledge that would allow them to understand what was being discussed in the group and enable them to make a contribution. Combined with a lack of confidence to engage in discussions with native English speakers in the group, Chinese students tended to perceive marginalisation within the group. Moreover, students also hold an intensely negative view about group assignments that require students to complete an assigned task as a group with shared marks (Campbell and Li 2006). This might be because the Asian education systems emphasise competition among students, and their teamwork skills are often neglected in student assessment (Huang 2005).

The differences of pedagogy between Western and Eastern countries have not been realised adequately by the host universities. Research has indicated that lecturers tended to assume that the learning process and activities valued in the host Western environment represent universal norms and that any deviations from it are cognitive, behavioural or social deficits (Volet

1999; Gu and Schweisfurth 2006; Campbell and Li 2006). They often ignored the training and time needed for Chinese students to adapt and to transfer their skills acquired in China. Thus, it became students' responsibility alone 'to adapt, to cross-culturally manage themselves ... to manage cultural differences at the interpersonal level ... and institutional level' (Sizoo and Serrie 2004: 161), sink or swim. Most Chinese students reported that they had adapted well to the new learning environments, and they simultaneously retained their own cultural traits, such as high learning expectations, achieving motivations, a strong sense of competition, and deep respect for teachers (Campbell and Li 2008). In the process of cultural adaptation, on the one hand, they made every attempt to adapt to the new learning culture; on the other hand, they tried to make best use of the learning skills acquired in China to succeed academically.

The Experience of Foreign Students in China

The earliest international students in China, following the founding of the PRC, were entirely from communist countries (Chen 1965). In 1950, Tsinghua University in Beijing received the first group of 33 students from East Europe, which represented the beginning of international student education in China (Dong and Chapman 2008). Since China became a member of WTO, the Chinese government has paid more and more attention to the development of international education. The number of foreign students recruited in Chinese universities has also increased steadily. In 2009, about 238,000 foreign students came to China to study, an increase of about 6.57 per cent from 2008. However, the development of international education in China is not satisfactory (Yao 2010; Xie and Jiao 2010). Firstly, the majority of the foreign students enrolled in Chinese universities and colleges came from Asian countries, although the number of students from Western countries has also increased (Yao 2010). As shown in Table 12.1, 67.8 per cent of the foreign students in China in 2009 were Asian. South Korea, the US, Japan, Vietnam and Thailand are the top five countries that have the largest numbers of international students in China (MOE 2011b). Furthermore, although the foreign students coming to China for degree education has increased significantly, the majority of them came for short-term training and other non-degree education (67.7 per cent in 2009). The percentage for language training is particularly high.

Compared with Western countries, international education in China was initiated quite late and there is still plenty of room for improvement. In-depth academic research on this topic is also inadequate. According to the published research papers, the main challenges that foreign students in China are facing also concentrate on the language barriers and the approaches of teaching and learning (Xie and Liu 2010; Ding 2010).

Table 12.1 Foreign students enrolled in China in 2009

Foreign students in China			%
Regions	Asia	161,605	67.84
	Africa	12,436	5.22
	America	25,557	10.73
	Europe	35,876	15.06
	Oceania	2,710	1.14
	Total	238,184	
Levels of training	Postgraduate	18,978	7.97
	Undergraduate	74,472	31.26
	Non-degree education	144,734	67.77

Source: MOE 2011b.

Language Barriers

Higher education courses provided in China are mainly taught in Chinese, and there are limited English courses. Studies in this field show that most of the foreign students in China had to overcome big language barriers (Xie and Liu 2010). The inadequate language proficiency hindered them in understanding the lectures and in achieving academic success, especially for students majoring in the subjects of linguistics, humanities and social science. It has also challenged them to communicate with domestic students, especially to make friends with them. Ding (2010) conducted a questionnaire survey in Shanghai and investigated about 450 foreign students studying there. He found that 84.8 per cent of the respondents were enrolled in Chinese programmes while only 11.0 per cent of them are in English programmes. Most foreign students were facing great language challenges, and only less than 10 per cent of the respondents thought it was easy to learn in Chinese. In this case, many researchers suggested that Chinese universities should develop English-teaching courses for international students. However, Ding's (2010) investigation shows that most foreign students still expected to learn in Chinese despite these difficulties, since learning Chinese is one of the most important reasons why they chose China as their study destination.

The foreign students reported that their Chinese language improvement was not as great as expected. In Ding's (2010) research, only 33 per cent of the respondents felt satisfied with their language improvement, while 29.9 per cent of them were not satisfied with it. Compared with listening, speaking and reading, students felt that their improvement in writing was relatively low (Xie and Liu 2010). They thought that the language training provided in their universities was far from adequate (Ding 2010). The training for writing was particularly weak (Ding 2010). Their low writing proficiency was a significant barrier for them in completing their assignments and theses. Thus, they indicated that it would be better if they could have more time to learn Chinese before they started their professional learning, and universities could provide more effective language training for them.

Teaching and Learning

The satisfaction of foreign students with the teaching quality in China is relatively low, compared with the perception of international students in Western countries, such as the UK and Australia (Ding 2010). In Ding's (2010) research, only 32 per cent of the respondents felt satisfied with the teaching quality provision in their universities. They felt that the teaching facilities, such as multimedia facilities in classrooms, were adequate and high quality (Xie and Liu 2010). However, the curriculum and teaching methods were very disappointing. They reported that there were very few interactive activities in the classroom, and students were expected to learn by rote. Teachers just followed the textbooks; in this case, students felt that they could just read textbooks instead of attending the courses. They expected to see diverse teaching methods, which would increase their learning motivation. In Chinese classes, students are expected to repeat what teachers have said, without any independent thinking. Foreign students, especially those from Western countries, felt particularly unsatisfied with this. On the whole, the difference in pedagogy became a great obstacle for the effective learning of foreign students in China.

Unlike the Chinese students studying in English-speaking countries, the foreign students in China did not think the teaching methods used by Chinese teachers were enjoyable or effective, and thus they did not have much motivation to adapt to the Chinese academic environment. As a result, some of them chose to be absent from classes. Foreign students' academic performance was fairly low, according to Ding's (2010) research. Chinese teachers and foreign students have different perspectives in terms of the low academic performance. According to Ding's (2010) investigation teachers thought that the foreign students were not as intelligent and diligent as domestic students. However, the foreign students did not agree with this. They felt that Chinese teachers discriminated against them; did not really understand their difficulties in making the intercultural adjustment; and did not provide sufficient support for them. In addition, the administration provided by the international offices in Chinese universities was particularly criticised by foreign students (Xie and Liu 2010; Ding 2010). For example, foreign students are divided from domestic students in accommodation, which aims to provide better accommodation for foreign students. It turns out that this strategy has made their intercultural adjustment more difficult (Ding, 2010).

According to the perspectives of the foreign students in China, on the one hand, they were interested in Chinese culture and language, and thus they were keen to come to study in China. On the other hand, they were not satisfied with the education quality provided by Chinese universities. They did not have much motivation to adapt to the teaching and learning patterns in Chinese classes. This might be one of the reasons why a majority of foreign students came to China for language training instead of learning professional knowledge.

The Experience of Domestic Students in China

The home students are also not isolated from the influence of internationalisation. In order to facilitate international communication and cooperation, Chinese universities have enhanced language training. Every Chinese undergraduate student has to pass the College English Test Band Four before they get their bachelor degree. Many scholars criticised Chinese students for spending too much time on learning English instead of professional knowledge and skills (He and Zhang 2005). The Western curriculum and pedagogy also have had a significant impact on Chinese classrooms. Universities have started to import foreign textbooks and initiated bilingual curricula. Many strategies have also been used to encourage teachers to use student-centred teaching approaches. This section takes bilingual curricula and student-centred teaching approaches as examples to explore the impact of internationalisation on the experience of domestic students in China.

Bilingual Curricula

In order to become more internationally connected, Chinese higher education institutions have begun to use bilingual instruction (in most cases, referring to Chinese and English) in teaching since the beginning of the 21st century. An initiative, *Some suggestions to improve the quality of undergraduate education* was launched by the MOE in 2001. It indicates that in the coming three years, from 5 to 10 per cent of all the curricula in universities must be taught bilingually, especially in such areas as biology, information science, international trade and law (MOE 2001). The establishment of bilingual curricula requires importing original English textbooks. Consequently, about ten of the top-ranked universities in China decided to buy and use the textbooks being used in Harvard University, Stanford University and MIT in 2002 (Huang 2003). The list of materials included natural science, engineering and medicine as well as law, economics and management.

From the students' perspective, compared with the textbooks compiled in China, they felt that the original English textbooks contained more cutting-edge knowledge and were illustrated with more examples (Su et al. 2002;

Chen 2007). These textbooks gave students a stronger learning motivation. The English textbooks were also more practice-oriented, which helped students to develop their problem-solving capabilities (Su et al. 2002). However, students also reported that some of the contents of the English textbooks were not related to the Chinese situation, which made it difficult for them to understand (Chen 2007). For instance, some cases provided in the law textbooks were difficult to understand for Chinese students without any Western background. In terms of the bilingual courses, most students were not satisfied with their quality (Wang et al. 2009). Students reported that they had to spend lots of time preparing for the bilingual courses, but they did not feel that their professional knowledge had been significantly improved. Without appropriate English skills, students had to pay more attention to understanding the language rather than the content. Thus, the border between 'learning through English' and 'learning English' has been blurred (Chen 2007; Wang et al. 2009). To some extent, the bilingual curriculum becomes another kind of English course. In addition, lacking qualified teachers is also regarded as one of the main reasons for the questionable quality of bilingual courses in China (Lu and Deng 2005; Chen 2007; Wang et al. 2009).

Student-centred Teaching Approaches

In the context of higher education globalisation, Chinese universities have made great efforts to produce high-level students with the capability of international competition. However, Chinese students' creative and practical capabilities are perceived to be particularly inadequate, compared with their Western counterparts (Liu 2011). In this case, the Chinese government and universities have encouraged teachers to abandon the traditional teaching and learning strategies and to apply the Western pedagogy in Chinese classrooms. The report, *The decision on deepening education reforms and enhancing the quality education* issued by the State Council in 1999 indicated that it was necessary to 'change the educational conceptions, reform the patterns of cultivating students, and use interactive teaching methods with discussions, to arouse students' independent thinking and creative spirits and to improve teaching qualities' (The State Council of People Republic of China 1999).

In this context, most Chinese universities have initiated their own regulations and/or incentive schemes to encourage teachers to use student-centred teaching approaches instead of the conventional teacher-centred approaches. Students are expected to learn by group discussion and team or independent work on research assignments. More innovative ways of student assessment have also been introduced, in order to develop students' critical thinking, creative spirits and practical abilities (Liu 2011).

The interaction between teachers and students in class was perceived as an interesting and beneficial experience by students and teachers, but the positive attitude towards student-centred teaching approaches did not result in a significant change of teaching methods. On the one hand, there are many difficulties in implementing the new teaching methods (Liu 2011). For example, the large class size makes it difficult for teachers to organise group discussions in classes. Teachers have been trained by the traditional teacher-centred methods and thus they do not like (or do not know how) to use the student-centred approaches. Students are also not active in expressing their own ideas in classes. This might be rooted in the traditional Confucius culture, which does not encourage students to challenge their teachers; and it could also be attributed to their school education, which adopted traditional teaching methods to train them.

On the other hand, it is debatable whether the interactive teaching and learning activities could produce better teaching effectiveness than the traditional methods (Liu 2011). Many Chinese teachers stressed that the traditional teaching approaches had their own advantages. The basic subject knowledge needs to be imparted to students. Without the basic knowledge, the communication between teachers and students would be shallow. This perception originates from the Confucian idea that understanding should be based on the reading of classics (Hammond and Gao 2002). Thus, Chinese teachers did not think a radical change from teacher-centred to student-centred teaching approaches was appropriate. The common consequence was that the new teaching methods were integrated into the traditional ones in order to develop an approach that was suitable and appropriate in their classes. The changing step was relatively slow, and depended largely on the intention of frontline teachers and their capabilities of doing this.

In summary, Chinese universities have strong ambitions to integrate themselves into the trend of internationalisation. Many strategies have been adopted by the Chinese government and universities to facilitate the process of learning Western curricula and teaching approaches. However, these strategies were not very effective at the level of classroom activities. On the one hand, teachers did not think the Western curricula and pedagogy were effective ways of delivering knowledge and they were not completely suitable for the Chinese classes. On the other hand, the conditions of adopting the Western curricula and pedagogy are inadequate. Both the capabilities of frontline teachers and the habits of students are very difficult to change in the short term. On the whole, the language training has indeed enhanced the international communication skills of Chinese students. However, the adjustment in terms of curricula and pedagogy did not go well.

Reflections

In the context of internationalisation, the three groups of students discussed in this chapter all face the challenges of language and pedagogy. International students, both the Chinese students studying in other countries and the foreign students coming to China, had to pass the language barrier and adapt themselves to the new academic norms. Influenced by the trend of internationalisation, English curricula and Western teaching approaches also entered Chinese classrooms, and challenged the habits of the domestic teachers and students.

Language and pedagogy are not isolated but interrelated factors influencing students' academic achievement. On the one hand, proficient language is the prerequisite for international students to understand new academic conventions and to enable them to get involved in the teaching and learning activities, such as group discussion and class participation. On the other hand, part of the language difficulties, especially writing, also originates from unfamiliarity with the new academic norms and requirements. Both the Chinese students studying abroad and the foreign students in China indicated that their language had improved to various extents.

Compared with the skills-related language improvement, the adjustment to new pedagogy was relatively slow. Pedagogy is shaped by the specific cultural values and ideology suited to the society where it originates (Barrow 1990). Teachers enacting pedagogies use the cultural conventions, norms and canons to transmit and reinforce the cultural values. International students, equipped with little knowledge of the new norms and conventions, found it difficult to make sense of it in the unmarked terrain. Meeting the entrance requirements of English language standards did not ensure that they were well prepared to make adjustments to succeed in the new educational system (Jepson et al. 2002). One of the ways of helping those adjusting to a new learning culture is to be aware of the difference between Western and Eastern pedagogies, and to provide intensive and ongoing training to international students to help them boost their levels of academic literacy, although the process of academic enculturation could never be completed.

Although the three groups of students discussed in this chapter all face the challenge of language and pedagogy, their experiences are not the same. In general, irrespective of the various difficulties Chinese learners had encountered in intercultural settings, their determination to learn and willingness to change were quite strong. The foreign students in China were keen to learn Chinese language and culture, but they did not regard the teaching and learning approaches used in Chinese classrooms as being effective, and so they did not have much motivation to adapt to the Chinese academic environment, thus their academic achievement was also not satisfactory. For the domestic students in China, the government and universities have initiated many strategies to give students access to Western textbooks and English curricula, and to encourage teachers to adopt Western teaching and learning approaches. However, these strategies seemed not as effective as expected; change at the teacher–student interaction level was not obvious.

The comparison between the experience of Chinese students studying abroad and the home students in China shows that the direct contact with the Western language and academic norms is helpful for the adjustment of students. The motivation of the Chinese students at Western universities to adapt is based in part on the fact that they have little choice: if they want to succeed, they need to understand and conform to the new learning environment. In this case, Chinese students choose to learn Western academic norms and approaches while keeping their own learning approaches that are beneficial to their academic achievement. In the Chinese settings, teachers are able to be selective in terms of how far they adapt the Western professional practice. They tend to integrate the new teaching methods into the traditional ones. To a large extent, whether the Western pedagogy can enter into Chinese classrooms is determined by the teachers' attitude to the Western teaching and learning approaches and their capabilities in using them. With the mediation of teachers, the chance of Chinese students to use Western learning approaches becomes relatively less and uncertain.

Furthermore, the comparison between the experience of Chinese students studying abroad and the foreign students in China reveals that the willingness and determination of students to make adjustment is significantly related to the extent to which students perceive the new teaching and learning approaches as being 'good'. Although it has never been proved that the Western pedagogy is more effective than the traditional Chinese way, this has become kind of common sense in the Western-dominated internationalisation. The opening up of China to the outside world, and, rightly or wrongly, the power of English language and education in Western countries, is part of the wider learning context. In this case, the adjustment of Chinese students to the Western academic environment can thus be seen as a highly rational response in a globalising world. In contrast, the willingness of the foreign students in Chinese classrooms to change is relatively low. There are more requests for the Chinese universities and teachers to adapt to the foreign students through establishing English programmes or changing teaching approaches.

By and large, the Chinese students in Western campuses have adapted to the Western language and teaching approaches relatively successfully. In contrast, the internationalisation of the domestic students in the Chinese campuses is kind of superficial, and the Chinese teaching approaches are not attractive enough for the foreign students coming to China to adjust to. In this case, it is necessary for Chinese universities to reform to enhance their internationalisation. On the one hand, part of the Chinese classes should adopt the Western teaching approaches. This could be mainly done by the teachers who have been trained abroad since they know more about the Western teaching approaches than the local teachers. As discussed above, teachers' attitude to the Western teaching approaches and their abilities in using them are very important factors determining the effectiveness of the Western teaching approaches in Chinese classes. In addition, English could be used as the teaching language and international textbooks might also be adopted in these kinds of classes, which is left for teachers to decide. Teachers should also be offered sufficient freedom to choose content and the ways of student assessment. In this case, the internationalisation of Chinese classes is expected to go deeper.

On the other hand, internationalisation has never been a one-way process of Westernisation; instead, it is a process of mutual learning. Thus, the traditional Chinese teaching approaches that are rooted in the Chinese culture should get more attention. More research should be done to find out the merits of the traditional teaching approaches and try to further develop them. In the long term, the advantages of Chinese teaching approaches are expected to be boosted and appreciated by the domestic and foreign students in Chinese campuses. Even though this would be rather difficult in the context of the Western-dominated internationalisation, Chinese universities should keep trying. If these reforms can be implemented successfully, two different kinds of teaching approaches, both Western and Chinese, will be available in the classes of Chinese universities. Which option will be left for students to choose. They could choose the teaching approaches that they prefer. As this research shows, only when students regard a certain kind of teaching approach as being effective, would they be willing to make adjustments.

Conclusions

In the context of higher education internationalisation, there are growing international flows of students. More and more Chinese students go abroad and increasing numbers of foreign students come to China to study. Originating from the different perceptions of knowledge and education, there is a big gap between the Western and the Chinese pedagogies. International students face the challenges of both language and academic norms. They need to learn the domestic language and to adapt to the new teaching and learning approaches. At the same time, the Western language, curricula and teaching approaches have also entered Chinese classrooms. This research shows that the skills-related language learning seems easier than the culture-related adjustment to new academic norms.

The Chinese students in Western campuses have adjusted to the new academic environment more successfully than the foreign and domestic students in Chinese campuses. The foreign students coming to China are interested in the Chinese language and culture, but they do not agree with the Chinese teaching approaches and are reluctant to make adjustments. New curricula and teaching and learning approaches imported from Western countries were not really accepted by the domestic teachers and students and thus have not resulted in a significant change. Therefore, there is still a long way to go before the Chinese universities could really become internationalised. This research shows that students' adjustment in the context of internationalisation is related to both their subjective intention and the objective conditions. Whether international students believe the language is useful and the teaching approaches are effective are two key factors determining their willingness to adjust to the new academic environment. Furthermore, whether the new academic norms are accessible and user-friendly is also very important, to enable the students to make adjustments. The effective training provided by universities is helpful for international students' adjustment. Based on the findings of this research, the author suggests developing two different academic norms simultaneously in Chinese universities and making both available. The option is left for students to choose the way they prefer.

References

Andrade, M.S., 2006. International students in English-speaking universities. *Journal of Research in International Education*, 5(2), 131–154.

Barrow, R., 1990. Culture, values and the language classroom. *In*: B. Harrison, ed. *Culture and language classroom*. Hong Kong: Modern English Publications and the British Council, 3–10.

Campbell, J.A. and Li, M., 2006. Asian Students' Perceptions of Group Work and Group Assignments in a New Zealand Tertiary Institution. *The Proceedings of EDU-COM Conference, Engagement and Empowerment*, 22–24 November 2006, Nong Khai, Thailand.

Campbell, J.A. and Li, M., 2008. Asian students' voices: An empirical study of Asian students' learning experiences at a New Zealand university. *Journal of Studies in International Education*, 12(4), 375–396.

Chan, S., 1999. The Chinese learner: A question of style. *Education + Training*, 41(6/7), 294–304.

Chen, S., 2007. The responses of university students to bilingual teaching: An investigation on a scientific and technology university. *Higher Education Exploration*, 3, 83–85.

Chen, T., 1965. Government encouragement and control of international education in communist China. *In*: S. Fraser, ed. *Governmental policy and international education*. New York: John Wiley & Sons, Inc, 111–133.

Cheng, R. and Erben. A., 2011. Language anxiety: Experiences of Chinese graduate students at U.S. higher institutions. *Journal of Studies in International Education*, 16 September.

China Academic Degrees and Graduation Education Information, 2011. *The list of the countries with agreement for the mutual recognition of academic diplomas and qualifications with China*. Available from: http://www.cdgdc.edu.cn/xwyyjsjyxx/dwjl/xwhr/ (accessed 1 November 2011).

Ding, X., 2010. What kind of education do international students in China need: On the basis of data from four universities in Shanghai. *Journal of Higher Education*, 31(6), 38–43.

Dong, L. and Chapman, D.W., 2008. The Chinese government scholarship program: An effective form of foreign assistance? *International Review of Education*, 54(2), 155–173.

Du-Babcock, B., 2002. Teaching a large class in Hong Kong. *Business Communication Quarterly*, 65(1), 80–88.

Ellsworth, E., 1997. *Teaching positions: Difference, pedagogy, and the power of address.* New York: Teachers College Press.

Gao, G. and Ting-Toomey, S., 1998. *Communicating effectively with the Chinese.* Thousand Oaks, CA: Sage.

Greenholz, J., 2003. Socratic teachers and Confucian learners: Examining the benefits and pitfalls of a year abroad. *Language and Intercultural Communication*, 3(2), 122–130.

Gu, Q. and Schweisfurth, M., 2006. Who adapts? Beyond cultural models of 'the' Chinese learner. *Language, Culture and Curriculum*, 19(1), 74–89.

Hammond, S. and Gao, H., 2002. Pan Gu's paradigm: Chinese education's return to holistic communication in learning. *In:* X. Lu, W. Jia, and R. Heisey, eds. *Chinese communication studies: Contexts and comparisons.* Westport, CT: Ablex, 227–244.

Hanban (Confucius Institute Headquarters), 2009. *2009 Annual Report.* Available from: http://www.hanban.edu.cn/report/pdf/2009_final.pdf (accessed 1 November 2011).

He, X and Zhang, X., 2005. The waste and harm of the 'great leap forward' of English. *China News Week*, 45. Available from: http://www.globalview.cn/ReadNews. asp?NewsID=6710 (accessed 1 November 2011).

Hills, S. and Thom, V., 2005. Crossing a multicultural divide: Teaching business strategy to students from culturally mixed backgrounds. *Journal of Studies in International Education*, 9(4), 316–336.

Hofstede, G., 1980. *Culture's consequences: International differences in work-related values.* Beverly Hills, CA: Sage.

Holmes, P., 2004. Negotiating differences in learning and intercultural communication: Ethnic Chinese students in a New Zealand university. *Business Communication Quarterly*, 67(3), 294–307.

Huang, F., 2003. Policy and practice of internationalization of higher education in China. *Journal of Studies in International Education*, 7(3), 225–240.

Huang, R., 2005. Chinese international students' perceptions of the problem-based learning experience. *Journal of Hospitality, Leisure, Sport and Tourism*, 4(2), 36–43.

Huang, R., 2008. *Critical thinking: Discussion from Chinese postgraduate international students and their lecturers. The Enhancing Series Case Studies: International Learning Experience.* Available from: http://www.heacademy.ac.uk/assets/bmaf/ documents/publications/Case_studies/huang.pdf (accessed 1 November 2011).

Jepson, M., Turner, T. and Calway, B., 2002. The transition of international students into the postgraduate study: An incremental approach. *Australian Association for Research in Education (AARE), International Education Research Conference*, 1–5 December 2002, Brisbane.

Kingston, E. and Forland, H., 2008. Bridging the gap in expectations between international students and academic staff. *Journal of Studies in International Education*, 12(2), 204–221.

Li, M., Baker, T. and Marshall, K., 2002. Mismatched expectations: A case study of Asian students in New Zealand. *New Zealand Journal of Applied Business Research*, 1(1), 137–156.

Liu, S., 2011. *Impact of the quality assessment of undergraduate education on university change in China.* Thesis (PhD). Institute of Education, University of London.

Lu, J. and Deng, J., 2005. The problems of bilingual curriculum in Chinese universities. *Journal of China Civil Aviation Flying College,* 16(2), 55–61.

Ministry of Education (MOE), 2001. *Some suggestions to improve the quality of undergraduate education.* Available from: http://www.edu.cn/ 20030804/ 3088968.shtml (accessed 1 December 2011)

Ministry of Education (MOE), 2009. *Chinese education yearbook.* Beijing: People's Education Press.

Ministry of Education (MOE), 2011a. *The statistics of various kinds of international students in 2009 published by the Ministry of Education.* Available from: http://www.moe.edu.cn/publicfiles/business/htmlfiles/moe/moe_851/201006/90108.html (accessed 1 November 2011).

Ministry of Education (MOE), 2011b. *The number of the foreign students in China exceeds 230,000.* Available from: http://edu.sina.com.cn/a/2010–03–23/1439186661.shtml (accessed 1 November 2011).

Robertson, M., Line, M. Jones, S. and Thomas, S. 2000. International students, learning environments and perceptions: A case study using the Delphi technique. *Higher Education Research & Development,* 19(1), 89–101.

Salter-Dvorak, H., 2004. Why can't I communicate with my British fellow students? Chinese learner perspectives; a rationale for pragmatic training. *Responding to the Needs of the Chinese Learner,* 16–18 July 2004, University of Portsmouth, Portsmouth, Hampshire, UK.

Senyshyn, R.M., Warford, M.K. and Zhan, J., 2000. Issues of adjustment to higher education: International students' perspectives. *International Education,* 30(1), 17–35.

Sizoo, S. and Serrie, H., 2004. Developing cross-cultural skills of international business students: An experiment. *Journal of Instructional Psychology,* 31(2), 160–166.

Su. Q., Yang, P. and Zhang, L., 2002. The investigation and analysis on the effects of bilingual teaching. *China University Teaching,* 10, 34–35.

The State Council of People Republic of China, 1999. *The decision on deepening education reforms and enhancing the quality education.* Beijing: The State Council.

Tian, M. and Lowe, J., 2009. Existentialist internationalisation and the Chinese student experience in English universities. *Compare: A Journal of Comparative and International Education,* 39(5), 659–676.

Tompson, H.B. and Tompson, G.H., 1996. Confronting diversity issues in the classroom with strategies to improve satisfaction and retention of international students. *Journal of Education for Business,* 72(1), 53–57.

Volet, S., 1999. Learning across cultures: Appropriateness of knowledge transfer. *International Journal of Educational Research,* 31(1), 625–643.

Wang, J., Fan, Y. and Gao, J., 2009. Investigation and analysis of bilingual education. *Human Resource Management,* 2, 72–74.

Ward, C. and Kennedy, A., 1993. Where's the 'culture' in cross-cultural transition? Comparative study of sojourner adjustment. *Journal of Cross-cultural Psychology,* 24(2), 221–249.

Xie. A. and Jiao, L., 2010. The opening-up to the outside world and development of Chinese higher education: A review and reflection since China's entry into WTO. *Teacher Education Research,* 22(5), 6–13.

Xie, Y. and Liu. Y., 2010. The measurement of the satisfaction of foreign students studying in China. *Modern Education Management*, 6, 57–59.

Yao, Y., 2010. The status quo and improvement of international students' education in central-affiliated universities. *Teacher Education Research*, 22(2), 71–75.

Zhang, Z. and Brunton, M., 2007. Differences in living and learning: Chinese international students in New Zealand. *Journal of Studies in International Education*, 11(2), 124–140.

Zhou, Y., and Todman, J., 2009. Patterns of adaptation of Chinese postgraduate students in the United Kingdom. *Journal of Studies in International Education*, 13(4), 467–486.

13

Broadening Students' Experience
A Singapore Perspective

DANIEL S. H. CHAN AND CHNG HUANG HOON

> The most valuable lesson I learnt from my education in NUS is that there is
> no one simple answer to many questions. In my home country, there is still
> a sense that there is a correct answer to every issue – I have learnt that this
> is not always true.
>
> (Full-time Vietnamese student in NUS, Year 3, Arts & Social Sciences,
> personal communication, December 2011)

This chapter discusses the nature of the student experience in Singapore,
using specific case examples from the National University of Singapore
(NUS). The analysis is contextualised within Singapore's socio-political
context and its national framework of education, which not only provides
the context for the student's journey and experience of university but at the
same time, as we will show, defines the various responses in curriculum
and pedagogical terms that a university like NUS has made. This broader
framing provides an understanding of the shifts in emphasis in university
experience in the last decade, and presents two noteworthy points. One is
the 'global but Asia' focus – a twin aspiration that speaks to extending NUS
globally but staying rooted to the local point of origin. Two, the transformation suggested in the mission statement includes cultivating a generation of Singaporeans who are able to think, live and work globally. Against
this broader socio-political context, Singapore's own brand of education
came into being.

Our chapter employs a combination of methods in providing a wide view of
one university's approach to broadening education. More specifically, we bring
both our experience in the system and our own reading of national education
trends and policies to bear in our account and we interviewed various groups
of students to get their first-hand experience of education, both in Singapore
and abroad. A brief description of this framework is provided in the next
section.

Singapore's Educational Framework

Apart from a small number of private schools and colleges, Singapore's education system is publicly funded. It comprises six years of compulsory primary education, followed by four years of secondary education or vocational school and two years of junior college or polytechnic education. Students from the junior colleges normally sit for either the Advanced Level or the International Baccalaureate examination, while students from the polytechnics graduate after three years with a professional diploma, which is valued by employers. Graduates from both the junior colleges and polytechnics can be admitted to the four publicly funded universities; namely NUS (est. 1905), Nanyang Technological University (NTU, est.1991), Singapore Management University (SMU, est. 2000) and Singapore University of Technology & Design (SUTD, est. 2010). There is also a private university, SIM University, which offers overseas degree programmes suitable for part-time studies. Except for NTU, which comes close to matching NUS in terms of size (student population of about 33,000), NUS, being the largest institution with 37,000 students and the most well established, has made relatively larger scale responses to many of the issues discussed in this chapter. So while the NUS responses are also echoed in responses made by the other universities in Singapore (e.g. on campus living arrangements for students, double degree programmes, etc.), for the most part, there are slight differences in details and scale.

Among the universities in Singapore, NUS is the most established. It assumed its present identity in 1979 from the merger of the University of Singapore and Nanyang University, but traces its history through its constituent colleges to 1905 when it began as a medical school. It was organised according to the academic traditions of the British universities, although much has changed since then.

The period from 1980 to 2000 were years of rapid growth for NUS and Singapore's university sector. This growth was driven by the restructuring of the Singapore economy, which resulted in the need for large numbers of graduates, especially in the professions. These years saw the building of universities and campuses to accommodate the growth in student numbers. The early 1980s saw the establishment of a new engineering school, Nanyang Technological Institute (the predecessor of NTU), and the year 2000 saw the establishment of SMU. At the same time, great efforts were taken to raise the academic and professional quality of the graduate output through frequent benchmarking and consultations with external examiners and international advisory panels. Throughout this period of growth, NUS's degree programmes were internationally respected for their academic rigour and it had strong enrolments of high quality. However, their academic requirements were sometimes seen as rather rigid and not fully able to meet the needs of all students in a large and increasingly diverse student population. There was also a sense that in this period of rapid growth in enrolment, wider aspects of a university education could be allotted greater emphasis through the shift towards developing a more holistic model of education.

The University and the Broadening of Education

Approximately 30 per cent of Singaporeans in each cohort pursue an undergraduate degree programme in a government supported university, with another 25 per cent pursuing degrees or diplomas in private institutions or an overseas institution. In 2010, there was an estimated 80,000 students enrolled in Singapore tertiary institutions (Yearbook of Statistics 2011). At any one time, NUS has about 27,000 undergraduate students; less than 20 per cent of these are international students.

In 1998, Singapore embarked on a national project to cast a vision for Singapore as a nation and society in the 21st century. Known as Singapore 21, this project involved broad-based discussion and consultation, and culminated in a final report that was wide-ranging in its perspectives. Among the recommendations was an aspiration for Singapore society to embrace a broader definition of success beyond just academic or economic terms (see Singapore 21 1999). The publication of these recommendations was followed by many significant changes in Singapore education that were aimed at fulfilling this aspiration. The ideal of a holistic education was promoted and an emphasis on national examination results was reduced. Multiple pathways were developed to cater to the different educational needs of the nation's children (see Ministry of Education 2012). Among the most visible of these implementations was the establishment of specialised schools where children who show early talent in the arts (i.e. School of the Arts), science (at the NUS High School of Mathematics & Science), sports (Singapore Sports School) and applied technology (Singapore School of Science and Technology) can develop their talent to the fullest while pursuing a school programme. Significant attention was also paid in these years to address the needs of a separate group of secondary school students who were less academically inclined, to succeed in industry-related vocations (see *The Economist* 2011; Northlight School 2012).

The broad changes at the national level soon percolated to the universities, with each university finding its own way to make suitable responses. In the first decade of the 21st century, major developments took place at NUS. With an enrolment of 27,000 undergraduates and 10,000 postgraduate students, NUS recognised that among such a large population of high academic achievers, there existed large differences in interests, talents and motivational levels. To enable as many of these students as possible to explore and develop their interests, NUS set out to develop numerous pathways to success and recognition, both in and outside the classroom.

Curricula at NUS went through major revisions to address the need for a more holistic education. For example, programmes were restructured that facilitated and encouraged students to go beyond their own disciplines and academic majors to read modules outside their own faculties. A general education requirement was put in place and different academic pathways were created outside the discipline-specific degree programmes. Students could read a minor in addition to their academic major, or pursue a double major, or a double degree concurrently, one from each faculty or a joint degree with some universities overseas. The University Scholars Programme (USP) for NUS undergraduates was set up in 2000 to offer exceptionally motivated and talented students the freedom to explore across disciplines, and a wide range of extra-curricular and overseas opportunities (cf NTU 2012). The first of its kind in Singapore, this interdisciplinary academic programme admits 180 students a year and aims to build a close community and produce graduates with the intellectual rigour, initiative and innovative spirit to make significant contributions to society. As part of efforts to build community, since 2011 USP students and academics have resided together in one of the university's residential colleges.

Singapore's small size means that most of NUS's Singaporean students live within commuting distance of the university. Historically, living at home has been the most cost-effective and practical option for most students. There is, however, the recognition that the student experience can be significantly enhanced through an extended period of campus residential living. New hostels were added to the existing halls of residences. These were structured along the lines of traditional university residences, each hall having its own student-led communal life involving extra-curricular activities, dinners and events. This traditional model was supplemented by the building of shared student apartment blocks that were largely self-catering, with more limited community activities within the blocks. Though space in these campus residences is limited, about 6600 students get to be part of such an on-campus community each year, and it has been widely acknowledged by hall masters and students alike that the 'hall experience' has yielded a deeper sense of belonging among this category of students.

Recently, a third model of student residential living was established in NUS, again a first in Singapore, and probably new to Southeast Asia. In this model, four residential colleges (RCs) were established in the new University Town campus. The aim of each RC, housing approximately 600 undergraduates, is to establish a learning residential community comprising undergraduate residents, Fellows and the Master. In addition to extra-curricular activities, incoming freshmen entering these residential colleges take five of their classes at the college over a two-year period, helping them to fulfil part of their degree requirements. In addition to this formal programme, the Colleges provide many informal opportunities for learning on a daily basis. Faculty members and visiting scholars from prestigious overseas institutions also live at the College and take meals in the same dining hall as students. There are regular 'Master's Teas' and other college events at which small groups of students can interact with distinguished visitors in a relaxed, informal setting. With the three models of accommodation, a total of 9000 students (including 1700 postgraduates) live on campus. If this residential programme at University Town works out well, the plan is to scale it up for the rest of main campus, barring cost constraints (University Town, 2012).

These changes in curriculum and possibilities of residential living were paralleled by other initiatives to provide opportunities for student experiences outside the classroom. The aspiration for more students to acquire international experience was met by major expansions in internationalisation programmes. Currently, 50 per cent of all NUS undergraduates spend part of their time overseas in various activities ranging from formal academic programmes, internships or attachments to summer programmes. Among this 50 per cent, half of the students spend at least one semester at an overseas university while the same number of students from overseas universities spends at least one semester in NUS. Another area of activity was in helping students who were interested to explore and develop their entrepreneurial skills in both the technopreneurship and the social entrepreneurship arenas. The NUS Overseas Colleges offer undergraduates opportunities to spend one year in a start-up company at eight overseas locations, while the iLEAD, which stands for innovative Local Enterprise Achiever Development, offers the same opportunities in local start-up companies. Besides these programmes, there is a very active student-driven NUS Entrepreneurship Society, running a range of activities promoting entrepreneurship in which industrial and alumni entrepreneurs participate to provide coaching and mentorship.

Support for student-run activities outside the classroom was given a boost by the setting up of an Office of Student Affairs (OSA). Working closely with the NUS Students Union, the OSA facilitates a range of activities for students to develop their talents beyond their studies. Achievements outside the classroom by individual students and groups are celebrated through the high profile annual NUS Student Achievement Awards (SAA), in sports, community service or in other student-led activities. The university's view on the value of such activities is best summed up by the Provost, Professor Tan Eng Chye, when he spoke at the recent 2012 SAA: 'Students who have taken advantage of these important learning opportunities outside the classroom environment will develop desired qualities of mind and character – namely, resilience, team work, confidence, interpersonal and leadership skills' (NUS Newshub 2012). These crucial personal attributes add real value to academic grades and prepare a student well for life and career, he noted, and emphasised that every nominee was a winner.

Through these continuing developments, NUS aspires to create diverse opportunities for personal growth among students, recognising that in the new workplace, an effective worker will require many skills and attributes that are beyond technical competence alone. It is the hope that students will avail themselves of these avenues of development in accordance with their interests and inclinations. As mentioned earlier, though these changes in expanding the curriculum and the enrichment of student life also take place in the other Singapore universities, the scale on which NUS has embarked on these is perhaps greater, given the student numbers and diversity within the NUS student population.

The Student Experience

Students' Experience of Curriculum

The NUS Law School revisited its admission policy in the interest of ensuring 'greater diversity in the backgrounds, abilities and interests of undergraduates' (*The Straits Times* 2012), motivated in part by the increased diversity in the general population, and in part by the increased number of high school students wanting to access university places. This news was received well by high school students. Two current law students, formerly from high schools that were under-represented in their law school said they welcome this move. We cite this article because it is among the most recent changes at NUS that is aimed at broadening experience for NUS students, by actively reflecting the diversity seen at the national level, opening access to all kinds of programmes through equalising the playing field, and generally encouraging social integration and intellectual growth across the board. This has not always been the case – student life has varied in the ways NUS students experience it and by 2012 it has come a long way.

To be a student in any university in Singapore, after 12 years of education in the Singapore school system, marks a culmination of hard-earned effort put into learning. Though not claiming all students did nothing else but studied hard, university life in NUS in the 1980s was definitely more solely focused on academic development. The highly structured nature of the university curriculum, consisting of compulsory and some elective courses, meant that most students went through the journey with a high degree of predictability and with little deviation from what would be considered a 'normal' route. In sum, apart from a standard curriculum, there were relatively fewer options for students to exercise, and, in the 1980s, there was only one university (i.e. NUS) in existence.

While the newer universities, like SMU, could frame themselves in different ways upon their more recent establishment, the century-old NUS had to make a few important shifts to make the students' varsity experience not just intellectually fulfilling and personally enriching, but also relevant to the 21st century workplace. These have included the conscious decision NUS took to position itself not just as a global university, but also one centred in Asia. This further translates into an overt focus on developing meaningful Asia–global perspectives in specific programmes. For example, the senior seminars offered at University Town defined themselves in exactly this way – to develop in students an understanding of Singapore/Asia's place in the world. Currently, heavier emphasis is also placed on different modes of continuous assessment and project work to cater to different styles of learning and to promote teamwork (as opposed to one final high-stakes exam), and added emphasis on oral skills. There is also more active deployment of technology (such as online forums, wikis, blogs and e-learning modes) within and outside the classroom. In short, students learn using different media, online and offline. Apart from the different housing options on campus, NUS, like the other universities, also devotes specific student spaces for self-study, sports, club activities and student functions, all designed with the dual objectives of enriching student life and integrating the diverse student population in mind. In addition to OSA overseeing these student matters, a recently created senior management position in 2010, the Vice Provost for Student Life, provides for the enhancement of student centricity on campus.

The above is not an exhaustive list of initiatives and shifts that have been affected in the university education and student life landscape, but it should be easy to see how significantly the university experience has changed in the past decade alone, as illustrated in a big public university like NUS, both in response to changes in the national landscape and in alignment with 21st century needs. To understand the impact some of these changes may have exerted on students, we spoke to small groups of students about the issue and, below, share some of these responses.

Singaporean Students' Experience of NUS

Twenty students we interviewed from June to August 2011 gave us some insight into their experience of NUS. Individual differences aside, there were easily identifiable themes that emerged as common patterns in their narratives. First, most came to the university as a natural progression in their educational development in Singapore – from primary to secondary, to post-secondary and then tertiary education. Many were already fully socialised into the Singapore system of education – highly intense culture of learning and single-minded pursuit of excellence. Second, most of these students, like many young people starting out in life, did not, however, think too deeply about their longer term career plans when they chose to come to the university. The focus was to obtain a degree (as opposed to an education experience) and, for many, they were motivated by pragmatic reasons (such as, 'to improve my job prospects') rather than by longer term personal development goals. For many, fortunately, the NUS experience turned out to be enriching. Several of these students said that they felt 'intellectually challenged'; some said they cultivated a good network of friends while in NUS. A few said that they did all the 'normal' things – i.e. studied, maintained a healthy CAP (i.e. Cumulative Average Point) and felt prepared to enter the workforce.

Some students spoke of the advantages they enjoyed in being part of a small programme (e.g. Japanese Studies has a relatively smaller student population in NUS; and the USP, by its very nature, allowed for small group interactions), and how this had effectively countered the isolation of a big campus because of the increased opportunity for interaction. In contrast, other students lamented about their classes being too big, and that their class experience had oftentimes proved impersonal, having experienced the much smaller class and school settings in their pre-tertiary days. Many of these students reflected that they were kept very busy during their stint in NUS – the continuous stream of assignments, the constant need to keep up with their studies, and the feeling they got that time flew quickly from semester to semester. In short, the common experience is of a kind of rat race that is reflective of life in Singapore.

A number of these students live on campus in a university hall of residence. Almost invariably, students who live in a hall of residence often reported a positive experience, with the opportunity to build tighter social networks through their hall activities. Of course, this does not mean that there were no negative stories – one female student in fact reported that she left her hall after the first year because she found it too noisy for her liking.

Every student said that it was good to reflect on their university experience with us – simply because they had not thought about their journey before we asked them explicitly about it. It was clear that in responding to our questions, these students became increasingly involved in actively reflecting on their NUS journey and belatedly but happily realised that the journey had been meaningful. It is hoped that the above highlights of our conversations with the 20 students provides a flavour of the students' journey in a big university like NUS, where different sectors would naturally undergo a slightly different experience even as they share some commonalities. The next section explores the foreign/international students' experience of NUS.

International Students' Experience of NUS

There are two types of international students in NUS – those who come to NUS on short-term exchange for a semester, and those who are fully enrolled in a degree programme in NUS and graduate with an NUS degree. Of the latter, there are two further subcategories – students coming in from China and India and students from the Association of Southeast Asian Nations' (ASEAN) countries, such as Vietnam and Myanmar. We have had many past encounters with international students and, recently, we interviewed four of them and surveyed another 11 via an emailed questionnaire to get a sense of their NUS experience.

The four students we interviewed are shown in Table 13.1.

Three salient patterns emerged from the interviews. One, all of them chose NUS because of the offer of a scholarship; NUS' reputation as a highly ranked university and that it offers a good degree programme in the subject of their study; and the proximity to their home country. Two, except for S4, who already has a good network of Singapore friends because of his immersion in Singapore's school system, these international students do not count many Singaporean students among their close friends. In other words, more often than not, except for S4, these students mix primarily with students from their home country or from other countries. Third, all of them have confidence that a Singapore degree will be useful to them as they prepare to live and work either in Singapore or elsewhere after their graduation.

The above findings are echoed by the survey we conducted with another group of 11 international students who opted to respond through email. The top three reasons that brought these students to NUS/Singapore were: NUS' academic reputation and world ranking; the offer of a Singapore or NUS financial aid or scholarship; and the reputable degree programme in the discipline of study. When asked what university they may have gone to if they *had not* come to NUS/Singapore, surprisingly, the majority said they would have stayed in their home country; some others said they would have looked first to Australia, then to the US or Canada to pursue their education. Cost seems to be the determining factor for most. As to what they hope to achieve beyond pursuing an NUS degree, many said: personal development; confidence in living independently in a foreign country (that is also close to home); and making new friends among Singaporeans and other international students. Some of them also responded with the aim to gain 'greater mastery' in English. The response, to 'make new friends among Singaporeans and other international students' is noteworthy – sadly, this goal goes unfulfilled for far too many students.

Table 13.1 International students interviewed

Student	S1 (Female)	S2 (Male)	S3 (Female)	S4 (Male)*
Nationality	Chinese	Indian	Vietnamese	Indonesian
Year of study	Year 1/PhD	Year 2/PhD	Year 3/BSocSc	Year 4/BBA
Subject major	Sociology	Physiology	Psychology	Finance

Note: *This Indonesian student has been in Singapore since he was 14, and has been part of the Singapore school system from secondary school (i.e. middle school) level.

These international students agreed about their main challenges – coping with the hectic pace of life in Singapore and the academic workload in NUS, and living up to the greater expectation for students to be independent learners. Many of these students also do not have a wide support network of friends, especially friends from Singapore. In spite of the range of student life opportunities instituted in NUS, many students said they do not mix much with Singapore students, because of busy schedules and some cultural barriers. For most, 'close friends' means only people from their own country. However, in spite of the challenges faced, all of them seemed agreed that a Singapore/foreign degree is well worth the effort as they expressed confidence that their Singapore degree will be valued elsewhere. The majority said they were likely to try to find employment in Singapore after their graduation, or pursue further studies elsewhere.

Among the benefits that were listed as the result of being in NUS, the salient point made by the students was the wide range of international opportunities that NUS offers – like Student Exchange Programmes (SEP), and the international mix on campus. While a number of students had various suggestions as to how student life could be improved in NUS (such as, creating more opportunities for different nationalities to interact), many of them felt that NUS provides many opportunities for student development, especially NUS' global programmes.

In short, it seems that the international student experience in NUS presents a relatively positive picture, though obviously there is room for improving the quality of the student experience, especially in providing better orientation for international students into Singapore/NUS life and in effecting better networking between international and Singaporean students.

NUS Students' Experience Outside NUS

According to data from the NUS International Relations Office, about 50 per cent of NUS undergraduates go overseas as part of their educational experience, and about 25 per cent spend one semester or more overseas on SEPs or other international programmes including Double and Joint Degree Programmes and NUS Overseas Colleges (NUS Overseas Colleges 2012). The three types of programmes that commanded the highest numbers in student participation in 2009 were SEPs, International Summer Programmes (i-SPs) and field trips. On the SEP front alone, NUS has over 200 overseas partner universities, and students go on exchange for at least one semester at partner universities in the Americas, Asia-Pacific Rim, Europe and UK. The top three preferred destinations are the US, Canada and the UK. The 'exotic' factor does come into play when students make choices on destination for their SEP – many Singaporean students still think of Asia-Pacific as too close to home, i.e. not exotic enough. There could, however, be other kinds of obstacles preventing some students from selecting China for instance – such as language barriers (cf. Student 1 below).

In December 2011, we interviewed three students who had gone on a semester-long exchange programme at a partner university in a small focused group discussion. We share the feedback gathered from two of the students because they provide a good contrast in terms of their profiles (see Table 13.2).

Our conversation with these two male students revolved around what motivated them to go on their SEP, what they were hoping to achieve through the SEP, and what they found most valuable or challenging about the experience. Like most other students that we got to know, the main motivation for going abroad on a short stint seems to be to experience a different living and learning environment and their decision of a host institution is based on the established reputation of the institution or the institution's strength in the particular discipline/programme. What was enlightening to us was the following:

- Student 1 chose China as the site of his exchange to experience another Asian university, and because of his scholarly interest in the politics of Northeast Asia. He also did some volunteer work on the side, his motivation being to gain a better understanding of the locale outside the safe shelter of Peking University. Having to operate in Mandarin was a challenge but he managed to cope with it sufficiently well. One challenge he named was coping with winter in Peking – it being his first winter abroad.
- Student 2 has been in Singapore for the past eight years, and wanted to experience living in a different place when he chose U Penn. He has thus lived in Singapore as a foreign student, and then went to Penn/US for the first time as an NUS student on SEP. On the one hand, he has sufficient experience living abroad given his life in Singapore; on the other hand, Penn/US provided him with a new living and learning experience that was different from Singapore. He identified the following successes in his SEP experience: experiencing a different learning environment and a different culture/country.

All three students said they felt they had succeeded in living independently and have grown personally during their SEP and though they rightly pointed out that one semester was too short a period to really learn all kinds of important

Table 13.2 Details of two students who went on a semester-long exchange programme

	Student 1	Student 2
Gender	Male	Male
Nationality	Singaporean	PRC Chinese
Faculty	Arts & social sciences	Engineering
Host institution	Peking University	UPenn

skills, they do feel slightly better equipped if they ever live and/or work abroad in the future.

Following the discussion with the three students, we designed a questionnaire and emailed it to 35 students (including the three we spoke to), all randomly selected from a university database, to seek more views on the quality of their SEP experience. We obtained 12 responses (including one each from the two students showcased above). Though the return rate was low, the responses to our questionnaire nevertheless provided some interesting insights about SEP from the student perspective. Below we provide some key findings of this survey.

The top three reasons for going on a SEP (in order of importance) were: to experience a different culture/country; to experience a different learning environment; and to enjoy a more independent lifestyle. It is noteworthy that at least two students said that the SEP provided a temporary relief from the stress of the Singapore education system. As one student put it, the SEP experience got him/her to 'rethink the sometimes unnecessarily stressful way of life and over-emphasis on academic achievement in Singapore'.

The top three most highly rated goals achieved through the SEP were that the student: experienced a different culture and country; experienced a different learning environment; and had a change from the monotony of the usual routine (at home and in the home institution). Students consistently said that the SEP gave them some measure of independence. As one student put it, 'I think NUS is doing a great job. It's good for NUS students to get out into the world and be independent!'

The top three activities that students gained from their SEP were that they: joined a student activity organised by students in the host institution; had gone on holiday (weekend or longer) with students from another country; and had made one/more friends from another country with whom they still kept in contact. Students, however, had differing ease in making new friends. For example, one student said he had developed 'a particularly strong friendship' with his South Korean roommate. Another reported the difficulties of breaking into 'the social circle of students from the host country'.

The top three benefits of the SEP experience were: better appreciation of the good and bad points of life in Singapore and NUS; better understanding of the society of the country where SEP was spent; and more confidence in communicating and working in a team with others outside their home country. Many students said they did not face any real challenges during the SEP. Those who encountered challenges said they had faced: problems in mapping modules (i.e. an NUS practice requiring students to match courses they took while on exchange to home institution requirements for credit transfer purposes); coping with extreme weather conditions and natural disasters like an earthquake while abroad; losing money through inexperience in dealing with people in the host country; and some misunderstandings due to differences in cultural practices. Some students said NUS could do with better crisis support for students on SEPs.

It is easily discernible from even such a small study that the SEP experience, though just one way of broadening students' intellectual and social horizon, has worked well for many NUS students. A more in-depth study needs to be done but what we have unearthed in this study provides a good starting point to think about the benefits of a global/broadened curriculum that allows students wider scope for personal and academic development. To the extent that such global exposure allows our students to emerge better skilled and more confident, we can conclude that these education initiatives are steps in the right direction.

The Role of International Degrees In and Beyond Singapore

Given the premium paid on education by Singaporeans, the role and value of a degree in general and an international degree in particular are significant for the Singaporean mindset. This explains both the growing demand for tertiary education by Singaporeans, not just at tertiary institutions in Singapore but also at universities abroad. And given the increasing number of international students who seek an education in Singapore, particularly from the ASEAN countries, the same may be said of international students' pursuit of international degrees. For both groups of students seeking degrees in Singapore and abroad, there is a strong belief that these will stand them in good stead for the future, however they envision it.

The rapid growth of NUS, in both size and curriculum terms, speaks to the response that an institution like NUS makes to cater to the needs of students and a globalised future. As we have already discussed above, students (both local and international) who come to NUS are given access to all kinds of programmes that may encompass a foreign dimension – the exchange and summer programmes, the joint/double degrees and so forth. But as students have themselves informed us through the interviews we conducted on different occasions, what they seek, in addition to a local or international degree that may set them on the road to a good career, is the opportunity to experience a different academic culture and living environment, and an experience in independence. As the Vietnamese student in the opening quote underscored, the value for her in coming to Singapore, apart from pursuing a foreign education and degree, is that she acquired a perspective that is markedly different, and valuably so, from the one she would have got in her home country. This, in a nutshell, is the value and role of an international degree for someone like her, and we daresay, from everything we have learnt from interviewing students and from our own experience of being foreign students once ourselves, that *this* is true of many Singaporean and international students who had the opportunity to go outside their home country to pursue a different educational experience.

Critical Reflections

The student population in a large, global campus like NUS is heterogeneous on several fronts: in terms of nationality, ethnicity, abilities and academic culture. In response to these variations and the size of such a population, the approach adopted by NUS may be characterised simply as providing a differentiated curriculum that caters to different sectors of students. This approach, while successful to a large extent, as is evident from the students' responses to their experience of NUS and NUS programmes, still presents a number of challenges that demand further considerations by university management. In this final section, we consider a few key challenges, namely: size of the student population; integrating the diverse student population; and integrating life skills into standard curricular spaces.

Size of the Student Population

As mentioned earlier, only NTU with its 33,000 students is almost as big as NUS, which has approximately 37,000 students, including both undergraduates and postgraduates. This large student population presents an immediate challenge to actively engage students and to prepare them to be globally ready. Many academic programmes have been put in place to allow students to extend their learning beyond NUS – there are various study abroad and internship platforms. But no matter how many programmes are instituted, not every student will have access to them, due largely to the high cost of education, space and other constraints. It is true that NUS has already met its target of having 50 per cent of its undergraduate students benefit from some form of overseas exposure, but, in a campus of this size, there is still the other 50 per cent (about 12,000) who could not access this global experience. Simply proliferating programmes is neither cost-effective nor sustainable. It is important to think in terms of scalability – to scale up the existing programmes to benefit more students.

Integrating the Diverse Student Population

The advantages of a global campus are easy to discern – students can richly benefit from peer learning in diverse group dynamics. A book by Winnifred R. Brown-Glaude on diversity has pointed out, for example, that a diverse student population helps to enable students to negotiate the world and the workplace. Instead of focusing on conflicts and discrimination, we should instead examine how we can reap the educational benefits of an ethnically diverse campus (2009).

However, the challenge of a global campus is a very real issue – how do we ensure that a campus with such a diverse population is fully integrated like a mini United Nations where distinct sub-groups, while maintaining their own group identities, do not feel excluded and subsequently alienated from other sub-groups? More importantly, how do we enrich and maximise learning from such a readily diverse global campus? This diversity, it should be noted, does not only encompass ethnic diversity – it also includes differences in academic cultures, i.e. students bring with them different practices from home institutions from around the world. This has resulted in issues like differences in student expectations, whether regarding aspects of their learning in NUS or aspects of living in Singapore. These issues are particularly in need of answers if we are to educate our students to operate effectively in a global economy; in short, to be globally ready.

Integrating Life Skills into Standard Curricular Spaces

In educating for global readiness, a third challenge relates to finding a balance in the standard curriculum to allow space for inculcating life skills. There is by now sufficient recognition that over and above domain-specific core skills, we also need to provide training for life skills – such as leadership, teamwork, communication and critical thinking skills. Finding space within an already crowded curriculum is no easy task, but yet is an issue that we constantly have to grapple with. We do know one thing and this we need to keep actively in view: we cannot talk about the importance of producing globally ready graduates for a global future without walking that talk – providing for relevant training on the life skills front – and the best way to teach these skills is to integrate them into the standard curriculum. How best to integrate them into the university curriculum, though a challenging issue, is one that all of us as educators, programme developers and university administrators must confront head on.

We add a final thought in relation to coping with the various constraints of education on a large and diverse campus, and that is the possibility of harnessing some form of technology-enabled education in NUS in the near future. Brooks' article about 'The campus tsunami' (2012) explained that online courses used to be seen as just 'interesting experiments', but are now 'the core of how [elite institutions] envision their futures'. Many of us have by now heard much about the fairly established Coursera online education resources, and the more recent EdX collaboration between MIT and Harvard. NUS has, for some time now, been looking into the ways in which we can implement some form of the 'flipped classroom' that will enrich the NUS's students' learning beyond the e-learning week experience that we implemented in 2009, riding on the high level of connectivity and internet access of the average student in Singapore, with an eye on the potential pedagogical outcomes that may be derived from freeing classroom time for higher order learning. This form of student engagement will need to be further explored and deliberated upon, but it is certainly one likely ingredient that may shape the approach to education in NUS in the future.

Conclusion

We began this paper with the observation that Singapore has rapidly transformed itself in its short history of nation building. The education system in Singapore has moved almost as fast and tertiary education in particular has made many significant shifts within the last two decades alone. These rapid shifts and changes in thinking and delivering quality education are in part the result of developments in the world but are also in part triggered by the Singaporean mindset that we have to quickly adapt and respond to our local and global environment. In our pursuit of global readiness for our graduates, the various NUS curricular developments in terms of increasing the number and flexibility of students' curricular options is just one institution's way of committing to a vision for a more student-centric and globally relevant education.

References

Brooks, D. (2012) 'The campus tsunami', *New York Times*, May, at http://www.nytimes.com/2012/05/04/opinion/brooks-the-campus-tsunami.html (accessed 30 July 2012).

Brown-Glaude, W. R. (2009) *Doing diversity in higher education*. New Brunswick, NJ: Rutgers University Press.

The Economist (2011) 'Go east, young bureaucrat', 17 March, at http://www.economist.com/node/18359852 (accessed 13 November 2012).

Ministry of Education (2012) Reply by the Ministry of Education to Mr Hri Kumar Nair, at http://www.moe.gov.sg/media/parliamentary-replies/2012/01/direct-school-admission-progra.php (accessed 26 February 2012).

Nanyang Technological University (NTU) (2012) University scholars programme. Available at http://news.ntu.edu.sg/pages/newsdetail.aspx?URL=http://news.ntu.edu.sg/news/Pages/NR2012_Jan25.aspx&Guid=2a85235a-ffa0-4cc1-b38b-01b9464e4756&Category=all (accessed 13 November 2012).

Northlight School (2012) at http://en.wikipedia.org/wiki/Northlight_School (accessed 13 November 2012).

NUS Newshub (2012) Academy style awards ceremony celebrates student achievements at http://newshub.nus.edu.sg/headlines/0212/awards_20Feb12.php (accessed 26 February 2012).

NUS Overseas Colleges (2012) http://www.overseas.nus.edu.sg/ (accessed 28 February 2012).

Singapore21 (1999) Internationalisation/regionalisation vs Singapore as home, Paragraph 52, at http://www.singapore21.org.sg/dilemma4.doc (accessed 26 February 2012).

The Straits Times (2012) 'NUS law school reviews student admission procedures', 25 January, Wednesday, at A3.

University Town (2012) National University of Singapore, at http://utown.nus.edu.sg/ (accessed 26 February 2012).

Yearbook of Statistics (2011) Yearbook of statistics Singapore, 2011. Singapore Department of Statistics.

14

The Student Experience in South Africa

JUDY BACKHOUSE AND FATIMA ADAM

South African higher education sits, somewhat uncomfortably, between what the introduction of this book describes as 'Western' higher education systems and systems in 'different cultural contexts'. South Africa's first universities were modelled by British and Dutch colonisers on 'Western' universities and newer institutions were developed along the same lines. The higher education system still looks to the United Kingdom (UK), Australia and Canada for leadership in policy and practice, and institutions strive to emulate the more prestigious 'Western' institutions. In many respects, the system is a 'Western' higher education system.

On the other hand, South African higher education has, since 1994, been forced to confront its position in Africa and is grappling with the meaning and practice of 'transformation' and 'Africanisation'. There are efforts at national, institutional and individual levels to explore alternative institutional structures and practices, as well as understandings of knowledge and approaches to research and teaching. However, there is not yet a sense that South African higher education is truly 'African' in anything but geographical location.

Understanding the student experience of internationalisation in the South African context is not a simple matter. The factors that influence experience are complex and include language, the race and class of the visiting student, the institution and the programme for which they enrol, and the degree of resonance between their previous experiences of education and the environment they find themselves in. Students studying in South Africa who have a good command of English and experience of education underpinned by similar 'Western' epistemologies and modes of learning are likely to feel at home and adapt easily to the educational context. Those who are less familiar with English and whose educational experience is significantly different are likely to find it harder to adapt. For South African students studying abroad, their experience differs depending on which country they travel to, particularly whether they travel to more or less developed countries. We conclude that results cannot be generalised and that discourses that homogenise the student experience are not useful.

This chapter is structured as follows: first we examine three aspects of the local context. We discuss the discourses around internationalisation in South Africa at a national level; we consider these discourses and practices at the institutional level; and we give some information about the numbers of international students and their reasons for travelling. Next we turn to student experience. We discuss the research base that we draw on to lay out a framework for understanding student experience. Then we reflect on the student experience, looking first at the experience of international students coming to study in South Africa, and then the experience of South Africans studying abroad. Included in these last sections are reflections on how student experience relates to other themes in this book, such as language, culture-specific approaches to learning, and globalised curricula. The conclusion draws together our observations of the key features of internationalisation of higher education as they relate to student experience in the South African context.

Contextualising International Higher Education in South Africa

A Postcolonial Perspective

As the only African country represented in this section, the authors feel an implied responsibility to represent Africa. Higher education in much of Africa has followed a similar path, being established by 'Western' colonisers, to mirror their own universities; and having to grapple, since decolonisation, with questions of how to create a locally meaningful higher education system that accommodates global expectations. However, South African higher education is different in two respects. Firstly, the success of African higher education systems since decolonisation relates to the extent to which ex-patriots in the country established themselves as permanent occupants, and supported higher education in their own interests (Lulat 2005). South Africa has a more substantial, well-established and well-resourced higher education sector than other countries in Africa. Secondly, South Africa's apartheid years included a period of extreme isolation from international contact and the divisions created during those years have resulted in unusual challenges for higher education.

Several authors position internationalisation as a 20th century phenomenon, linked to globalisation (Groening 1987; Davies 1997; Tiechler 1999; Altbach 2000), and driven by economic rationales towards increasingly intensive international activities around staff and student mobility, internationally relevant curricula, and institutional linkages and networks (De Wit 2002). From the South African (and African) perspectives, these analyses make little sense.

South African higher education began as an imported education system, teaching international curricula. Not only were institutions of higher learning modelled on European universities, members of the academic staff were trained in Europe and curricula were geared to the needs of the European settlers. Student mobility was common as European settlers seeking higher degrees and black intellectuals who were denied access to local institutions travelled abroad to study (Cross and Rouhani 2004; Sehoole 2006). In the late 1800s and early 1900s the system was more international than it was during the second half of the 20th century, or, arguably, is at present.

During the apartheid years (1949 to 1994), higher education in South Africa experienced growing isolation as the international community stopped collaborating with South African institutions and prevented academics from travelling. Local institutions became more clearly divided by language as those with stronger ties to Britain, and English as an international language, still aspired to international ties. Afrikaans was more strongly associated with the struggle for national identity and Afrikaans institutions were more inclined to adopt a stance of defiant self-sufficiency. It was during this period that separate institutions were set up for African, 'coloured' and Indian students, the former positioned in the rural 'independent homelands' that were established in support of the policy of 'separate development' (Szanton and Manyika 2002). The result was a fragmented higher education system divided along lines of race and language. Few institutions were able to sustain international linkages and few international students travelled to South Africa.

Since 1994, higher education in South Africa has been preoccupied with creating a coherent national higher education system. This process has included policy developments (National Commission on Higher Education [NCHE] 1996; Department of Education [DoE] 1996, 1997, 2001a, 2001b; Higher Education Act of 1997) and institutional mergers, carried out over 2004 and 2005. The result is greater coherence and uniformity in policy, and some blurring of the divisions between the 23 public universities, but historical legacies and positionings are still evident. A second preoccupation has been with access. Although African students now make up 67 per cent of the student body in public universities, young white people are significantly more likely to enrol and more likely to succeed in higher education than African students (Council on Higher Education [CHE] 2009; Department of Higher Education and Training [DHET] 2012a). In addition to physical access to the university, many African students have had poor schooling, lack strong skills in English, and have not developed the sets of values, practices, cultures and identities that allow them to become effective participants in the university environment. Questions of socio-cultural and 'epistemological access' (Morrow 1992) are thus also of national concern (Cross and Johnson 2008; Cross et al. 2009; CHE 2010).

South Africa has been welcomed back into regional and international academic circles. Networks have been re-established, scholars are able to travel and increasing numbers of international students have been enrolling in South African higher education institutions. However, internationalisation of higher education has received relatively little attention in South Africa. This is due to the enormity of the changes that the higher education system has been grappling with and the more obviously pressing need to expand higher education access, in all senses, to more black South Africans (Kishun 2007). In addition, common discourses around internationalisation have been rejected as having simplistic conceptions of nationhood (Sehoole 2006) and being 'concerned with legitimizing universalizing concepts and approaches to internationalisation emanating from the experiences of West European and North American countries' (Cross, Mhlanga and Ojo 2009: 76). Postcolonial African countries, used to being short-changed in international engagements, are justified in approaching internationalisation with caution and must interpret and reconstruct ideas of international education to take into account local histories and concerns (Cross, Mhlanga and Ojo 2009).

During the 1990s many foreign universities attempted to establish a presence in South Africa, but by 2000 regulations were tightened to limit this (Kruss 2004). There are currently only five foreign institutions registered with the Department of Higher Education and Training as private providers of higher education (DHET 2012b). Such institutions have been viewed with suspicion in South Africa as being primarily concerned with profit, as competitive threats to local universities, and as working for individual benefit, rather than for the benefit of the wider society (Kruss 2004).

Rationales for internationalisation of higher education tend to be political, economic or socio-cultural/academic (Cross and Rouhani 2004). One of the drivers towards internationalisation is regional cooperation across the Southern African Development Community (SADC). The 1997 SADC Protocol on Education and Training aims at sharing resources, reducing constraints and facilitating the movement of students and staff across the region. However, in spite of political commitments to greater ties with Africa and regional development, South African universities' international linkages have been mostly with institutions in Europe and North America, reflecting traditional trade ties (Cross and Rouhani 2004; Sehoole 2006). At this stage it is not possible to establish whether this pattern is changing as there is little systemic information about university partnerships. What information there is, relates to partnerships with specific regions, such as the South Africa – U.S. Higher Education Partnerships Project (2012).

International students in the country benefit local economies (du Plessis and Fourie 2011), but they are not a major source of revenue for universities, and are a cost to government because most (70 per cent) are from SADC countries and, in terms of the SADC Protocol, are charged the same fees and enjoy the same government subsidies as local students (DHET 2012a).

What policy statements there are about internationalisation are at a high level. The National Plan for Higher Education (2001) and the recent Green Paper (DHET 2012a) both recognise the economic and political benefits of international students, but the socio-cultural rationale for internationalisation, evident in the National Plan, is missing from the 2012 Green Paper, which combines long-term political and economic rationales:

> Hosting tens of thousands of SADC students represents a major contribution by South Africa to the development of the sub-continent. It is also making a major contribution to the development of South Africa, because all countries in our region are interdependent and the strengthening of Southern Africa economies must inevitably result in the strengthening of South Africa's own economy.
>
> (DHET 2012a: 51)

Internationalisation as Relocalisation and Africanisation

How do these national concerns play out at the institutional level? Institutional responses to internationalisation vary from strong financial imperatives and reactive responses to the arrival of foreign students, to proactively exploring internationalisation as a means to add diversity, 'new dimensions to academic scholarship' (Cross and Rouhani 2004), and expanding research agendas. South African universities understand internationalisation to include international activities (including staff and student mobility), the delivery of education programmes to other countries and the integration of an international, global or intercultural element into curricula, but these understandings come with four local 'qualifiers' (Cross et al. 2003; Cross, Mhlanga and Ojo 2009; Ojo 2009).

Firstly, internationalisation incorporates relocalisation, the opportunity to incorporate local knowledge into what has until now been a European institution. Academics explain how social divisions of race and class result in ignorance of local conditions; 'most of my faculty have no clue of what it's like growing up in a township; they haven't been to a township' (Cross, Mhlanga and Ojo 2009: 83). There is a sense that international knowledge has, until now, been foregrounded at the expense of local knowledge. Secondly, internationalisation is not just about international students. It is about 'providing a unique local and global experience to all staff and students' (Cross, Mhlanga and Ojo 2009: 84). This experience is aimed at enabling them to engage across cultures, on global and local levels, benefitting from local and global knowledge and experience. Thus, at the institutional level socio-cultural or academic rationales for internationalisation are more evident.

Thirdly, there is a view that internationalisation has to be about 'Africanisation', a contested term meaning one or more of: developing curricula responsive to the African context, pursuing an African epistemology (although there is little agreement on what that might be), and creating an African identity for the university. Africanisation seeks to locate African knowledge in its rightful place, with universities on the continent being uniquely positioned to become centres of expertise on Africa. Finally, internationalisation is about an end to the isolation of apartheid. Academics and students look forward to greater contact with the outside world, broader horizons and exposure to international perspectives.

These understandings have been used to frame internationalisation in terms of an environment that encourages the use of local experiences and advantages to produce knowledge that addresses local and global problems (Cross et al. 2003).

Manifestations of Mobility

At present South Africa is host to some 70,000 international students, both in the country and studying South African programmes in distance mode, while some 6,000 South Africans study abroad.

Inward Mobility

In 2010 South Africa ranked 11th in the world as a study destination, attracting 1.9 per cent of all international students (Organisation for Economic Co-operation and Development [OECD] 2011). In 2012 there were 66,113 international students in South Africa's public universities and an estimated 6,000 in private institutions. Most come from neighbouring SADC countries (46,191 or 70 per cent), followed by countries in the rest of Africa (11,130 or 17 per cent), Europe (3,653), Asia (1,813) and North America (1,737), with small numbers from the Australia/Oceania region and South America (Higher Education Management System [HEMIS] 2011). In 2009, the SADC countries that had the highest number of students studying in South Africa were Zimbabwe (14,359), Namibia (7,264), Botswana (4,849), Lesotho (4,849) and Swaziland (3,453).

There is a common perception that most international students come to South Africa for postgraduate study, but this is not the case. Some 60 per cent of foreign students in the country are enrolled in first qualifications (Table 14.1).[1] However, there are proportionately more international students than local students doing master's and doctoral degrees. For example, 5 per cent of all international students, and 7 per cent of international students not studying through University of South Africa (UNISA),[2] are doctoral students, compared to only 1 per cent of the total student body. In part this is because few black South Africans (the majority of the population) continue to higher degree study (Herman 2011).[3]

Table 14.1 Enrolments (headcount) in South African public universities, by level of study

	All international students		International students without UNISA students		All students in public universities	
Occasional study	3,016	5%	2,157	6%	24,613	3%
First qualification	38,355	66%	22,714	60%	684,472	82%
Postgraduate diplomas/honours	5,718	10%	3,558	9%	74,442	9%
Master's	7,628	13%	6,511	17%	43,723	5%
Doctorates	3,072	5%	2,768	7%	10,529	1%
Totals	57,789	100%	37,708	100%	837,779	100%

Source: Higher Education Management System, 2009.

Most international students come to South Africa to study programmes in science, engineering and technology (see Table 14.2). Such programmes are often not offered at their home institutions and South African institutions often cannot fill places with local students because of low levels of achievement in mathematics at South African schools.

International students come to South Africa because they expect a better learning experience, better curricula and improved career prospects; because facilities are better than in their home country; or to study courses not offered in their home country. Many choose South Africa because it is cheaper than studying in Europe or the United States (US) and some are prompted to study abroad

Table 14.2 Enrolments (headcount) in South African public universities, by field of study

	Including UNISA students		Excluding UNISA students	
	Headcount enrolled	Percent of international students	Headcount enrolled	Percent of international students
Science, engineering and technology	18,113	31%	15,748	42%
Human and social sciences	17,968	31%	11,291	30%
Busines, commerce and management	15,719	27%	6,503	17%
Education	5,989	10%	4,166	11%
Totals	57,789	100%	37,708	100%

Source: Higher Education Management System, 2009.

because of available funding (Sam 2001; Cross and Rouhani 2004). Postgraduate students are motivated by access to research infrastructure and cultures, the level of supervision, and wanting to do research that is relevant in the African context (Cross and Rouhani 2004; Kahn et al. 2004; Cross et al. 2009).

Outward Mobility

Relatively few South Africans leave the country to study abroad. In 2009, only 6,062 South Africans travelled to study, primarily in the US (1,675), the UK (1,582), Australia (875), Cuba (387) and Ireland (161) (UNESCO 2011a, 2011b). Other data sources include New Zealand, Canada, Germany, Portugal, The Netherlands and France in the favoured destinations (OECD 2011).

There have been no in-depth studies as to why these students study abroad. We do know that some are sponsored to travel for specific training to address local skills shortages, such as medical students who are sent to Cuba to be trained (Department of Health [DoH] 2010). Others travel for postgraduate study to institutions more closely engaged in their chosen research field or 'to work in large research environments that offer greater challenges' (Kahn et al. 2004: 54). Still others travel to institutions in the US and UK that are considered more prestigious than local institutions and which will give them better access to international labour markets (Kruss 2004).

Student Experience

Framing Student Experience in Terms of Three Conceptual Domains

While there is a growing body of research into student experience in South Africa (Cross et al. 2003; Cross and Johnson 2008; Cross, Mhlanga and Ojo 2009; Academy of Science of South Africa [ASSAf] 2010; CHE 2010; Strydom and Mentz 2010), we have found little that focuses specifically on the experience of international students – either those coming into South Africa or those leaving to study elsewhere. Research into student experience almost always considers the student body as a whole, local and international. Where these studies make explicit mention of international students as a subset of the student body, we have been able to draw on them (Cross et al. 2009; CHE 2010; Strydom and Mentz 2010). Elements of student experience can also be deduced from studies on understandings of internationalisation (Cross and Rouhani 2004; Cross, Mhlanga and Ojo 2009; Ojo 2009).

When it comes to South Africans studying abroad, the little research available tends to group South African students with others from Africa or from developing countries.[4] This means that it is not possible to separate out the experiences of South Africans, but we extrapolate from such studies the experiences of South Africans.

Several South African studies of student experience (Cross and Johnson 2008; Cross, Mhlanga and Ojo 2009; CHE 2010) make use of a framework of conceptual domains, adapted from Bernstein's (1990, 2000) analysis of intellectual fields and pedagogical identities, and we have adopted the same framework in our discussion here. This framework explains student experience as being shaped by the dialectic between three conceptual domains – the official, pedagogic and social domains. The official domain is concerned with the artefacts, processes and common ways of doing things that shape and reproduce the dominant culture of the institutions with which students interact. The pedagogic domain is concerned with the academic culture and includes discourses, curricula and teaching and learning practices, as well as explicit and implicit rules for interactions in the academic space. The social domain is concerned with the norms and assumptions about people and their social interactions in the broader society, as well as in the campus microcosm. These domains position students in different ways, and impact their sense of agency and the interactions between the domains result in the student experience. This framework has proved useful in understanding the different aspects of student experience as well as the role of student agency in student experience.

Experiences of Students Studying in South Africa

Official Domain: Bureaucratic Hindrances with some Irritation Value

International students studying in South Africa interact with two official domains – the government departments and offices that regulate their cross-border movement, and the official structures at the university. In both domains, students report mixed experiences.

Students coming to study in South Africa need a valid passport, a study permit as well as medical and police clearances. While studies have not been able to conclude that these requirements constitute significant obstacles to studying in South Africa, they have been called 'bureaucratic hindrances with some irritation value' (ASSAf 2010: 97) and students do complain about the process (Ojo 2009). It seems that policy statements on internationalisation have not translated into a coherent approach to dealing with students across the various government departments (Cross and Rouhani 2004; ASSAf 2010).

A particular problem is that the study permit expressly forbids work in South Africa[5] so that students in financial difficulties do not have the option to take up part-time work. About a third of the international students in one study reported financial difficulties (Cross et al. 2003).

Institutions have set up international offices and programmes to better inform students, welcome them on arrival and ease their settling in, but these support mechanisms are often under-staffed or staffed by poorly trained people, and under-resourced (Ojo 2009), and students are mixed in their views of the services provided (Cross et al. 2003). For some the process is simply inefficient:

> They are not making it easy for us at all. For example, I applied here in 2006. I desperately wanted to come and study. I had put money aside and everything aside to come. But, they are not just efficient. Everything was just delayed.
>
> (Ojo 2009: 106)

For others, accommodation is unsatisfactory (Cross et al. 2004) or is not provided as some individuals expected:

> Can you imagine coming from ... a neighbouring country with no relatives here and been told there is no accommodation for me? Why did they give me admission in the first place when they have not arranged an accommodation for me?
>
> (Ojo 2009: 106)

And, as might be expected, international students experience the official domain as disempowering:

> As an international student, I have strictly adhered to the stipulated rules by paying my fees and obtaining my study permit. So for me, this is a clear experience of internationalisation. They make the rule and either I like it or not, I just have to obey.
>
> (Ojo 2009: 106)

Pedagogic Domain: Familiar Language, Curricula and Pedagogies

Two key factors influencing student success in the pedagogic domain are language and the teaching and learning approaches in use (Church 1982 in Sam 2001). How do foreign students in South Africa adapt?

LANGUAGE IS A LOCAL ISSUE

English is the medium of instruction in South African universities and the majority of visiting students do not have a problem with the language: 'Almost all the African students have had English as their medium of instruction at school' (Ayliff and Wang 2006: 27). A minority of international students, from Asian and Francophone African countries, find it difficult integrating into the education system because language serves as a barrier to their full participation in teaching and learning activities (Ayliff and Wang 2006). Even when students have learned English they find the accents in South Africa difficult to understand and lecturers report that their knowledge of English is not sufficient for university study (Ayliff and Wang 2006).

However, the few visiting students that struggle with English pale into insignificant in the South African context. Language is one of the major educational challenges in South Africa where there are 11 official languages and many South Africans get to university without having mastered English. Students who have not studied in English or been in environments where English is commonly spoken, struggle to participate in class:

> To be honest, I just listen ... you see some kids having a nice time in the lectures ... and on the other hand here you are struggling to conceptualise what is being delivered in the lectures and catch each and every English word.
>
> (CHE 2010: 75)

Thus the focus of the language concerns in South Africa is not on the difficulties of foreign students, but rather on the significant problems amongst South African students.

EUROCENTRIC CURRICULA

Research suggests that international students adjust to curricula depending on the extent to which the curriculum philosophy resonates with their prior experience (Lee and Rice 2007). Curricula in South Africa are informed by two dominant discourses: the traditional liberal discourse and the utilitarian or responsiveness discourse (Adam and Cross 2011). The traditional liberal arts education is underpinned by Eurocentric conceptions of knowledge, and values the enculturation of the mind and knowledge as an end in itself. By contrast, the utilitarian discourse values knowledge for its relevance and application to local and global concerns in the social and economic world. Depending on the particular universities or programmes students will experience different curriculum philosophies (Adam 2009).

At many South African universities students are exposed to curricula similar to those in Europe:

> We don't do Indian philosophy, we don't do Jewish philosophy, and we don't do African philosophy. We just practice philosophy in the classical, analytical, Western tradition which is sceptical-based rather than building up, as it were, theories about what particular people might have thought about.
>
> (Head of the School of Philosophy, University of the Witwatersrand, reported in Adam 2009: 168)

International students from SADC and many other African countries that have similar colonial histories, as well as those from Europe, find that such curricula resonate with their experience and adjust easily. Students that have been exposed to the utilitarian curriculum discourse have greater variation in their experience because this approach attempts to combine global and local contexts and the extent of global versus local focus in programmes affects their experience (Adam 2009; Ojo and Booth 2009).

For example, courses that make use of South African case studies create difficulties for foreign students who lack the detailed and nuanced knowledge of the socio-political and economic environment. Social science and education programmes in South Africa have developed a strong focus on local policy issues as a means of being responsive, and research has identified curricula in political science and education courses that exclude foreign students (Adam 2009). This problem is less evident in the science and engineering fields where practices and examples tend to be more globally applicable.

THE FOREIGNNESS OF CRITICAL PEDAGOGIES

There are two distinct approaches to pedagogy in South Africa. On the one hand a critical pedagogy that encourages debate and dialogue, critical thinking and non-absolutist knowledge; and on the other, fundamental pedagogy underpinned by rote learning, absolutism and authoritarianism (Sedibe 1998). Critical pedagogy has been foregrounded in national and institutional policies and is slowly becoming the dominant discourse in the country (Adam 2009).

Students who come from critical pedagogy traditions integrate well into programmes that promote critical engagement. However, many students from African and Asian cultures that encourage obedience and respect for authority find the pedagogy in tension with their own identity and struggle to adapt. For example Chinese students experience a 'learning shock' because in China they are expected to gather information and attend lectures but they are not expected to debate concepts and ideas with their tutors as this is viewed as disrespectful (Ayliff and Wang 2006).

Again, this is not only a problem for visiting students. The same 'learning shock' awaits South African students whose educational experience is of fundamental pedagogy and whose culture is more authoritarian. These local students face the same difficulties adjusting as foreign students and both groups report feeling ignored, isolated and discriminated against (Sam 2001; Ayliff and Wang 2006; CHE 2010).

Social Domain: Acquaintances Sharing the Same Space

International students studying in South Africa have mixed experiences in the social domain. Some experiences are common to international students in many countries, like feeling homesick (Cross et al. 2003) and not 'belonging' (Ojo 2009), while others are specific to being in South Africa.

The divided nature of South African society goes against the ideal of inter-nationalisation providing cross-cultural interactions. Foreign students say that they find it difficult to meet South African students and they tend to mix mostly with other foreign students (Cross et al. 2003); this is reflected in the proliferation of country-based student organisations (CHE 2009). Although students say that they would welcome opportunities to interact socially with people from different cultures, interactions appeared to be of the nature of 'acquaintances sharing the same space' (Cross et al. 2003: 20) rather than deep relationships.

Foreigners are often struck by the racial divides in South African society: 'They cannot make friends with each other; my black friends and white friends do not relate with each other' (Ojo 2009: 115), as well as the more complex ethnic divisions: 'Like yesterday I had five of them here, and she's Sotho, she's Xhosa, she is whatever … so I'm saying, but you're South African!' (CHE 2010: 85).

Xenophobia is evident in South African society and, although less blatant at universities, it does impact on foreign students (Cross and Rouhani 2004; CHE 2010). In 2008 the country experienced a wave of violent attacks on foreigners, some of these in places where international students were living. One student said: 'Can you imagine the killing of foreigners these past weeks? They accused neighbouring Southern African nationals of being criminals and of taking their jobs and wives. Does that make sense?' (Ojo 2009: 115). Unfortunately some South African students do resent foreigners because they are perceived as competitors for scarce university places and for scarce government finan-cial resources (Cross and Rouhani 2004).[6] In addition, foreign students have generally enjoyed better quality school education and often do better in their studies.

Students value the varied cultural experiences that universities offer, supportive environments for international students, and gaining national and international perspectives that are valued in a globalised world (Cross, Mhlanga and Ojo, 2009). Students were also aware that their experiences in the social domain were related to their own sense of agency:

> First time I thought nobody likes me. I just felt like that. Or maybe it was in my behavior too – I was shy, in a new country and because I couldn't speak good English. I was always waiting for somebody to come to me.
>
> (Ojo 2009: 107)

South Africans Studying Internationally

It is difficult to discuss the experience of South African students studying abroad, not only because of a dearth of research, but also because experience obviously differs depending on the destination country. Here we could find no research that reflected on the official domain and we have combined the discussion of the pedagogical and social domains since what studies there are focus on language and social issues, but not on curricula and pedagogy.

Pedagogic and Social Domains: Cultural Carriers of Unwanted Gifts

We can identify two types of South Africans studying abroad. The first may or may not have financial resources, but did not meet the academic requirements to enter high demand programmes like medicine in their home country. These students generally study in other developing countries including Cuba, India and even the United Arab Emirates. These students are likely to experience languages, cultures and educational contexts that are significantly at odds with their own experience. Medical students in Cuba, for example, say that they found it difficult to learn in a foreign language and a foreign culture (DoH 2010).

The second group are high achievers who earn world class scholarships to top institutions in developed countries. These students generally have come through schools and universities that are similar to the developed world institutions that they go to study at. If they go to English speaking countries, they do not have difficulties with language; neither do they experience academic literacy, curriculum or epistemological barriers. Studies suggest that these students are more likely to encounter social problems than academic ones, including perceived discrimination and having few friends (Sam 2001).

Language (including accent), race and the culture of their country of origin play a part in the experience of international students and whether they feel welcomed or isolated. Prejudice and stereotyping of students by race, region and culture is common and affects students' experiences of academic life (Lee and Rice 2007). Lee and Rice found that students are in the US treated with different degrees of prejudice based on neo-racism – a hierarchy of race and the state of 'development' of their home countries, with students from less developed countries often being viewed in terms of academic deficit models. White international students face less discrimination than their 'coloured' counterparts, and people from Asia and the Middle East are treated worse than those from Mexico (Lee and Rice 2007). From this one can extrapolate that white South Africans are likely to have better experiences of international education than black South Africans, and that students from other parts of Africa are likely to have worse experiences than South Africans, because South Africa is considered more 'developed' than other African countries.

As a result of neo-racism, as well as the tendency worldwide for students to mix with students from their own country first and nearby countries second (Volet and Ang 1998), the internationalisation discourse that positions students from developing countries as resources and cultural carriers in developed countries, encouraging links between cultures, reducing prejudice, hostility and discrimination, is not reflected in the experience of students. It seems that few students and staff in developed country institutions have any desire to understand and learn from foreign cultures or have their pre-existing opinions of these countries challenged (Lee and Rice 2007). This has led some researchers to conclude that the underlying motivation for internationalisation is indeed financial (Lee and Rice 2007; Cross et al. 2009).

Conclusion

We make five key claims about students' experiences of internationalisation from a South African viewpoint. Firstly South African higher education is characterised by three significant phases in terms of its international orientation. Initially it exhibited many of the characteristics now associated with international education; during the apartheid years it became isolated from the international community and fragmented along lines of race and language; and since 1994, South Africa has enjoyed greater access to international linkages, including increasing numbers of international students from Africa.

Secondly at the national level, there are political and economic rationales for internationalisation of higher education, but these have not resulted in any coherent way of dealing with international students. Universities in South Africa understand internationalisation of higher education in terms of relocalisation and Africanisation, which includes the pursuit of African identities and epistemologies, but also in terms of enriching the educational experience and knowledge base by engaging across cultures and ending the isolation of the apartheid years.

Thirdly higher education in South Africa attracts substantial numbers of foreign students, particularly from other countries in Africa, but internal challenges have preoccupied the higher education system and internationalisation has received little attention. In South Africa concerns with learning in unfamiliar languages, with cultural difference, and globally and locally meaningful curricula are not regarded as issues related to internationalisation, but are central concerns of higher education as it applies to local students. The tension between local versus global content in the South African context is complex. Important drives to 'relocalise' and 'Africanise' curricula conflict with understandings of internationalisation as presenting alternative world views, teaching knowledge and skills that have global application, emphasising international dimensions of programmes and dealing with international issues. Local priorities may, at least for a time, leave foreign students feeling excluded.

Fourthly for students coming to study in South Africa, the experience varies according to their command of the English language, and their prior experience of curricula and pedagogy. Many international students that come from very similar education systems find it easy to adapt. Those who don't form an insignificant group as large numbers of local students are also struggling to make these adjustments. As a result international students seldom receive special support, but they are able to take advantage of the support structures put in place for local students.

Fifthly there is little research on the relatively small number of South Africans who study abroad. Their experience is likely to depend on the country, institution and programme they study. In particular, indications are that student experience differs depending on whether the destination country is perceived as more or less 'developed' than South Africa and on neo-racist rankings in terms of culture and language. The idea that students from less developed countries can enrich the learning of students at the host institution is not reflected in practice.

From these claims we conclude that universalising conceptions of internationalisation that seek to impose Western models of higher education are not applicable to the South African context or indeed in other postcolonial situations. South African higher education is located in a complex web of competing imperatives including the need for increased access for black South Africans, the educational and social challenges faced by local students, and the struggle for a locally meaningful higher education, as well as pressure for international recognition and acceptance. At the same time it is inevitably engaged with internationalisation as African students come to the country in search of better opportunities. Their experiences are shaped by the local reality: at both policy level and in the institutions, their concerns compete with and are overshadowed by those of local students.

Notes

1 Undergraduate diplomas and certificates, general academic bachelor's degrees, three- or four-year professional first degrees and bachelor of technology degrees.

2 Thirty-six per cent of international students are enrolled at UNISA, a distance education institution. Since our focus is on students who travel to study, we exclude the UNISA students, where appropriate.

3 Herman's research attributes this to insufficient funding, lack of interest in higher degrees, family commitments and the lure of employment, and alienating institutional cultures at historically white universities.

4 Often quite legitimately, because the number of students spread across many countries becomes insignificant as a unit of study.

5 Those who need to complete practical work components as part of their study programmes apply for a practical training permit.

6 While in the broader society, immigrants are viewed as competition for low-skilled jobs, this is not a specific source of resentment towards international students as study permits do not allow them to work while they are in South Africa.

References

Academy of Science of South Africa (ASSAf) (2010). The PhD study: An evidence-based study on how to meet the demands for high-level skills in an emerging economy. Pretoria: Academy of Science of South Africa (ASSAf).

Adam, F. (2009). Transformation of higher education. A humanities case study. PhD thesis, University of the Witwatersrand, Johannesburg.

Adam, F. and Cross, M. (2011). Utilitarianism and the fate of the humanities in South African higher education-the Wits experience. In Bitzer, E. and Botha, N. (eds.) Curriculum inquiry in South African higher education. Stellenbosch: SUN Media. pp. 113–134.

Altbach, P. (2000). What higher education does right. International Higher Education, 18(Winter), 2.

Ayliff, D. and Wang, G. (2006). Experiences of Chinese international students learning English at South African tertiary institutions. South African Journal of Higher Education, 20(3), 25–37.

Bernstein, B. (1990). Class, codes and control. Volume IV: The structuring of pedagogic discourse. London, Routledge.

Bernstein, B. (2000). Pedagogy, symbolic control and identity. Oxford: Rowman & Littlefield.

CHE (2009). Higher education monitor 8: The state of higher education in South Africa. Pretoria: Council on Higher Education (CHE).

CHE (2010). Higher education monitor 9: Access and throughput in South African higher education – three case studies. Pretoria: Council on Higher Education (CHE).

Cross, M. and Rouhani, S. (2004). Vanishing borders and new boundaries: Student and staff mobility and the internationalisation of South African higher education. In Zelesa, P. T. and Olukoshi, A. (eds.) African universities in the twenty-first century, Volume 1, Dakar, Senegal: CODESRIA, pp. 234–249.

Cross, M. and Johnson, B. (2008). Establishing a space of dialogue and possibilities: Student experience and meaning at the University of the Witwatersrand. South African Journal of Higher Education, 22(2), 302–321.

Cross, M., Mhlanga, E. and Ojo, E. (2009). Emerging concept of internationalisation in South African higher education: Conversations on local and global exposure at the University of the Witwatersrand (Wits). Journal of Studies in International Education, 15(1), 75–92.

Cross, M., Sehoole, T. et al. (2003). University experience in the 21st century: Perception of global and local exposure at the University of the Witwatersrand. Johannesburg: University of the Witwatersrand.

Cross, M., Shalem, Y. et al. (2009). How undergraduate students 'negotiate' academic performance within a diverse university environment. South African Journal of Higher Education, 23(1), 21–42.

Davies, J. L. (1997). A European agenda for change for higher education in the XXIst century: Comparative analysis of twenty institutional case studies. Creation, 111, 47–92.

De Wit, H. (2002). Internationalisation of higher education in the United States of America and Europe. London: Greenwood Press.

DoE (1996). Green paper on higher education transformation. Pretoria, South Africa: Department of Education (DoE).

DoE (1997). Education white paper 3: A programme for the transformation of higher education. Pretoria, South Africa: Department of Education (DoE).

DoE (2001a). National plan for higher education. Pretoria, South Africa: Department of Education (DoE).

DoE (2001b). Restructuring the higher education system in South Africa (Report of the National Working Group to the Minister of Education). Pretoria, South Africa: Department of Education (DoE).

DHET (2012a). Green Paper for post-school Education and Training. Pretoria, South Africa: Department of Higher Education and Training (DHET).

DHET (2012b). Register of private higher education institutions. Pretoria, South Africa: Department of Higher Education and Training (DHET). Retrieved 9 April 2012 from http://www.dhet.gov.za/LinkClick.aspx?fileticket=6l07VCUmDjc%3d&tabid=36

DoH (2010). Public health set to receive human resources (HR) boost. Statement issued by the Department of Health (DoH), 5 July 2010. Retrieved 17 January 2012 from http://www.info.gov.za/speeches/2010/10070608251002.htm

Du Plessis, E. and Fourie, J. (2011). Higher education exports in South Africa: A case study of Stellenbosch University. South African Journal of Higher Education, 25, 460–475.

Groening, S. (1987) The impact of economic globalization on higher education. Boston, MA: New England Board of Higher Education.

Herman, C. (2011) Elusive equity in doctoral education in South Africa. Journal of Education and Work, 24(1), 163–184.

Higher Education Act of 1997. Republic of South Africa. Available from: http://www.che.ac.za/documents/d000004/Higher_Education_Act.pdf

Higher Education Management System (HEMIS) (2011). Republic of South Africa: Higher Education and Training.

Kahn, M., Blankley, W., Maharajh, R., Poue, T. E., Reddy, V., Cele, G., et al. (2004). Flight of the flamingos: A study on the mobility of R&D workers (p. 54). Cape Town, South Africa: HSRC Press.

Kishun, R. (2007). The internationalisation of higher education in South Africa: Progress and challenges. Journal of Studies in International Education, 11(3–4), 455–469.

Kruss, G. (2004). Chasing credentials and mobility: Private higher education in South Africa. Cape Town, South Africa: HSRC Press.

Lee, J. and Rice, C. (2007). Welcome to America? International student perceptions of discrimination. Higher Education, 53, 381–409.

Lulat, YG.-M. (2005). A history of African higher education from antiquity to the present: A critical synthesis. Westport, CT: Praeger Publishers.

Morrow, W. (1992). Epistemological access in university. Academic Development Issues, 1, 3–5.

National Plan for Higher Education (2001) Ministry of Education. Republic of South Africa. Available from: http://www.cepd.org.za/files/pictures/National%20Plan%20%20for%20Higher%20Education%20in%20South%20Africa.pdf

NCHE (1996). A framework for transformation. Pretoria, South Africa: National Commission on Higher Education (NCHE).

OECD (2011). Education at a glance: 2011 OECD indicators. Retrieved 10 January 2012 from http://www.oecd.org/dataoecd/61/2/48631582.pdf

Ojo, E. (2009). Internationalisation of higher education at the University of the Witwatersrand: A phenomenographic study of students' perspectives. Thesis, University of the Witwatersrand, Johannesburg.

Ojo, E. and Booth, S. (2009). Internationalisation of higher education in a South African university: A phenomenographic study of students' conceptions. Education as Change, 13, 37–41.

Sam, D. L. (2001). Satisfaction with life among international students: An exploratory study. Social Indicators Research, 53(3), 315–337.

Sedibe, K. (1998) Dismantling apartheid education: An overview of change. Cambridge Journal of Education, 28(3), 269–282.

Sehoole, C. (2006). Internationalisation of higher education in South Africa: A historical review. Perspectives in Education, 24(4), 1–13.

South Africa – U.S. Higher Education Partnerships Project (2012). Available at: http://africa.isp.msu.edu/AHEPI/

Strydom, J. F. and Mentz, M. (2010) South African Survey of Student Engagement (SASSE) – focusing the student experience on success through student engagement. Pretoria, South Africa: Council on Higher Education (CHE).

Szanton, D. L. and Manyika, S. (2002) PhD programs in African universities: Current status and future prospects. Berkeley, CA: University of California.

Tiechler, U. (1999). Internationalisation as a challenge and for higher education in Europe. Tertiary Education Management, 5(1), 5–22.

UNESCO (2011a). Top five destinations for mobile students and outbound mobility ratio. UNESCO. Retrieved 17 January 2011 from http://www.uis.unesco.org/Education/Pages/tertiary-education.aspx

UNESCO (2011b). Numbers of mobile students by region of origin and inbound mobility rates. UNESCO. Retrieved 17 January 2011 from http://www.uis.unesco.org/Education/Pages/tertiary-education.aspx

Volet, S. and Ang, G. (1998). Culturally mixed groups on international campuses: An opportunity for inter-cultural learning. Higher Education research and Development, 17(1), 5–23.

15

Growing Pains
The Student Experience in Chile

MARÍA JOSÉ LEMAITRE AND RAÚL ATRIA BENAPRÉS

Cross culturally speaking, the prevailing approach to higher education as a priority area for national development is built on the assumption that investment in education at the highest level of the system is the path for both individual advancement and sustained upward mobility of the students that can enter the system and attain the corresponding technical or professional credentials. In the context of an increasingly open market global economy the 'employability' of graduates is at the core of this crucial assumption. This is probably the major factor that explains the massive growth of the student population in the higher education systems everywhere. National higher education systems are being shaped according to different public policy combinations or 'models' through which the concerned official agencies face the challenges emerging from this generalised assumption. The student experience in each national context cannot be understood without taking into consideration the impact these policy models have on the students and their families.

Chile is certainly a notable case for examining these impacts as the country has experienced during the last three decades profound changes in the design and implementation of its higher education policy models. At the background of these changes there have been important structural trends that must be taken into account for evaluating the performance of the higher education system as regards the basic social mobility assumption mentioned above.

Survey data collected at the Center for Research in Social Structure (CIES 2011) at the Sociology Department of the University of Chile in 2009 show that the peak of upward mobility for respondents' fathers, as measured by intergenerational advancement in education at the higher education level, was reached by the cohorts born in the 1950s and 1970s. In this survey, respondents who were born, for example, in the 1970s, were accessing higher education in the 1990s and were reporting on the educational level their father had reached 20 years earlier. Proportions of 47 and 36 per cent of respondents born in the 1970s and 1980s respectively had fathers with higher education. For those born in the 1940s and 1960s, the proportions were 19 and 22 per cent. These ups and downs show that there is a sort of 'stop and go' succession of educational mobility waves, which most probably are related to the impact of governmental educational policies adopted during specific political and ideological periods in the country since 1920. At the secondary education level, the upward mobility flow has three peak decades, namely the 1940s, 1960s and 1980s, showing a similar intergenerational pattern. In the case of higher education, upward mobility flows of sons and daughters are also observed in the 1960s and particularly in the 1980s after the deregulation of the higher education system, the strong entrance of private providers and the ensuing expansion of enrolment.

This is a firm indication of the complex interplay of politics, public policies and social structure. In addition, and this is most remarkable, there is a sort of 'rollercoaster' pattern in the flows of upward mobility when educational comparisons between fathers and sons/daughters are concerned. There is a lesson in this picture: in Chile, for each generation, educational upward social mobility is not a solid upstairs escalator; it can also have painful downward steps even at the uppermost part of the ladder. In this paper, an attempt is made to relate the student experience to some of these trends.

Context of the Country's Higher Education System

Until 1980, the Chilean higher education system was made up of two state universities and six private ones, all equally funded by the government. It was a relatively homogeneous system, in which universities focused on the three traditional functions of teaching, research and public service, were very selective in terms of students and staffed with highly qualified academics. The educational reform of 1981 introduced dramatic changes, which can be essentially summarised in two main aspects: differentiation and funding.

Differentiation happened in two directions:

- Horizontal differentiation, meaning the emergence both of new public universities, established on the basis of the regional branches of the existing ones, and a new breed of private provider, with an explicit or implicit profit goal and mainly focused on absorbing demand.
- Vertical differentiation, through the establishment or public recognition of non-university institutions: professional institutes (PI), offering professional degrees, and technical training centres (TTC), offering two and three year technical–vocational programmes, such as computer programming, public relations or teacher assistant.

For the sake of simplicity and easier understanding, we will refer to the original eight universities, plus those created on the basis of their regional branches, as the 'public' sector. This includes 16 state universities and 9 private ones, all of which receive public funding on a regular basis. Institutions created after 1981 compose the private sector, with very limited access to public funds. We will use the concept of higher education, even though we will be referring to a three tiered system, which is closer to the idea of tertiary education.

Funding changes meant that the government significantly reduced its contribution to higher education, shifting the bulk of funding to students and their families. Higher education institutions – both public and private – were asked to become 'self-funding', which meant asking them to act following market rules and, in practice, introduced a privatising rationale even in those higher education institutions owned by the State.

Higher Education Institutions

Higher education institutions grew in number during the eighties and nineties, but both quality assurance requirements and market considerations led to a reduction in number at the end of the nineties, as can be seen in Table 15.1.

However, even though the numbers were quite stable, institutions grew increasingly differentiated in most of their main features, such as their age, location, size, ownership, quality, functions, selectivity or the characteristics of the student body, the academic or teaching staff. Therefore, they have been grouped according to some of these features.

Universities were classified on the basis of their selectivity (that is, whether they accept students over or below an above average score in the entrance test) and their main functions (classifying them as research universities; universities with research; teaching universities with some research; and teaching universities). These categories were further refined adding size (using 15,000 students as the cut-off point) and quality, using the results of the accreditation processes. The classification for universities is shown in Table 15.2.

Professional institutes were classified on the basis of their accreditation results, their size (large: over 10,000 students; medium: between 2,000 and 9,999 students; small, below 2000 students) and the number of areas they covered, designating specialised those institutions that cover three areas or less. The results are shown in Table 15.3.

Table 15.1 Higher education institutions in Chile, 1980–2010

	1980	1985	1990	1995	2000	2005	2010
Public U	8	20	20	25	25	25	25
Private U	0	3	40	45	39	36	35
PI	0	1	76	73	60	43	44
TTC	0	132	161	127	116	102	73

Source: CNAP, 2007.

Table 15.2 Categorisation of universities, by function, quality and size

Selective universities	
Research universities	5
Universities with research activities	6
Teaching universities with research activities	6
Teaching universities	10
Non selective universities	
Small teaching universities, mid or high quality	13
Small teaching universities, low quality	12
Large teaching universities, low quality (one exception)	6

Source: Torres and Zenteno, 2011.

Table 15.3 Categorisation of professional institutes by quality, size and level of specialisation

High or medium quality				Low quality		
Large	Medium		Small	Large or medium	Small	
Non specialised	Specialised	Non specialised	Specialised	Non specialised	Specialised	Non specialised
6	1	2	2	7	14	12

Source: Torres and Zenteno, 2011.

Technical training centres present a much more varied situation. They were classified first in terms of size (large, over 5000 students; medium, between 2000 and 4999 students; small, below 2000 students) and then in terms of their accreditation and licensing status. However, since accreditation is voluntary, some TTC have not applied for accreditation. It can be assumed that the better ones have sought the recognition associated with accreditation, but it is an assumption that is difficult to verify. In any case, only 11 are accredited, and 62 either have not been accredited or have not applied for accreditation.

Describing this classification is not trivial, since the features of the student body and their experience is very different depending on the type of institutions where they enrol. This is analysed in the next section.

Student Population

Enrolment grew during the eighties and nineties mostly in the private sector, but since 1998, it has grown in both sectors, with a marked concentration on universities, which have steadily concentrated over 60 per cent of the enrolment. While there may be different reasons for this concentration, it is mostly associated with a more traditional approach on the part of the students, who tend to associate quality and prestige with a university degree (see Figure 15.1). However, this trend may be slowly changing: in the last two years, enrolment in technical programmes has exceeded that of universities.

The growth in enrolment initially focused on students from the upper income groups (deciles 5–10) but, since 2000, the focus of most policy decisions has been on improving opportunities for access to lower income groups. This means that increasing numbers of lower income students are entering higher education, but inequities are still apparent, as can be seen from Table 15.4, which shows the percentage of the potential student population enrolled in higher education.

Comments on the Description of the Chilean Higher Education System

Higher education in Chile has experienced substantial changes in the last 30 years, which must be taken into account in any analysis of its operation and of the student experience. Institutional diversification is one of them; while there

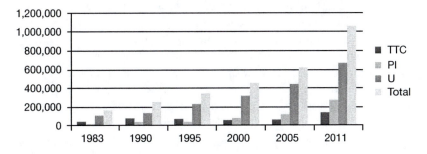

Figure 15.1 Changes in student enrolment, by institutional type, 1983–2011

Source: www.mineduc.cl.

Table 15.4 Net coverage by income quintile (1990–2009)

Quintile	1990	2000	2009
I	3.7	7	16.9
II	6.6	12	21.4
III	10.1	21.7	25.2
IV	18.2	32.2	35.1
V	35	53.2	57.3

Source: Orellana, 2011.

is only one formal group of universities – that of public funded universities, which belong to the Council of Rectors – there are clear categories, which have been described previously in this chapter. Following that categorisation, it is possible to say that prestige is closely associated with the public/private divide, and with the level of selectivity of higher education institutions. Universities in the first two categories all belong to the public sector; private universities appear only as selective teaching universities with research activities. Among professional institutes (all private), prestige is linked to size and quality, with the two larger institutions clearly surpassing the others.

A second significant change is the increased demand for higher education, which goes together with the emergence of a new student population, very different from the traditional male, young, urban, highly qualified students. A third important aspect is the reduction of public funding, and increased privatisation of higher education institutions through the need to access private sources of funds (mainly student fees). An Organisation for Economic Co-operation and Development (OECD) study puts Chilean public funding at a rate of 15 per cent of the total social expenditure in higher education (OECD 2008). While this may not take into account all public funds that go to higher education, Chile is probably one of the countries with the lowest rate of public funding in the world, which means that most of the resources must come from students and their families. Since all higher education institutions charge fees and these tend to be quite high, students who cannot afford to pay them out of their personal or family income must take loans, which carry different levels of subsidy but which, in general, impose a heavy burden on new graduates.

Another feature is the distinct 'marketisation' of higher education provision, that is, a strong dependence on market rules for the main decisions that must be made in institutional management (e.g. definition of programmes to be offered, level of fees charged to students, salary levels). The need to look for and to find private sources of funding makes institutions highly dependent on market opportunities, which can be quite different from the institutional priorities, set in their mission statements, or even contradict their stated purposes. This has also had an impact of the level of fees, which show a wide spread, as can be seen in Figure 15.2.

In order to put these figures in perspective, average per capita income by quintile is reported in Figure 15.3.

Most students in Chile stay in their own city to study (only 13 per cent report moving to a higher education institution located in a different city). They tend to live at home, in part because of cultural patterns, but also because living away from home involves additional expense, almost impossible to cover for most students in addition to the tuition fees.

Finally, it is important to mention that quality assurance processes have been in place in Chile since 1990. Quality assurance has been seen as an essential component of higher education policies, initially focused on licensing of

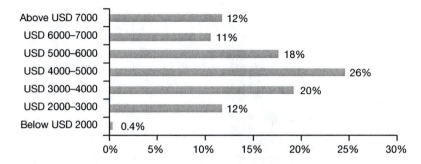

Figure 15.2 Distribution of enrolment by level of annual fees
Source: CNED, INDICES, 2011.

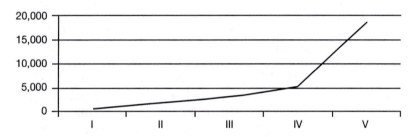

Figure 15.3 Average per capita income in US dollars (2009) by quintile
Source: CASEN, 2009.

new, private institutions, but later expanded to cover both programme and institutional accreditation. The latter is required for students to be eligible for subsidised loans to cover fees, which means that most institutions have applied for accreditation.

The Student Experience

The Student Experience in the Country

As mentioned above, enrolment has more than doubled in the last ten years. This means not only more students, it also means a different type of student. While in the 1990s and early 2000s access was centred on upper income students, by the end of the first decade of this century the rate of expansion was explained mostly by the increasing access of the poorer 50 per cent of Chilean society (see Figure 15.4).

As a consequence, it is impossible to speak of 'the student experience'. There are many experiences, which depend on the entry qualifications of the student,

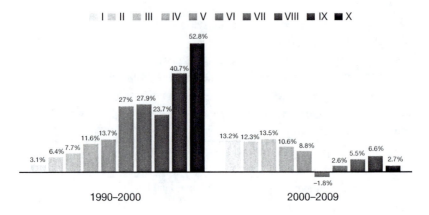

I   II   III   IV   V   VI   VII   VIII   IX   X

Figure 15.4 Rate of growth of coverage in higher education, by income deciles

Source: CIES, 2011.

his/her cultural background, and, of course, the income level. These are closely linked with the experience in secondary education, the institutions where it is possible to study, the quality of the programme offered, the probability of completing a course of study and earning a degree in a reasonable period of time, and, finally, with the opportunities for employment or further study.

For those students able to enter a selective university – and this depends mostly on the quality of secondary education – higher education opens up many opportunities. Teaching staff are, in general, highly qualified; programmes are updated frequently; and teaching and learning resources are readily available. Students in these institutions tend to complete their studies (although they take longer than expected) and, after graduation, they show twice the rate of employment of non-university graduates, and earn about four times as much. If they want to continue studying, they have ample opportunities, both in Chile and abroad. Enrolment in these universities accounts for 56 per cent of all university students, and, roughly, represents one third of all higher education students.

Students who enter the better non-selective universities, or professional institutes with good accreditation results, also tend to have a positive experience. They are less likely to complete their studies than the first group, and the probability of employment and of a higher salary is also less, but it is clearly much higher than that of other members in their age cohort who do not have a degree. These students represent between 25 and 30 per cent of the total student population.

The situation is very different for the rest of the students. Some of them come from middle income families, but most are part of an emergent and increasing lower middle class, who attended relatively poor public secondary schools, with weak social and cultural networks – many of them are the first generation in their families able to enter higher education – who study part-time and enter non-selective universities, for-profit professional institutes or technical training centres with low accreditation results. Their rates of attrition are very high, and only about 40 per cent of them manage to graduate.

National policies have focused mostly on increasing access, through funding for student aid (some scholarships and two complementary loan schemes to cover tuition fees). As a result, enrolment, as seen in Figure 15.1, has grown significantly, reaching a figure of over one million students in 2011. Of course, to enrol is only the first step in a complex itinerary, which includes the choice of institution and programme, the chances for progressing through the study plan, graduation and, finally, employability.

Access carries with it a large set of expectations, which are probably greater the lower the social position of the student. The problems mentioned for the third group of students outlined above are probably one of the main reasons that explain the significant level of student and social unrest associated with higher education in the country.

Not surprisingly, students tend to concentrate in universities (university degrees carry more prestige than other degrees), but those in the lower end of the scale – low selectivity, large numbers of students, low accreditation results – are the ones that show greater rates of growth, as they offer places to students who do not have the needed qualifications for other types of universities. Non-selective universities represent 44 per cent of the university enrolment, with between 20 and 40 per cent of part-time (mostly evening) students, who tend to choose programmes in education or in the area of health. At the level of professional institutes, six of them represent 64 per cent of the enrolment, but smaller institutions are growing, mostly though the offer of technical or vocational degrees: over 40 per cent of the students enrolled in professional institutes are following technical programmes, and 45 per cent do so in evening classes, while at the professional level, this percentage falls to 38. Larger institutes enrol students mostly in the areas of technology and business administration, while medium sized institutes tend to focus on education and technology.

The increase in enrolment in evening programmes is linked to a higher proportion of adult students, who wish to upgrade their credentials. These usually hold a full-time job, and, therefore, are able to devote a smaller portion of their time to study.

Another aspect of access is the type of programmes chosen by students. At the university level, it is possible to identify which programmes are selected as first choice for enrolment, further classifying students according to the occupation of the main breadwinner in the family, as a proxy for socio-economic status.

Table 15.5 lists in order of preference the programmes students enrol in, by social group. They are ranked from highest to lowest (e.g. business administration is the top priority for three of the four groups considered in the data). The two upper categories fill in the places offered in the more traditional, high prestige and high income programmes. The two lower categories find enrolment in less traditional, middle or high income programmes, and in business administration and law, which have expanded their offer to cover demand. One problem that is not evident from this distribution is that programmes that offer the same nominal degree can vary widely in terms of the actual opportunities they offer: learning outcomes from a degree that enrols higher income students, granted by a highly selective university charging high fees will be quite different from the same degree offered to less qualified students, with very different teaching conditions, in terms of learning requirements, qualifications and dedication of the academic staff or availability of learning resources. This is the case of business administration and law, seen in Table 15.5. Unfortunately, many students, especially those who are the first generation to attend higher education (over 60 per cent in 2010), are not aware of this, and they expect to obtain equal or very similar benefits.

A secondary effect of increased access is the opportunity higher education gives students to use information and communications technologies (ICT). Ninety per cent of the students belonging to families in the professional and managerial category declare that home is the main space for the use of the internet; this is the case for only 59 per cent of students from the unskilled worker group. For 23 per cent of these, their place of study offers the main opportunity for access to the internet.

The real problem students face becomes apparent when looking at retention rates, which are very different depending on the type of institution, but which are consistently low at those institutions enrolling lower income students (see Table 15.6).

Table 15.5 Ranking of the first choices of students, by social group

Managers and professionals	Technicicans and mid level professionals	White and blue collar workers	Unskilled workers
• Business administration • Law • Engineering • Medicine • Physiotherapy • Engineering • Dentistry • Architecture • Psychology	• Business administration • Physiotherapy • Law • Informatics • Psychology • Teacher training in physical education • Nursing • Dentistry • Construction	• Business administration • Physiotherapy • Law • Engineering • Teacher training in physical education • Construction • Construction • Psychology • Nursing	• Physiotherapy • Business administration • Law • Informatics • Engineering • Teacher training in physical education • Construction • Risk prevention • Auto mechanics

Source: Orellana, 2011.

Table 15.6 Rates of retention in universities, by institutional category

	Percent rate of retention after 1st year[1]	*Percent Rate of retention after 2nd year*[2]
Selective universities	80	70
Non selective universities with high accreditation rates	78	60
Non selective universities with low accreditation rates	53	40
Large PIs, with high accreditation rates	68	48
Large and medium PIs with low accreditation rates	47	35

Notes:
1 Percentage of students enrolled in first year who re-enroll for the second year.
2 Percentage of students enrolled in second year who re-enroll for the third year.

Source: Torres and Zenteno, 2011.

This means that while many students enter higher education, over 50 per cent of them have failed at least in one programme by the end of their second year. Those who graduate – and there are no reliable figures, but the overall estimate is about 50 per cent – take one to two extra years to complete their programmes, with the corresponding cost both in terms of time and fees to be paid. It is interesting to note, however, that there is a group of institutions that seem to be doing a better job in retaining students: those non-selective universities, with high accreditation results, show rates that are not far behind the selective institutions. While no studies have been carried out in this respect, it is highly likely that these outcomes are the result of improved curricula, which take into account the requirements of the actual students; of support mechanisms (such as mentoring); and a close supervision of student progression. Therefore, these cases should be analysed carefully, since they seem to provide students with an effective learning experience.

The situation is aggravated by the fact that all students must pay tuition fees, although the government has provided some scholarships and a wide ranging loan programme. However, students who leave their studies without getting a degree must still pay their loans.

It used to be unusual for students to work in Chile. While this is changing, since many students from the lower income groups cannot afford not to work during their years of study, still the proportion of students who hold a job while studying is relatively small (between 10 per cent, mostly part-time in the upper group, and 16 per cent in the unskilled workers group, where at least half of those hold a full-time job).

Table 15.7 Distribution of income from salaries, according to higher education institution, in individuals coming from families in the blue collar and unskilled labour groups

	% Below US$1000	% Between US$1000–2000	% Over US$2000	% Total
Research universities	40.0	25.0	35.0	100
Selective universities	57.1	28.6	14.3	100
Non selective universities	60.0	33.3	6.7	100
PI or TTC	83.0	15.1	1.9	100
No higher education	93.2	5.7	1.1	100
Average income in Chile	88.0	8.9	3.1	100

Source: Orellana, 2011.

Finally, a few words about life after higher education. While information is scant, and not related to the degree obtained, it is possible to find some data about the impact of higher education on salary levels, which can be seen in Table 15.7 above.

It is clear that for those lower income students who manage to access a high level university, and graduate from it, opportunities increase significantly. In fact, 4 per cent of children from working families are now part of the upper professional group. When taking into consideration that children from working families are the largest social group, 4 per cent is a very high figure. But the table shows that graduates from all types of higher education institutions can expect to earn higher salaries than the average and much higher than those with no higher education at all.

In summary, Chile is going through a difficult period. Its main effort has been to increase access, and it has achieved its goal. Access to higher education, for those who manage to graduate, is linked to social recognition, higher salaries and a better quality of life. The challenge now is to make the provision increasingly relevant to the new type of students, who require different curricular and pedagogical arrangements, different programmes and, most of all, opportunities not only for access, but also for permanence, progression and timely graduation.

The Experience of International Students in the Country

Internationalisation has become a priority for higher education around the world, but it is a rather marginal concern for Chilean higher education institutions. In this sense it is clear that Chilean universities have tended to look at themselves and to plan their institutional development from a largely inward perspective. The main reason for this view is probably related to the pressing challenge of rebuilding the universities after they were submitted to forced intervention and tutelage during the authoritarian military regime in the 1970s and 1980s.

In order to put things in a proper perspective, it must be underlined that the military assumed total control of the country after the coup of 1973, banned political parties, suppressed political and social mobilisation and made a radical change in the political, economic and social bases of the development model that had been installed in the country since the late 1930s. In that context, public policies and practically all the institutional fabric of the country were drastically affected. The educational system, and, in particular, higher education institutions, were not an exception. The government took de facto control of all the universities and designated new academic authorities that carried out repressive actions aimed at the eradication of all possible forms of resistance or dissent in the campuses. This restrictive scenario changed with the return of democracy in 1990. Accordingly, academic priorities during the following two decades were predominantly focused on the reconstruction of institutions in a context of intense massification and diversification.

In recent years, the realities of global trends have slowly gained increased attention in the strategic planning of higher education institutions in the country. International organisations are changing the way in which higher education student mobility is measured. From a broad approach that measured all foreigners that are studying in the recipient country, the measurement that prevails nowadays narrows down to those international students that are expressly admitted as students by the recipient country. The advantage of this narrower measurement is that 'net' student migration can be more precisely quantified. Some observed discrepancies in the sources of data (e.g. OECD versus United Nations Educational, Scientific and Cultural Organization [UNESCO] statistics) are due to this change of focus. Chilean data on the matter only recently started to reflect this situation and now uses the narrow definition as stated above. Table 15.8 shows how results vary according to the way in which international student mobility is measured.

Table 15.8 shows the two different international distributions of higher education for the year 2008: one refers to all foreigners that are enrolled as students (6,896), and the other counts international mobility based on those foreigners that were admitted in the country as registered students (2,041). To try to avoid overestimation of the international flows of student mobility, we will rely on the latter figure. Irrespective of the figure used, the discrepancies of the two distributions are mainly in the kinds of programmes of enrolment, particularly in technical and professional programmes. Data for the international student migration are not available before 2008.

According to data in Table 15.9, provided by UNESCO that uses the narrow approach to measuring international student mobility as stated above, the majority of foreign higher education students in Chile come from the regional

Table 15.8 Foreign students and student mobility in Chile (2008) (% of enrolment)

	% Foreigners as students	% Internation student migration
Type B programmes	0.7	0.2
Type A programmes	0.9	0.2
Advanced research programmes	10.8	10.4
Total tertiary enrolment	0.9	0.3
Total foreign enrolment (frequency)	6.896	2.041

Source: OECD 2011.

Table 15.9 Inflow of higher education foreign students, by region of origin (2010) (in percentages)

Regions	Inflow of HE foreign students
East Asia and the Pacific	1.3
Latin America and the Caribbean	54.8
North America and Western Europe	4.6
Southwest Asia	0.1
Sub-Saharan Africa	0.1
Unspecified	39.1
Total	100.0

Source: UNESCO 2010.

neighbourhood (54.8 per cent), although it can be seen that there is a sizable number (almost 40 per cent) of unspecified region of origin. Apart from the 4.6 per cent coming from the northern hemisphere, the figure for the rest of the world is negligible. It is also clear that in the Latin American context only Argentina and Chile are relatively important destinations in the region, attracting 3.8 per cent of all students studying abroad in the region (UNESCO 2010). A tradition of regional higher education student mobility is simply non-existent.

The Experience of Chilean Students Internationally

The international outflows of students are still limited and they tend to concentrate in selective groups of Chilean students moving abroad to pursue post-graduate studies. The official scholarships programme known as 'Becas Chile', funded through the National Commission for Science and Technology (CONICYT is the acronym in Spanish) has been the key policy instrument for the successful implementation of the programme. In general, the geographic destinations of these outflows follow the priority pattern prevailing in internationalisation policies in Latin America in which Europe is the first priority, followed by Latin America and the Caribbean and North America. There are no other significant destinations as far as internationalisation is concerned (IAU 2010: 93). The transnational marketing of European higher education after the Bologna Process may explain the high positioning of European institutions as a destination of students abroad.

Destinations

In 2008, Chileans studying abroad amounted to 6,664. There are two countries that were preferred by Chilean students studying abroad that year: Spain and the USA (see Table 15.10). After democracy returned to Spain, the political opening of the country coupled with the commonality of language were certainly the main factors explaining the rise of Spain to the top of the list. The USA, on the other hand, has had a long history as an environment of reference in the academic and educational communities in Chile. France and Germany, and the UK to a lesser degree, have a strong influence in the cultural conformation of the traditional middle and upper classes in the country, which may explain the relative attraction they still have for Chilean students moving abroad. The interesting case is the presence of Australia, which is clearly a rising newcomer in the context of international student mobility.

Table 15.10 Outflow of higher education students, by country of destination (2008), in frequencies and percentages

Countries	Frequency count		%	
Australia		227		3.4
Europe		2,799		42
France	473		7.1	
Germany	420		6.3	
Spain	1,659		24.9	
UK	247		3.7	
USA		1,193		17.9
Total of OECD		**5091**		**76.4**
Brazil		267		4.0
Other non-OECD		1,306		19.6
Total of non-OECD		**1,573**		**23.6**
Total		6,664		100.0

Source: UNESCO 2010.

As shown in the UNESCO statistics, the net higher education student mobility flow is positive in the case of Chile as the country receives more foreign students than Chilean students moving abroad. In 2008 there were 6,664 Chileans studying abroad and 2,041students whose motivation for migration was solely educational. It must be remembered that the total enrolment of foreigners was 7,946, corresponding to 0.3 per cent of the national higher education enrolment figure, but this includes many students who are not necessarily looking for a Chilean higher education – they just happen to be here. There is certainly significant room for improvement in the inflows of higher education student mobility.

Quality of Experience

There are no precise OECD or UNESCO data on the distribution of Chilean students abroad according the level of studies (undergraduate and graduate). Information on awards of official governmental scholarships provided by the National Commission for Science and Technology (CONICYT) may help in that respect. From that source, in 2008 there were 1,069 scholarships assigned to either MA or PhD eligible candidates, which amounts to 16 per cent of the total number of Chileans pursuing tertiary studies abroad (CONICYT, 2011) (see Table 15.11).

A graphic representation of the data in Table 15.11 may help in order to grasp the trend in the assignment of scholarships through CONICYT since 2000 (see Figure 15.5). As shown in the curves of the graph in Figure 15.5, a major increase in the number of scholarships was attained in 2007–2008 when 'Becas Chile' reached a peak of 1,600 awards for both MA and PhD studies.

Table 15.11 Scholarships for post-graduate studies abroad, selected years 2000–2010; 2011–2014 projected figures

Year	PhD	MA	PhD complement
2000	56	26	–
2002	72	46	–
2004	110	30	–
2006	183	80	–
2008	827	777	110
2010	446	371	145
2012	450	300	250
2014	50	300	350

Note: Includes all types of scholarships administered by this State Agency.

Source: CONICYT 2011.

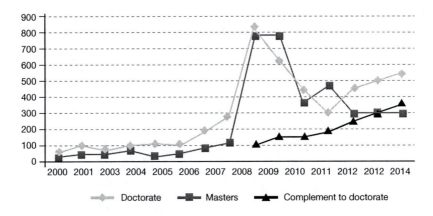

Figure 15.5 Scholarships for post-graduate studies abroad 2000–2010; 2011–2014 projected figures

By 2009–2010 the programme seems to have stabilised in the range of 300 to 500 awards for both types of graduate programmes, adding a new subsidy that operates as a complement to PhD candidates.

As far as areas of knowledge are concerned, during the period under scrutiny, there are two trends that must be highlighted from Table 15.12. The first one is the tendency of the social sciences to maintain a dominant position in the process of high human capital formation, which may be also related to the upward move of the humanities. The two areas combined represent 60 per cent of the total doctoral scholarship assignment. There are cultural dimensions and preferences that are surely at the basis of this positioning. The second trend relates to the upward move of the natural sciences up to 2010 with a strong diminution in 2011. Although the fall to 15 per cent is still an 'isolated' point it calls for a certain concern if it were a point of inflection in the curve.

Finally, a sample from data on doctoral scholarships awarded by CONICYT in 2011 combined with the Shanghai ranking of universities available for the same year, seen in Table 15.13, shows the potential of Chilean students for admission to top level post-graduate programmes offered abroad.

With respect to quality recognition of the recipient higher education institution abroad, it should be mentioned that up until 2010 candidates for 'Becas Chile' were requested to specify the institution and the graduate programme to which they were applying for admission, providing proof of their application. The quality ranking of the institution that was available to CONICYT was given a significant weight for the evaluation of the candidates. Starting in 2010 the programme introduced an important change as the candidates were now expected to provide certification that they had been formally admitted at the international institution of their choice, with the same assessment of the

Table 15.12 Areas of knowledge for assigned post-graduate scholarships (2008–2011)

Knowledge area	2008 %	2009 %	2010 %	2011 %
Social sciences	49	44	44	48
Natural sciences	19	28	33	15
Engineering and technology	13	15	10	14
Humanities	9	6	6	12
Agrcultural sciences	5	5	4	6
Medical sciences and health	5	3	3	5
Total	100	100	100	100

Source: CONICYT 2011.

Table 15.13 Doctoral Scholarships awarded by the 'Becas Chile' Programme, 2011

Shanghai Ranking 2011	Percentage of scholarships awarded
1 to 50	17.9
50 to 100	25.0
101 to 500	46.4
Out of ranking	10.7
Total	100

Source: CONICYT 2011.

institutional quality. In other words, the burden of proof of the quality of the recipient higher education institution abroad is now on the shoulders of the student. The new procedure has been subject to strong criticism and debate.

Role of International Degrees Within and Beyond the Country

Chile has a well regulated system for the recognition of undergraduate (professional) degrees from other countries. Universidad de Chile, the main public university in the country, is in charge of assessing, recognising and validating international degrees, which can only be done through a thorough analysis of the curriculum and the actual learning experience of the candidate, plus a review of the alignment of the contents of the degree with its equivalent in Chile. This makes it a cumbersome, relatively slow and expensive process for the applicants and its revision is under discussion. In addition to this, Chile signed a number of international agreements providing recognition of degrees of specific countries. These agreements can be classified in two groups: those signed at the beginning of the 20th century, when higher education in Latin

America was very different from that available today, and those signed in the last few years. The first have also come under close scrutiny, since they do not include any provision for checking on the quality of the programme or the learning contents, and, in many cases, have been subject to additional requirements. The second set of agreements link recognition to the result of accreditation processes in the country where the degree was obtained; while these agreements are still in their initial stages, they point to a significant change in the way in which international degrees are recognised.

Graduate degrees are not regulated, and their recognition depends exclusively on the prestige of the granting institution, and on the value the market allocates to them.

Chilean degrees, on the other hand, are widely recognised in many other Latin American countries, even though they are formally required to go through procedures that are similar to those described in the Chilean case for undergraduate degrees. Most Latin American countries are still in the very initial stages of development of graduate programmes; Chile, which has a long experience in this area – together with Argentina and Brazil – is therefore a source of higher degree opportunities for other Latin American countries, which show the value assigned to the teaching offered both through the acceptance of Chilean graduates abroad, and through the enrolment of Latin American students in graduate programmes in Chile.

Conclusions

Higher education in Chile has served as a reference point for most Latin American countries. In Colombia, for example, there is at present a debate on new legislation for higher education and the Chilean experience has been carefully and critically examined. The development of quality assurance mechanisms, starting from 1990, was a model for many other countries in the region and beyond, and the policies leading to the development and expansion of higher education have been acclaimed and disseminated by the World Bank and other international organisations. Higher education in the country has made significant progress, and its prestige in the Latin American region is well deserved.

However, a closer look at the system makes it easier to understand the underlying reasons for the student unrest that occupied front pages during 2011: increased access involves significant challenges in terms of quality, equity and relevance; market rules lead to high fees and unacceptable levels of graduate indebtedness; accreditation, as applied in the last five years, has been unable to provide the needed assurance of basic levels of quality; and neither the government nor the political system were able to ensure that the demands of students, their families and large segments of the population would be taken into consideration and that acceptable solutions would be found.

Higher education in Chile faces a difficult challenge: its student population is characteristic of a mass higher education system, including highly qualified students, with rich cultural capital and strong social and academic networks, and many first generation students, without the needed qualifications or support systems to perform in a competitive higher education system. The response from the system is consistent with these strong differences: elite higher education institutions, which cater to a selected population of students, with very good results, nationally and internationally; a few good quality teaching institutions, both within and without the university sector, which are developing new models for curricular arrangements and teaching practices in order better to serve a new student body; and a number of profit-making, poor quality institutions, which enrol large number of students, with mixed – and generally poor – results, both in terms of effectiveness and efficiency.

The future depends mostly on policy definitions, by the government and by other state agencies – those in charge of funding and of quality assurance procedures. A key word in any discussion of higher education in Chile is autonomy, and institutions jealously defend their right to define independently the type of programmes they offer, the curricular arrangements, the teaching methods and the mix of functions that they perform. The main challenge now is to redefine the concept of autonomy, to include a measure of responsible innovation and the commitment to make higher education a significant experience for all those students who are admitted and encouraged to spend years of their lives, and large portions of their current or future income, in studying towards a degree. All involved stakeholders must work towards a new definition of quality (or several ways of looking at it) and make all institutions responsive to these new demands. Diversity – a key feature of Chilean higher education – cannot be confused with mediocrity, and cannot be achieved without strong measures involving regulations, funding schemes and clear guidelines for the future.

References

CASEN, Encuesta de Caracterizacion Socioeconómica (Socioeconomic Characterization Survey), 2009, http://www.ministeriodesarrollosocial.gob.cl/casen2009/ (accessed 14 November 2012).

CIES (Center for Research in Social Structure), 2011, Tabulados básicos de la Encuesta Nacional de Estructura Social, Documento de Trabajo, Departamento de Sociología, Universidad de Chile, Santiago, Chile.

CNAP, 2007, El modelo chileno de acreditación de la educación superior, Ministerio de Educación, VERDE, Santiago, Chile.

CNED, INDICES, 2011, Compendio estadístico, Santiago, Chile, www.cned.cl (accessed December 2012).

CONICYT, 2011, http:// www.conicyt.cl (accessed March 2012).

IAU (International Association of Universities), 2010, Internationalization of Higher Education: Global Trends, Regional Perspectives, 3rd Global Survey Report, Paris.

OECD, 2008, *Tertiary Education for the Knowledge Society,* Vol 1, OECD, Paris.

OECD, 2011, Education at a Glance 2011: Highlights, OECD Publishing. http://dx.doi.org/10.1787/eag_highlights–2011-en (accessed March 2012).

Orellana, V., 2011, 'Nuevos estudiantes y tendencias emergentes en la educación superior. Una mirada al Chile del mañana', in M Jiménez and F Lagos (eds), *Nueva Geografía de la educación superior y de los estudiantes*, Aequalis. Foro de Educación Superior, Santiago, Chile.

Torres, C. and Zenteno, M.E., 2011, 'El sistema de educación superior: una mirada desde las instituciones y sus características', in M Jiménez and F Lagos (eds), *Nueva Geografía de la educación superior y de los estudiantes*, Aequalis. Foro de Educación Superior, Santiago, Chile.

UNESCO, 2010, Unesco Global Education Digest. Comparing Educational Statistics Around the World, Unesco Institute for Statistics, Montreal, Canada.

16

Conclusion

The Changing Landscape and Marketisation of Higher Education

MARK WEYERS

There are a multitude of pressures on contemporary higher education, including the Bologna Process, mass enrolment, privatisation, quality assurance and accountability, internationalisation/globalisation and decreased public funding. These have led to new government agendas and the development of national and international policies around internationalisation, research-led education, key skills and employability, entrepreneurship and student mobility. As Scott (1998) argues, universities are agents of globalisation; research intensive institutions are fundamental nodes in a global knowledge network that crosses borders and spans nations (Castells 2001; McCarney 2005).

There is a strong positive correlation between the higher education enrolment of a nation and its global competitive performance (Bloom 2005: 23–24). Higher education has become central to the cultural and economic transformations that are occurring across the globe and is the precursor for the new knowledge economies of the future. The global influx of people, information, technology and finance are having an impact at both local and national levels in many countries. Cross-border cooperation and competition are central themes at the institutional level and are driven by international student mobility, global rankings and the internationalisation of higher education (Marginson and Van Der Wende 2007). However, as Scott asserts, 'Not all universities are (particularly) international, but all are subject to the same processes of globalisation – partly as objects, victims even, of these processes, but partly as subjects, or key agents, of globalisation' (1998, 122). Regardless, the transformations that are occurring at all levels are having a major impact on the policies and strategies of the higher education sector.

However, globalisation is not a level playing field as demonstrated by the unequal cross-border flows of students. The US and the UK have a huge impact on global higher education and at the same time seem less affected by other systems that they engage with. For some institutions, the international agenda has become the central guiding strategy for development and growth. In Europe, the development of a common higher education area and European research networks are increasing cooperation and assisting in expansion.

Global research networks are rapidly developing in countries such as China, Singapore and Korea, which are already key countries in international student mobility. However, the emerging economies (outside the Organisation for Economic Co-operation and Development [OECD]) now produce half of the world's economic wealth. China is expected to overtake the US's gross domestic product (GDP) by 2025 and India is growing rapidly as well (Marginson and Van Der Wende 2007).This will have profound implications for both research and education in the global higher education arena.

Currently, Britain and America are world leaders in higher education provision and each attracts more students than any other country in the world. They also top the global university rankings and hold a large majority of the top 20 places. However, the increase in fees in Britain has led to a drop in university applications, and changes in the national higher education landscape in countries like China are seeing less student movement into Britain and America. The international agenda has been an important agenda for many institutions and attracting international students tends to top this agenda. International students generally pay higher fees than home students and their impact on the national economy is great.

In the US international students contribute almost $21 billion dollars (US Department of State 2011) to the economy. Similarly, in 2009 international students in the UK contributed £8 billion to the economy and this is expected to increase to £17 billion by 2025 (*The Economist* 2012). The growth of cross-border education has the potential to drastically transform an institution's mission. In 2005 Oxford University reported that it planned on cutting the number of home and EU undergraduates to expand its non-EU overseas intake. The motivation was to improve its financial situation and provide a more multicultural learning environment. It made clear that international student fees allowed institutions to run, as they do not make enough money to run a global institution on public investment and home fees (Marginson and Van Der Wende 2007).

OECD statistics (2012) suggest that there are 4.1 million internationally mobile students, up from 2.1 million in 2002. According to the United Nations Educational, Scientific and Cultural Organization (UNESCO 2011) 60 per cent of those students were studying in North America and Western Europe. A further 20 per cent were studying in East Asia with another 10 per cent studying in Central and Eastern Europe. The higher education system in China is going through a major development. From 1998 to 2004 the total number of undergraduates rose to 20 million (from five million) making the Chinese higher education system the largest in the world (Liu 2006: 1). China is committed to raising the quality and global competitiveness of its leading research intensive universities and is investing heavily in the university sector. They are also increasing PhD admissions, which will reduce their dependence on doctoral training abroad and will support China's goal of becoming a global centre of research activity. Graduate students in China are first authors on almost half of all journal articles published (Liu 2006: 2–6).

Globally there has been major expansion of branch campuses and multi-institution joint degrees. However, some universities are also starting to rethink their approaches to student recruitment as branch campuses in foreign countries have brought their own share of difficulties. Britain has not been very active in the overseas campus market while the US has 78 foreign campuses and has been operating abroad since 1955. Johns Hopkins University opened a satellite campus in Italy (1955) and in China (1986) catering to both local and international students. The first British university satellite campus was established in Malaysia in 2000 by the University of Nottingham. Australian universities have had a strong international profile with campuses in Malaysia, Singapore and the United Arab Emirates (UAE).

Niche degree programmes and distinctive curricula are now common place across the higher education sector. At the institutional level trademark graduate attributes (e.g. global citizenship) are used as marketing tools as well as innovative approaches to course design (e.g. problem-based learning; inquiry-led education) that promise the kind of unique education that will give its graduates an edge in the graduate employment market. Many small institutions that have traditionally not engaged extensively in the global higher education market are now rebranding themselves and are competing for their own local students. As Gwinnett (2011) reported on an investigation in strategies for promoting a unique institutional ethos and identity, the fundamental element universities were using was the 'unique student experience'. Contemporary students are consumers and given the substantial fees they pay for tuition they are well aware of the typical quality indicators. They are increasingly astute when it comes to researching and comparing institutions on these indicators and they place a high importance on teaching quality along with the assessment processes within programmes and institutions. Likewise, institutions are becoming more attuned to the importance of offering a unique student experience.

Cross-border accreditation is also becoming more popular as institutions seek accreditation outside their national context (Altbach 2003; OECD 2004). The rationale behind this approach can be factors such as the lack of accreditation opportunities in their home countries; international accreditation can enhance an institution's position within their own nation; to avoid the requirements of national accreditation; or to enhance their institutions global recognition through their relationship with a reputable foreign accreditation body (Marginson and Van Der Wende 2007).

There has been a global movement of higher education from public to private, which has stemmed from the discussions surrounding the inclusion of education in the General Agreement on Trade in Services (Altbach 2003). This has generally resulted in reduced public funding; research funding being streamed into select areas focused around science and technology; and a shift to entrepreneurialism and corporate funding (Slaughter and Leslie 1997). As Currie and Newson point out, 'Globalization has brought the free market into universities but with serious ramifications and significant costs' (1998: 6). This is causing concern that academic disciplines will be segmented based on their perceived economic worth (Slaughter and Leslie 1997) demonstrated by a programme's attractiveness to international students. Slaughter and Rhoades (2006) note that the research intensive disciplines in the well-funded hard sciences (e.g. biomedicine, biotechnology) are in a healthy position while disciplines in the arts and humanities are in an increasingly difficult position.

The Impact of the Bologna Process

The drive to be a 'world-class university' has led to a convergence of institutional policies and practices with a dedicated attention to 'The Student Experience'. This convergence in many respects has been positive as it enhances international cooperation, and allows institutions to be globally competitive, transparent and easier to manage. In the late 1990s, in response to the growing global competition from the US and Asia, 30 countries in Europe participated in a harmonisation process and the European Area of Higher Education was formalised via the Bologna Declaration. This process ensured a more coherent higher education system with increased comparability and transparency. The basic framework outlined three cycles of a higher education qualification (bachelor, master, PhD) through the European Credit Transfer and Accumulation System (ECTS). It outlined the modularisation of courses, set credit hours and has led to the initiation of a liberal arts-style 'general education' that allows for a four-year degree with a major in one discipline and a minor in another. This has made way for the introduction of a grade point average (GPA) on a four-point scale that has begun to be adopted by universities in the UK and abroad. Other countries are also adopting the principles and tenets of Bologna and aligning themselves to the European processes so that they can compete globally using the same metrics, and can compare themselves to other institutions using international league tables and rankings.

The Bologna Process has also been instrumental at encouraging a shift to a learning outcome-based approach to curriculum development with the aim of encouraging active, student-centred learning. This push moves higher education from a content-knowledge framework to a competency-based approach. These structural and policy changes are intended to better serve the needs of a modern knowledge society. Quality assurance is now a global concern for institutions with the enhancement of the student experience central to that agenda. The Bologna Process has been instrumental in driving enhancement, not just in Europe but around the world.

Employability and the Development of Key Skills

As higher education has expanded, there has been increased emphasis on the skills students need once they complete their degrees. These skills are considered crucial for employability and include communication (written and oral), time management, information technology, problem solving and teamwork; furthermore business and entrepreneurial skills are also now considered crucial in the new knowledge economy.

Maintaining a competitive advantage through demonstrating that expected skills gains are translated into positive labour market outcomes is essential. The role of higher education in preparing graduates for the labour market is becoming increasingly important. This agenda is also central to the recruitment of international students as the marketing of degree programmes now often highlight the unique aspect of their degrees through the key skills that students will develop. However, this has raised issues about how generic and subject-specific key skills may be taught and assessed within academic programmes.

Another factor that has contributed greatly to student mobility is the drive by international students to acquire English as a second language. English is the language of business and the global language of research and academic publishing and is therefore central to the global knowledge economy. However, we are starting to see a trend as the emerging economies (e.g. Brazil, Russia, India and China) start to take a more global hold, and the need for native English speakers to acquire a second language is becoming more important.

Experiences and skills gained, especially the use of a foreign language, while studying internationally can give students an 'employability advantage'; however, how these skills transfer to other international labour markets is sometimes difficult to anticipate. Intercultural sensitivity and acquiring a global perspective in one's discipline has been noted by many to be fundamental to living in a global community (Crossman and Clarke 2010: 602) and for working in international companies where a global perspective and the ability to work with other cultures is crucial (Bosch 2009).

The Digital Student

Contemporary higher education operates in a digitally enhanced world with a global network of peers and a multitude of tools to engage with both their teacher and fellow learners. However, learners need a particular set of skills to be able to use this technology in what Jenkins (2009) calls a participatory culture. While an obvious benefit of technology is that students can access their course material at any time of the day, virtual learning environments (VLEs) have been slowly moving away from being an online repository to environments that are more interactive and engaging. Learners today are immersed in technology, and the creation of global learning communities contributes locally relevant knowledge to the learning experience. There has been a pedagogical shift from didactic methods of teaching to more student-centred constructivist and socially situated pedagogies (Conole 2010). New technologies allow modern online learning to occur in networked socially mediated environments that emphasise and enhance collaboration (Siemens 2005).

A learning community that includes both geographic and cultural diversity exposes all the members of that community to a mixture of approaches and experiences. While working with learning groups across time zones can be challenging, a situation faced by many internationalised student cohorts, asynchronous computer-mediated technologies (e.g. online discussion groups) can minimise the common difficulties encountered by online courses that are spread across temporal boundaries and large geographical distances. These developments and enhancements in technology have led to what is now becoming much more prevalent in global higher education – fully online virtual learning. In this environment students engage predominantly with their institution through the university's VLE. This has changed the student experience dramatically, especially for international students, and has enabled students to engage with programmes and institutions far removed from their own geographies, as demonstrated by The Open University in the UK. These technologies are not just important for studying across national borders, they are also proving to be instrumental for institutions that have populations of students who have difficulties moving within national boundaries. For example, the University of South Africa (UNISA) is transitioning from a distance education model to online learning through a VLE to reach out to students that have been traditionally isolated. This new model is being implemented through local study centres and contractual arrangements with local internet cafes to allow students with no internet connection at home to access their online courses.

While traditional VLEs have been designed for desktop computing, the new trend in higher education learning is mobile technologies. New smart phones and tablets provide students with the opportunity to learn on the go and the improving conditions of connectivity in many countries is making it possible to use these mobile devices for learning regardless of location. Another new trend that is emerging and is expected to have a dramatic impact on higher education learning and teaching is massive open online courses (MOOCs). MOOCs represent a fundamental shift in the evolution of higher education and higher education internationalisation. While there is limited teacher facilitation, student interaction and peer support are prominent. They award certificates rather than academic course credits. Most importantly, the course resources and the expertise are free. Similar to other online pedagogies, students have the opportunity and flexibility to move through the course at their own pace. The scalability of these courses is one of their defining features and courses such as the Stanford Artificial Intelligence course had more than 90,000 participants in 2011. While we are seeing the emergence of new start-ups, such as Coursera, edX and Udacity, the true impact these approaches will have on the higher education sector are yet to be seen.

Similarly, Open Educational Resources (OER) is becoming more prominent in global higher education. OER are freely available educational materials that can be reused and repurposed for educational purposes often through creative commons licensing. Massachusetts Institute of Technology (MIT) popularised this agenda in 2002 when it introduced its Open Courseware initiative and made all of its teaching material freely available online. Its stated purpose was to enhance human learning worldwide and the initiative inspired a number of other governments, non-profits and institutions to make their course materials available as OER (e.g. the China Open Resources for Education was introduced in 2003 to encourage international collaboration between China and other international organisations). While students can of course access the material for their own use, it is more appropriately aimed at educators for use in their own teaching. However, pessimistically, the clear message that MIT is sending through this initiative is that you do not come to MIT for subject content; you come for the experience of learning in a world-class institution.

Summary

A global hierarchy within international higher education will continue to become more prominent as the desire of students to gain a world-class university education increases and the impact of university rankings become more widespread. However, the student experience is becoming much more important to universities as students are increasingly aware of the quality indicators needed to make informed choices about their study destination. The choice of institution based on teaching quality is now slightly more important than the reputation of the institution. Higher education has become truly global. However, educational systems that are congruent with the needs of a knowledge society are crucial. The international student experience continues to change as the relationships between teacher and student, institution and learning environment, continue to evolve.

As the impact of the emerging economies increases, national borders are becoming less important to students as the reduction in government funding for higher education and new fees structures are introduced. Students are now looking outside local geographical areas and are considering international study beyond that which they have previously considered. While branch campuses have provided students access to an international education within their national context, the advances in technology mean digital migration is now possible when international mobility is not. The knowledge society is truly global. As the higher education landscape continues to grow and adapt to the political, social and cultural pressures of a globalised world, the impact of technology continues to open up higher education to prospective and current students around the world in ways never before imagined.

References

Altbach, P. (2003) American accreditation of foreign universities: Colonialism in action, *International Higher Education*, 32, 5–7.

Bloom, D. (2005) Raising the pressure: Globalization and the need for higher education reform, in G. Jones, P. McCarney and M. Skolnik (eds.), *Creating Knowledge: Strengthening Nations: The Changing Role of Higher Education*, University of Toronto Press, Toronto, pp. 21–41.

Bosch, G. (2009) The 'internationalisation' of law degrees and enhancement of graduate employability: European dual qualification degrees in law. *The Law Teacher* 43(3), 284–296.

Castells, M. (2001) *The Internet Galaxy: Reflections on the Internet, Business and Society*, Oxford University Press, Oxford.

Conole, G. (2010) Review of pedagogical frameworks and models and their use in e-learning. Available at: http://cloudworks.ac.uk/cloud/view/2982/ (accessed 14 November 2012).

Crossman, J. and Clarke, M. (2010) International experience and graduate employability: stakeholder perceptions on the connection. *Higher Education* 59(5), 599–613.

Currie, J. and Newson, J. (eds) (1998) *Universities and Globalization: Critical Perspectives*, Sage Publications, Thousand Oaks, CA.

The Economist (2012) Learning without frontiers. Available at: http://www.economist.com/node/17363377 (accessed 12 September 2012).

Gwinnett, A. (2011) Distinctiveness as a route to sustainability for higher education institutions. Society for Research into Higher Education (SRHE) Annual Research Conference. 7–9 December 2011, Newport, Wales.

Jenkins, H. (2009) Confronting the challenges of participatory culture: Media education for the 21st century. The John D. and Catherine T. MacArthur Foundation Reports on Digital Media and Learning. Cambridge, MA: MIT Press. Available from: http://digitallearning.macfound.org/atf/cf/%7B7E45C7E0-A3E0-4B89-AC9C-E807E1B0AE4E%7D/JENKINS_WHITE_PAPER.PDF

Liu, N. (2006) The differentiation and classification of Chinese universities and the building of world-class universities in China, Presentation at the seminar at Leiden University, 13 September 2012.

Marginson, S., and Van Der Wende, M. (2007) Globalisation and higher education. Education Working Paper Number 8, Organisation for Economic Co-operation and Development, Paris.

McCarney, P. (2005) Global cities, local knowledge creation: Mapping a new policy terrain on the relationship between universities and cities, in G. Jones, P. McCarney and M. Skolnik (eds.), *Creating Knowledge: Strengthening Nations: The Changing Role of Higher Education*, University of Toronto Press, Toronto, pp. 205–224.

Organisation for Economic Co-operation and Development (OECD) (2004) Internationalization and trade in higher education: Opportunities and challenges. OECD, Paris.

Organisation for Economic Co-operation and Development (OECD) (2012) *Education at a glance 2012*. OECD, Paris.

Scott, P. (1998) Massification, internationalization and globalization, in P. Scott (ed.), *The globalization of higher education*, The Society for Research into Higher Education/Open University Press, Buckingham, pp. 108–129.

Siemens, G. (2005) Connectivism: A learning theory for the digital age. *International Journal of Instructional Technology and Distance Learning* 2(1), 3–10.

Slaughter, S. and Leslie, L. L. (1997) *Academic Capitalism: Politics, Policies and the Entrepreneurial University*, The Johns Hopkins University Press, Baltimore, MD.

Slaughter, S. and Rhoades, G. (2006) Academic capitalism and the new economy: Privatization as shifting the target of public subsidy in higher education, in R. A. Rhoades and C. A. Torres (eds.), *The university, state, and market: The political economy of globalization in the Americas*, Stanford University Press, Stanford, CA, pp. 103–140.

United Nations Educational, Scientific and Cultural Organization (UNESCO) (2011) *Global education digest 2011*. UNESCO Institute for Statistics, Paris.

US Department of State (2011) Open doors 2011: International student enrolment increased by 5 percent in 2010/11. Available at: http://www.iie.org/en/Who-We-Are/News-and-Events/Press-Center/Press-Releases/2011/2011–11–14-Open-Doors-International-Students (accessed 13 September 2012).

Index